"Brimming with positivity and compassi[on] *[Adulting]* *on the Spectrum* reads like a blueprint for [...] ture of personal stories, practical strateg[ies and ...] questions, Sandison inspires and motivates. Whether you're a teen or an adult on the spectrum, this book will not only help you better understand yourself but also provide valuable insight for navigating the future."

AMY K. D. TOBIK, editor-in-chief of *Exceptional Needs Today* and CEO of Lone Heron Publishing

"*Adulting on the Spectrum* is a must-read for adults with autism, the families that love them, and the professionals who support them. In this book Sandison covers the gamut, from leaving the nest to college life, from dating to learning the ins and outs of the workplace, and so much more. You will find personal stories from his own life and from other awesome adults with autism who share their challenges and successes. Sandison offers useful strategies for overcoming a 'hopeless complex' to become a fierce self-advocate, and tips for handling the top hindrances many people encounter when transitioning to adulthood. Take it from Sandison—someone who lives with autism, understands the potential pitfalls, and has overcome them to achieve his dreams with abundant faith and optimism."

WENDELA WHITCOMB MARSH, CEO of Adult Autism Assessment & Services and author of *Independent Living with Autism*

"In his new book, Ron Sandison articulates how he navigates life as an adult with autism. He understands what adults with autism need. Sandison powerfully illustrates many important practical concepts for young and mature adults on the autism spectrum. This book is a gift not only to people with autism but also to their families and friends."

LAWRENCE FUNG, MD, PhD, director of the Stanford Neurodiversity Project and assistant professor of psychiatry and behavioral sciences at Stanford University

"*Adulting on the Spectrum* is a great resource for people who are transitioning to adulthood. Parents, educators, and professionals who help young adults with autism prepare for college will also greatly benefit from this book."

ANTHONY IANNI, self-advocate, motivational speaker, and author of *Centered*

"This is a very practical guide to addressing employment and other life and mental health issues for adults with autism (and their families). Sandison is able to draw on his own experiences and writes in a lively and accessible style."

MICHAEL BERNICK, former director of the California State Department of Labor and author of *The Autism Job Club*

"Finally, a book I feel I can share with young adults with autism! The direct approach of lists, acronyms, and activities offers clear and concise steps for implementation. Sandison not only delivers practical life hacks but shares stories highlighting learning curves, which I hope will help others not feel so alone when navigating the largely neurotypical world."

DESIREE KAMEKA GALLOWAY, director of the Autism Housing Network and lead consultant of Neuro-Inclusive Housing Solutions

"Ron Sandison's description of himself as 'a force to be reckoned with' could not be more spot-on. In *Adulting on the Spectrum*, Sandison's stories depict relentless self-advocacy, starting with the support of his mother during his childhood and flourishing in adulthood. As a result, Sandison has attained personal and professional goals that many experts predicted he could never achieve. By writing this book, he has become an advocate to other adults with autism, providing a wealth of practical strategies in each chapter."

RUTH ANAN, PhD, BCBA-D, professor at the Michigan School of Psychology

"Ron Sandison addresses the importance of youth knowing their own strengths for a job or a career. I fully agree. When youth discover the various kinds of strengths and the ways they can use strengths as leverage in challenges, they gain a powerful tool that increases inner security. I strongly recommend Sandison's book."

JACKIE MARQUETTE, PhD, autism employment researcher, author, and parent of an adult son with autism

"When my son, Sam, was diagnosed on the borderline of severe autism at age two, there were few resources available. Ron Sandison's book has come at the perfect time for Sam, who is now transitioning to adulthood. It is such a relief to finally have a book to help young adults navigate life after high school, prepare them for college or a trade school, and learn skills for independence. Next spring, Sam graduates from high school, and it feels scary. As a parent, I can't tell Sam what's going to happen or predict his future. We must handle issues as they come, from figuring out a college to deciding on a career to understanding relationships. Launching my son into the world is full of uncertainty, excitement, fear, and hope. This book is a godsend and provides families and individuals on the spectrum with the knowledge to navigate life's circumstances from the perspective of an adult with autism whom I trust. Thank you, Ron, for writing this book that every parent and their young adult with autism desperately needs!"

SARAH BROADY, author, speaker, and parent of a young adult on the spectrum

Also by Ron Sandison

Views from the Spectrum:
A Window into Life and Faith with Your Neurodivergent Child

AN **INSIDER'S GUIDE** *for*
NAVIGATING LIFE WITH **AUTISM**

adulting
ON THE SPECTRUM

Ron Sandison
Foreword by Dr. Barry M. Prizant

KREGEL
PUBLICATIONS

Adulting on the Spectrum: An Insider's Guide for Navigating Life with Autism
© 2025 by Ron Sandison

Published by Kregel Publications, a division of Kregel Inc., 2450 Oak Industrial Dr. NE, Grand Rapids, MI 49505. www.kregel.com.

Ron Sandison is represented by and *Adulting on the Spectrum* is published in association with The Steve Laube Agency, LLC. www.stevelaube.com.

The author and publisher are not engaged in rendering medical or psychological services, and this book is not intended as a guide to diagnose or treat medical or psychological problems. If medical, psychological, or other expert assistance is required, the reader should seek the services of a health-care provider or certified counselor.

Some of the content included in this book was originally published in articles on the Art of Autism's blog (www.the-art-of-autism.com). The articles are owned by Ron Sandison and are used with permission.

All Scripture quotations, unless otherwise indicated, are taken from the Holy Bible, New International Version®, NIV®. Copyright © 1973, 1978, 1984, 2011 by Biblica, Inc.™ Used by permission of Zondervan. All rights reserved worldwide. www.zondervan.com. The "NIV" and "New International Version" are trademarks registered in the United States Patent and Trademark Office by Biblica, Inc.™

Scripture quotations marked NKJV are taken from the New King James Version®. Copyright © 1982 by Thomas Nelson. Used by permission. All rights reserved.

Scripture quotations marked NLT are taken from the *Holy Bible*, New Living Translation, copyright ©1996, 2004, 2015 by Tyndale House Foundation. Used by permission of Tyndale House Publishers, Carol Stream, Illinois 60188. All rights reserved.

Cataloging-in-Publication Data is available from the Library of Congress.

ISBN 978-0-8254-4933-8, print
ISBN 978-0-8254-4935-2, epub
ISBN 978-0-8254-4934-5, Kindle

Printed in the United States of America
25 26 27 28 29 30 31 32 33 34 / 5 4 3 2 1

For my dad, Chuck Sandison, who taught me the skills necessary to transition to adulthood and has modeled the attributes of being a man of God. I learned from my dad the qualities of integrity, hard work, faithfulness, and the importance of trusting Christ. Thanks for shaping me into who I am.

When I was a child, I talked like a child, I thought like a child, I reasoned like a child. When I became a man, I put the ways of childhood behind me.

1 Corinthians 13:11

For my mom, Janet Sandison, who quit her job as an art teacher when I was diagnosed with autism at age seven. She then became a full-time "Ron teacher." I learned from my mom to seek God first and foremost and never give up.

Be diligent in these matters; give yourself wholly to them, so that everyone may see your progress.

1 Timothy 4:15

For my daughter, Makayla, who brings me joy each day with her dancing and songs.

Children are a gift from the LORD; they are a reward from him.

Psalm 127:3 (nlt)

For my wife, Kristen Sandison, who loves me unconditionally and believes in my dreams.

The man who finds a wife finds a treasure, and he receives favor from the LORD.

Proverbs 18:22 (nlt)

For my mother-in-law, Sue Boswell, for her love and support.

And do not forget to do good and to share with others, for with such sacrifices God is pleased.

Hebrews 13:16

Contents

Contents

Foreword

RON SANDISON IS A REMARKABLE man who has lived and continues to live a remarkable life. So when he asked on my *Uniquely Human* podcast whether I would be willing to contribute a foreword for his latest book, I said without hesitation, "I would be honored to do so." Ron and I have enjoyed each other's work for many years, and I continue to learn so much from him as he generously shares his journey and his achievements. With *Adulting on the Spectrum*, you, the reader, can do the same.

The autism revolution that we continue to experience is driven primarily by autistic people sharing their stories. By *revolution*, I am referring to the systematic demolishing and dismantling of so many harmful and inaccurate narratives about autistic individuals that persisted for decades following Leo Kanner's and Hans Asperger's first descriptions of autism in the 1940s. Ron's life story debunks harmful myths about autistic people, such as their not being interested in having friendships and loving relationships, lacking empathy, not being able to contribute to society, and not having a spiritual life, just to name a few. Concurrently, the revolution is contributing positive narratives about the special qualities and unique attributes of individuals living on the autism spectrum. These include their resilience, distinctive learning styles and passions, honesty and loyalty to others, and integrity and commitment to justice and truth—qualities all descriptive of Ron's character.

Foreword

The autism revolution is fueled by the stories we hear that are now being told by hundreds, if not thousands, of autistic individuals in lectures, writings, and artistic endeavors. These first-person insights, directly or indirectly, are the primary force serving to right the wrongs of misinformation fabricated by neurotypical researchers and clinicians that have endured for decades. Thankfully, they are also building positive, humane impressions of autistic people as invaluable members of society. Ron has been a significant and major contributor to this movement through his books, presentations, and online presence. When looking at the breadth and depth of his work, it's clear that his contributions stand out as unique and vital in the burgeoning landscape of works by autistic people.

Like so many of his autistic compatriots, Ron has been challenged, misunderstood, and discriminated against by a society that has yet to understand and embrace the humanity of neurodiversity. What is exceptional about Ron's journey is how, with his unrelenting thirst for learning, his passion for excellence, and his hard-earned confidence, he implores us to benefit from the lessons he has learned in dueling with his personal challenges and in overcoming adversity. Another special characteristic that Ron brings to his work is his fascination with the lived experience of other autistic people. He has interviewed hundreds of people on the spectrum, and he shares what he has gleaned to drive home the crucial point that those who share the same diagnosis are still first and foremost individuals with different experiences and personalities. Ron's deep faith and knowledge of Scripture allow him to put his special imprint on his work. With these tools in hand, Ron teaches us the fundamentals of constructing a life of extraordinary quality that clearly is relevant for both autistic people and neurotypical folk.

To do this, Ron turns his attention to navigating the difficult, critical, and risk-laden transition to adulthood. He accomplishes this by diving into topics that have been either ignored or glossed over because of the historically disproportionate focus of research and literature on autistic children. Ron addresses crucial challenges faced by autistic teens and adults in areas as critical and diverse as health and well-being, friendships and romantic relationships, mental health, advocacy, employment, managing emotions, and executive functioning. Through personal experiences and stories of others on the spectrum, Ron is frank and forthright in documenting intrapersonal and interpersonal challenges that are too often barriers to living a productive and happy life. But the great gift of this book, given Ron's natural optimistic propensity, his solution-oriented drive, and his motivation to help others, is that he shifts to practical recommendations and wisdom-based strategies that clearly will be helpful to others in addressing their specific challenges. By infusing reflection questions and fun activities, Ron engages the reader to develop self-awareness through a strengths-based, positive learning perspective.

In this manner, *Adulting on the Spectrum* can be seen as an essential quality-of-life handbook for teens and adults on the autism spectrum, as well as for those who love and support them at home, in school, and at work.

BARRY M. PRIZANT, PhD, CCC-SLP
Adjunct professor at Brown University and author of
Uniquely Human: A Different Way of Seeing Autism
and the SCERTS Model® manuals

Introduction

No mortal man can knock me off my journey.

—Tarik El-Abour, a professional baseball player with autism

As someone with autism, I encountered many struggles in my transition to adulthood, including: lacking confidence to take risks, needing self-efficacy to accomplish my dreams, finding courage to move out of my parents' house, developing coping methods to control my sensory issues and meltdowns, acquiring social skills to maintain gainful employment, and understanding boundaries for healthy relationships. Acquiring these skills, which are needed for successful transition to adulthood, required perseverance and patience from me and my parents.

Transition in my life was difficult and took me longer than it did for my peers and brothers. I graduated from high school at the age of twenty. I was thirty-two before I had stable employment, thirty-five before I had a long-term relationship, thirty-six when I moved out of my parents' home, thirty-seven when I got married, forty-one when I became a father, forty-two when my first book was published, and forty-five when my third book, *Views from the Spectrum*, made it into print.

As Jesse A. Saperstein, author of *Getting a Life with Asperger's:*

Lessons Learned on the Bumpy Road to Adulthood, wrote, "Success with any disability is dependent upon reaching for the skies in the steadiest of increments. Wade into the ocean of self-confidence and resist the urge to plunge."[1]

Too often in my transition to adulthood, I plunged, which caused me to crash and burn with feelings of depression and despair. When I got fired from a ministry position, or when a girl I was crazy about broke up with me, I felt hopeless.

If only the transition to adulthood for those with autism were graceful, like it is for eaglets. The bald eagle empowers her eaglets to transition from the nest to the sky by slowly removing her feathers that line the nest, uncovering sharp, thorny branches, and making the nest feel uncomfortable for her young. After enough feathers are removed, the eaglet leans slightly over the side, gently spreads its wings, and soars.

Trust me—if you try this trick on a young adult with autism, instead of a soaring eagle, you will get a raging Tasmanian devil or, even worse, an agitated honey badger. Just ask my parents—they tried it with me. They tried removing the comfortable "feathers" by no longer purchasing my favorite snacks and not allowing me to watch television all day and ride with my friends in their cars. It was a futile attempt to motivate me to search for a job and leave their nest.

Transitioning to adulthood took years of perseverance before I saw the fruits of my labor—a master's degree, a wife, a family, a career in the medical field and as a professor of theology, and three published books.

I wrote this book to empower young adults with autism to be able to have a smoother journey and to help them learn practical ways to transition to adulthood. Twenty years ago, as I crashed and burned into adulthood, the lessons contained in this book could have saved me from the many tearful, lonely nights I experienced because I lacked the social skills to maintain friendships, and they could have provided me with the clarity I desperately sought by providing me with a game plan to achieve my goals.

One social crash-and-burn incident this book could have saved me from happened while I was in college. For three years I had a crush on a girl to the point of obsession. Whenever I was around her, my mind went into overdrive. I could not think about anything but her. The church we both attended had a weekend college student retreat at a campground. The pastor offered a free ticket to the event as a prize for the first student to read 1 Corinthians 9:24 from the Bible.

I raced down the aisle and jumped onto the stage. The pastor looked at me in shock and asked, "Where's your Bible?"

"I am a walking Bible!" I replied as I proceeded to quote 1 Corinthians 9:24: "Do you not know that in a race all the runners run, but only one gets the prize? Run in such a way as to get the prize." The pastor then handed me the ticket.

The first night of the retreat, I approached this girl while she was chatting with her friends by the campfire. "I would love to go out on a date with you. I think you're amazing and beautiful," I blurted out. She freaked out, and later that night she had one of her guy friends warn me: "Look, man, she's not at all interested. You need to leave her alone and back off!"

The following night there was a barnyard dance, and a pretty blond girl—who was more attractive than the girl who spit me out like liver the night before—asked me to dance. Putting her head on my chest while dancing, she looked up at me and said, "Wow, I saw how you can quote the Bible! You're amazing! Do you have a verse on dancing?"

I quoted Lamentations 5:15 to her: "Joy is gone from our hearts; our dancing has turned to mourning."

For forty-five minutes, without seeming to take a break, I told this pretty blonde about the girl I had a crush on and how she had broken my heart. Having autism, I missed every social clue of this blonde's disinterest in this topic. She checked her watch every few minutes and twirled her hair. Looking back now with the social knowledge I've gained, I realize this pretty blonde was interested in me and I blew my opportunity because of my autistic obsession and inability to decode her body language. The chapter on dating and relationships would've prevented this romantic-triangle catastrophe.

I also wrote this book to provide hope and encouragement for young adults with autism and their families. Throughout this book, I share inspiring stories of individuals with autism who use their gifts to achieve their dreams. My life is an example that with support, love, and acceptance from family and friends, autism cannot hold us back from reaching our goals in life.

Autism does not have to hinder your transitioning to adulthood and gaining independence and freedom from your mom and dad. You will learn the steps necessary to become an adult. Each chapter will provide easy-to-follow instructional teaching, reflective questions, and fun activities. You can do these activities on your own, but I recommend that you go through the book with a group. This will help you put into action what you're learning. The activities sections follow a four-step structured learning style:

- Didactic instruction (explanation of the skills and steps to perform them)
- Modeling of skill steps
- Role-playing skills with corrective feedback
- Practice inside and outside a group

The structured learning style will help you generalize the skills learned in this book and apply them to your life. I also share my personal struggles with transitioning to adulthood and the knowledge I gained on my journey to becoming an adult. And each chapter ends with a real-life story in which a person shows the use of these skill steps in life to reach his or her dreams.

My goal is for you to live a happy and productive life on the spectrum. Autism quirks and interests make you unique, and refining these qualities will enable you to gain freedom and enjoy independence. Our uniqueness creates a beautiful world. As Saint Thérèse de Lisieux said, "The splendour of the rose and the whiteness of the lily do not rob the little violet of its scent nor the daisy of its simple charm. I realised that if every tiny flower wanted to be a rose, spring would lose its loveliness."[2]

We can accomplish our dreams by perseverance, self-determination, and intrinsic motivation. By opening this book, you have already taken the first step to learn the skills necessary for relationships and employment, and to live free.

Chapter 1

Leaving the Nest

*Leaving home in a sense involves a kind
of second birth in which we give birth
to ourselves.*
—ROBERT NEELLY BELLAH, American sociologist and author

AS SOMEONE WITH AUTISM, I experienced extreme difficulty transitioning from adolescence to adulthood. Those who are neurotypical may not understand the unique challenges, and I often explain using the nightmare COVID-19 pandemic as an example.

I tell them to imagine this scenario: You worked for a gym that is now permanently closed, leaving you unemployed and broke. Wearing a mask creates sensory issues with facial itching and a rash on your forehead. Since a significant portion of communication is body language, not words, you miss nonverbal social clues because of everyone wearing masks—making you feel socially awkward.

Barbershops and salons are closed—your new look is Captain Caveman with unkempt hair and poor hygiene. Social distancing of six feet combined with the prohibition of shaking hands, high fives, and hugs causes your body to cease production of oxytocin, the cuddle hormone, causing you to feel depressed and disconnected from society. Congratulations—this is your new normal for COVID-19.

Then I tell them to imagine COVID-19 continued for twenty years, and people start to understand why my transition from adolescence to adulthood was challenging.

The hardest part of my transition was leaving my parents' home. It required self-efficacy and self-confidence for me to move out. *Self-efficacy* is the belief that when you set a goal, you can accomplish it. I was reminded of the importance of self-efficacy and the ability to adjust to life's transitions by a patient I'll call Jeff. In his early forties, Jeff was admitted to the hospital because his elderly parents were unable to care for him. Jeff's siblings advised their parents to place him in an adult foster care (AFC) home because after they passed, he would not be able to care for himself.

For the next three months, while Jeff was in the hospital, his mom brought him food from McDonald's, Tim Hortons, or a local restaurant three times a day. A fellow patient, who was eighteen, noticed the care and good food Jeff's mom gave him and said, "Man, Jeff, you have it made."

Jeff replied, "No, you have it made. You're only eighteen, so you have another twenty-five to thirty years you can live with your parents. My time is almost up!" Finally, just in time for the holidays, Jeff was placed in an AFC home—upset and angry because he could no longer live with his parents.[1]

Jesse Saperstein, an advocate with autism, described self-efficacy, stating that "living with Asperger's is an understanding that victory comes in knowing that the new problem is less of a problem than the one that has just been eradicated."[2]

Planning for transition from home is important and requires addressing issues and problems you will encounter. In this chapter we will examine transitioning from home to college. There are five main ways you can transition from your parents' home to a new living arrangement: moving in with a roommate or friend, finding a spouse and moving in together, moving into your own apartment or house, going away to college (dorm life), or transitioning to a group home.

My transition from my parents' house, unlike the eaglets leaving the nest, was not due to discomfort but to pursuing my special interests in academics and theology at Oral Roberts University (ORU). Halfway through my junior year of high school, my special interests changed from track and cross-country to the Bible and theology. I became obsessed with memorizing Scripture, and I memorized more than two thousand verses in less than a year. When I had entered my junior year of high school, before discovering an interest in theology, TV evangelists, and memorizing Bible verses, my GPA was only 1.7. During my final three semesters I averaged a 3.3 GPA and graduated from high school with a 2.5 GPA.

During my senior year of high school, my dad and I visited ORU in Tulsa, Oklahoma, for college weekend. I stayed in the dorms with the students while my dad stayed at a local hotel. My dad and I toured the campus, and he helped me locate the student cafeteria, resource center, chapel, and classrooms. We met with the theology department professors and staff, and my dad explained to them my learning disabilities due to autism and the accommodations I would need to succeed away from home.

I was determined to attend ORU and study the Bible and theology. After high school, I received a full-tuition athletic scholarship for track and cross-country from nearby Michigan Christian College (now Rochester Christian University). My dad thought it was best for me to attend MCC for a year and transfer to ORU. With my father's encouragement, we decided that my living at home for a year and having two semesters of college completed would prepare me for ORU.

For a young adult with anxiety issues, a large university was intimidating. I was scared to death to travel 950 miles away from Michigan, alone, to go to college in Tulsa. My parents traveled with me to Tulsa and helped me get my dorm room set up, complete my class schedule, find my classes, and connect with the student resource center. They also introduced me to student leadership at ORU and the resident adviser (RA) and chaplain for my dorm. The purpose of an RA is to create a safe and comfortable environment for the dorm residents. My parents being with me made my transition from home to college smooth.

I learned fourteen valuable lessons transitioning from home to college life. The first nine apply to moving out on your own, and the other five relate to college life in general.

1. Make sure you're ready to leave your parents' home—don't jump ship (leave) too early.

Even if living at home as an adult feels embarrassing, don't jump ship too early. Be sure you have the necessary experience and skills to live on your own or with a roommate. Some of the skills required for me to live on my own were learning to prepare my own meals, washing, ironing, cleaning, and maintaining employment to pay my bills. I developed these skills by working from an early age and attending college out of state.

2. When you first move out on your own, choose a place two to three miles from your parents' or guardians' home.

Having an apartment or house close to your family's home offers a safety net. If you have an emergency, help and support are near. This also enables your family to help you with shopping and cooking.

Transitioning to adulthood can be difficult and may occur in progressive stages. I was thirty-six years old before I moved out of my parents' house. I moved out a month before I got married. For the first two years of my marriage, I would go directly from work to my parents' home to do my two hours of Bible memory work. I did not get home until 6:30 p.m., but now I do my memory work at my apartment.

3. When you first live on your own, find a roommate willing to help.

A good place to find a roommate is at college. Social work, psychology, and theology majors could be a good fit. Offer the roommate a discount in rent for the help they can provide.

4. Be ready to handle change in your routines.

Many individuals with autism hate change. I love to follow my set schedule. Every workday I get up at 5:47 a.m. I spend thirty minutes before work doing Bible memory work in my car, and at 6:54 a.m. I clock in for work. After work, at 3:45 p.m., I do more Bible memory work for two hours, and then I eat dinner. I also hate change in my environment. My wife, Kristen, loves to move the furniture in our apartment—this drives me nuts. When she moved the couch in the living room from the right side to the left, it took me three days to adjust. Having a roommate will require you to adjust your schedule and routines.

5. Your parents are still a great resource for knowledge.

When you move out of your parents' house, there is a transition from your parents being benevolent dictators to trusted advisers. Even as an adult you will still need your parents' wisdom and encouragement. During my first semester of graduate school at ORU, I was taking Greek class and felt overwhelmed and wanted to give up. I called my dad, who gave me sound advice: "Everyone feels intimidated taking a new language, so make friends in the class and study with your new friends." His advice worked. I went on to take three years of Greek and translated two-thirds of the New Testament from Greek into English.

6. Keep your dorm room or apartment clean.

No roommate wants to live with a slob.

Zosia Zaks, who has autism, recommends five areas of home-care tasks in order of priority:

- Sanitation: Remove your garbage, recycling, and pet waste.
- Safety: Fix major hazards.
- Body care: Maintain a place to shower and a place to eat.
- Everyday objects: Clean rooms and furniture, organize house or apartment.
- Optional activities: Decorate, upgrade, and do home-related hobbies.[3]

Keeping your living space clean involves daily maintenance. The two easiest ways to accomplish chores are to have a schedule or time for them posted on your refrigerator and to multitask with your chores. For example, while you are on the phone, wander around straightening things up. If you've put something in the microwave or under the broiler, spend those three minutes wiping counters or doing dishes. While waiting for the bath to fill or the shower water to heat, wipe down the sink and the outside of the toilet.

Example of a cleaning priority list
- Take out the garbage regularly.
- Scrub bathroom: tub, shower, sink, floor, toilet.
- Wipe down kitchen: counters, floor, fridge, microwave, stove, dishes.
- Do laundry: clothes, sheets, blankets, towels.
- Vacuum the carpet and mop the floors.
- Dust and wipe surfaces (TV, windows, mirrors, doors).
- Clean furniture (couches, bookshelves).
- Pick up items around the house (magazines, books, video games).
- Perform seasonal maintenance (mow lawn, rake leaves, shovel snow).
- Take on special projects (painting walls, replacing windows).[4]

7. Maintain hygiene.
While at ORU, my friend Chip had a roommate with autism who refused to shower. The students in his dorm nicknamed him the Mad

Scientist due to his thick, slimy hair and his habit of wearing a flasher trench coat in one-hundred-degree heat. The stench was so unbearable that Chip quickly moved to another room.

Temple Grandin, an autistic person and well-known author, offers advice on hygiene: "When I started living on my own I was a slob. My new boss . . . made it very plain to me that my grooming had to improve. . . . It is perfectly fine to be a little eccentric but dirty or ragged is not acceptable."[5]

Reasons hygiene is important
- Good hygiene prevents disease and infection. Lack of cleanliness can serve as a breeding ground for viruses and bacteria.
- Hygiene affects your social desirability.
- Minimal conformity may allow you to avoid ridicule and be accepted by peers, prospective employers, or a romantic partner.

Rules of hygiene
- Regularly shower and/or wash.
- Use deodorant.
- Brush your teeth.
- Comb your hair.
- Sneeze into a tissue.
- Use a restroom when passing gas.
- Don't burp or belch in public.
- Dress in clean clothes that don't have any stains or funky smells.
- Women should shave legs and underarms, and men with facial hair should keep it well trimmed.

8. Unless you want to starve, learn to prepare a few different meals.

Now that you've moved out of your parents' house, your mom is no longer your personal gourmet chef, so unless you want to live on ra-men noodles the rest of your life, you better learn how to make a few meals. The easiest meal to make is a sandwich. One meat, one cheese, and two pieces of bread; or even easier, make a peanut butter and jelly sandwich.

You can learn to make meals from friends and family, cookbooks, or the easiest way—searching recipes online. Recipes nearly always work, but you must follow the directions, especially while baking. No one is allowed to go out on a limb while baking unless he is a professional chef, because there is a huge difference between a quarter tablespoon and a quarter teaspoon of baking powder, and your meal will taste horrible with the wrong amount of an ingredient. I find following directions difficult, so when making a new meal, I have a friend help me prepare the dish the first time.

My two favorite sandwiches are peanut butter and grilled cheese. Both are quick lunches.

9. Budget your money—college and living on your own are very expensive.

The key to saving money is to spend less than you make. Keep in mind that you can save money by taking all your general education classes at a community college before transferring to a university.

While in college, my friend Jeff ate at diners and restaurants three nights a week and went to the movie theater twice a week—charging his entertainment bill to his credit cards. By the time he graduated from ORU, he owed $80,000 in student loans and an additional $30,000 on his credit cards.

Should you use cash or credit? If you want to save money, buy things with cash or check rather than a credit card. You can find yourself in financial trouble if you spend more money than you make or have saved.

Understand the difference between good debt and bad. Good debt helps finance things you need, such as a home or car for transportation to work. Bad debt funds a flashy lifestyle beyond your means and puts you in financial ruin. When receiving a loan, ask yourself, *What will this debt accomplish?*

Before any big purchase, ask yourself, *Do I need this new? Do I need this exact model? What is a low, reasonable, and high price on it? How much is it selling for in stores locally compared to online?*

Three ways to decide if something is worth spending money on

- How reliant am I on this good or service?
- Is this something I might be able to do by myself but could mess up and cause costly damage? (For example, car repairs or fixing a household appliance.)
- Is this something that will last me four times as long if I spend twice as much? (For example, purchasing a new laptop or TV versus a used one or cheaper model.)

I save money by buying items out of season. Buy summer things at the end of summer, when they're on clearance. If you love decorating for holidays, go to stores five days after the holiday when everything is marked down 90 percent.

10. Earn your bachelor's degree in a field in which you can have gainful employment after graduating and your master's degree in the field you're passionate about.

During times of economic recession, you will be glad you did this. Also, do not choose a degree in which you will owe lots of money in student loans and have no financial means to repay it.

Some good jobs for people with autism and Asperger's

- Computer programing: This career allows you to focus on creating codes and programs without a great deal of human interaction. It also builds on some typical autism spectrum disorder (ASD) strengths, including strong pattern recognition and tech savviness.

- Engineering: Aspies are overrepresented in this field, which also builds on the strengths of pattern recognition, mathematical manipulation, attention to detail, and understanding technology.
- Writing, editing, and copyediting: Some people with autism love words and writing and enjoy the detail-oriented, solitary work of editing.
- Web page design: This growing occupation requires people with skills in art, design, technology, and attention to detail.
- Accounting: Working with numbers allows people with autism to use math skills and attention to detail.

11. Develop mental toughness to prepare for academic challenges.

Mental toughness is acquired by developing good study habits and limiting distractions. This mental toughness requires you to learn to control your impulses and not procrastinate. Mental toughness will cause you to study for exams when you'd rather play video games and manage your disappointment when you receive a bad grade. It also allows you to complete assignments on time when you feel tired from staying up late and you just want to nap. Mental toughness empowers you to manage stress, control your emotions, and adapt to adverse circumstances.

12. If you live on campus, choose a dorm with an environment in which you feel comfortable to study and live.

Many college students with autism cannot handle loud bass and music and students staying up all night. During my sophomore year at ORU, I lived in the academic dorm—it was perfect. There was no loud noise and no pranks, and the students on my floor were great proofreaders and study partners. During my junior and senior years, I lived in Remnant—a dorm known for its funny pranks, such as catching a squirrel and letting it go in another dorm or putting superglue on toilet seats.

While living in Remnant, I had a honey-badger meltdown. At about 3 a.m. one day, I heard some 2 Live Crew rap as my walls were shaking from the blaring bass. My sensory processing went haywire. I ran down three flights of stairs to where the music was coming from, wearing only my white underwear. In my pre-meltdown condition, I screamed at the six-foot-four college basketball player, "You must be lost! This is ORU! Tulsa University is about thirty minutes due east!"

The basketball player came aggressively toward me. Lucky for him, an RA broke up the skirmish before the player was injured. This RA and I were in a theology class together, and the next day he told me, "Don't worry—this guy won't be listening to rap in his room anytime soon!"

13. Take advantage of every available resource from the government or college.

During my sophomore year of college, Michigan Rehabilitation Services donated money for me to purchase a $1,500 computer, and I received $1,200 a semester for tuition from them. When I was in Greek class, I took advantage of unlimited test time. Taking the test without a time restriction enabled me to experience less anxiety and helped my mind to process the information easier.

14. Find a roommate who is understanding of your autism quirks and sensory issues.

The first year of my master's degree program, I was still living in the dorms, and we had Big Dave on our floor—a six-foot-three football player. He never knocked on our door but just threw it open and walked on in. I posted a sign quoting Proverbs 25:17 on my door: "Seldom set foot in your neighbor's house—too much of you, and they will hate you."

Over a two-year period, Dave and I became best friends. In 2002 Dave's American Heroes organization flew me to Washington, DC, for an event celebrating the lives of the victims of September 11. (During the event, I met Muhammad Ali.) Even though Dave and I were best friends, I could never have had him as a roommate—he drove me nuts.

Finding an understanding roommate will help you enjoy your college journey, which will go fast.

Closing Thoughts

Transitioning from your parents' house is difficult and may take you a few tries. When a hang glider pilot prepares to leap from a cliff, he patiently waits for the right gust of wind so he can soar gracefully across the sky. Having a safety net support team and learning basic life skills will be your gust of wind to successfully transition from your parents' house. College life in the dorm can help you learn social skills and prepare you for independence.

REFLECT

1. Going away to college helped me learn life skills necessary for independence. What are some life skills you need to develop to live in an apartment or attend college?
2. Transitioning from your parents' home to a college dorm or an apartment can be challenging and rewarding. What are some challenges you think you would experience living in a college dorm or an apartment? List three qualities you would like in a roommate.
3. I budget my money by purchasing clothes and items out of season and using cash rather than credit cards. What are some ways you can also budget your money and save for the future?

FUN ACTIVITIES

Talk to friends or family members who attended college or a trade school and have them share their favorite memories. In your group or with a family member or friend, visit a college or trade school you would like to attend. Write some questions to ask during your tour, and meet with some faculty and students to gather more information.

With your group or a friend, write five things you desire in a home or apartment and three things you don't desire. For example, "I desire an apartment with a pool and nature trails, and I don't desire noisy neighbors who play loud bass or a living arrangement that does not allow pets."

At the top of the list, write, "Home Sweet Home." Next to each living-arrangement desire, paste or draw a picture that represents the thing you want, and next to each thing you don't want, paste or draw a picture of that thing. For example, I want a pool, so I would paste or draw a picture of a pool; or I want a pet, so I paste or draw a picture of a pet I would like.

Discuss your desired living arrangements with your group or a friend or family member, and share some challenges you may experience and the steps necessary to live on your own or with a roommate.

FURTHER READING

Parties, Dorms and Social Norms: A Crash Course in Safe Living for Young Adults on the Autism Spectrum, by Lisa M. Meeks and Tracy Loye Masterson

A Freshman Survival Guide for College Students with Autism Spectrum Disorders: The Stuff Nobody Tells You About!, by Haley Moss

Students with Asperger Syndrome: A Guide for College Personnel, by Lorraine E. Wolf, Jane Thierfeld Brown, and G. Ruth Kukiela Bork

Sydney Holmes's Story
Preparing for College Life

*I think I had a typical college experience. It was my first time
on my own and I had to restart and make new friends.*
—Sydney Holmes

During elementary school, Sydney Holmes was suspended for
more than fifty days for what the school called "meltdowns" or "escape
behaviors." She was expelled from or asked not to come back to three
different Christian schools. This made her feel misunderstood and unwanted by the schools and even the church, so in her elementary years,
she was often confused.

In fourth grade Sydney's mother left her career temporarily to
homeschool her and fill in the gaps from the missed school days and
to teach her social skills and emotional regulation. Sydney received
therapy to further help her develop social skills.

The Holmes family moved to another state for a school system
with better resources. In elementary school Sydney had a few friends,
and her mom had the Autism Society teach inclusion lessons to those
friends. Sadly, some parents and professionals lacked an understanding of autism.

In middle school Sydney developed the tools for socializing and
advocating, and her teachers were understanding of autism—but her

peers were less compassionate. She was bullied and felt excluded. When adults were present, Sydney's Girl Scout troop acted cordially, but at school these same girls were mean to her. One girl cruelly informed her, "I cannot be your friend because you're holding me back from the popular crowd."

Middle school and high school were tough for Sydney. In high school she focused on academics to prepare her for college and to avoid teen drama. While still in high school, she attended a community college and considered which career to pursue.

After community college, she attended Shorter University in Rome, Georgia, and received a bachelor of arts degree in history and a minor in education. "I was anxious about being too far away from home," Sydney says, "so I knew I did not want to be out of state. I was nervous about being too far away from my parents in times of an emergency."

Sydney wanted the freedom of experiencing life without feeling as if her parents were looking over her shoulder, so she wanted to be at least an hour or two driving distance away. She wanted a small Christian college with like-minded people with whom she could interact. She also wanted to learn from professors who could help her when her overthinking, anxiety-prone brain kept her from understanding assignments.

Sydney's biggest fear of college was not being able to graduate. She was terrified of being the stereotypical Aspie living in her parents' basement until she was thirty. This fear is what ultimately drove her toward success, because she still felt a need to prove to everyone that she was capable of being a fully independent adult. "My mom was my biggest supporter. She toured the college with me. We got to walk around and learn the layout, so I was not anxious about getting lost. Finding a new church home was scary, but my mom helped me find a place where we both felt I was going to be safe and loved."

Her mom also helped her learn the city—the locations of the grocery stores, urgent care, hospital, and diners. This eased her anxiety.

Her dad practiced the drive to and from school with her so she could feel comfortable navigating the route on her own.

Sydney pursued a history education major. She loved working with kids and wanted to work in a classroom. During the program, she realized that classroom and teacher politics were not for her, but she still desired to work with kids. After an internship at a local historic house, Sydney switched her major to history with an education minor. She developed skills to work with kids in a different and more creative setting: museums.

In college she learned to advocate and be more independent. Her biggest challenges were her anxiety from overanalyzing and her perfectionism. She was afraid of disappointing her professors with her work. "I asked the same questions about papers and assignments multiple times just to make sure I was doing the right thing."

Another challenge was friendships. "I don't think I really understood how to be a good friend until my junior year of college." Past relationships had taught her wrong and childish behaviors that she had thought were normal. She did not handle her first roommate situation well, as she was not quite sure how to communicate her feelings without sounding coldhearted and blunt. She also had to learn how to consider other people's feelings when expressing feelings of hurt, anxiety, burnout, and being left out.

Sydney learned to turn her OCD (obsessive-compulsive disorder) into a strength by being extremely well organized and having excellent time management. She was usually two weeks or, in some cases, a month ahead on assignments. She set her own deadlines for when she wanted things done. She was able to look ahead and see when multiple assignments would be due around the same time, and she planned accordingly, which reduced her stress.

Sydney's only college regret was in her sophomore year, which she calls her "prodigal year." She was friends with people she should have stayed away from and got into situations she should not have walked into. This was where her autism mind-blindness was a problem: "I could not tell when I was in danger or when people were trying to manipulate and hurt me. I dated a few guys my mother warned me to stay away from, which led to a whole catastrophic nightmare."

The most valuable lesson she learned was that she could not trust blindly. She wanted to see the good in people, but she learned that some people would take advantage of that. She had to learn whom she could trust.

In addition, she had to learn to read social situations. While she is still not great at reading social cues, she does think her time in college helped her grow in that area. She was able to become more self-reliant, trust her gut, and defuse situations if she messed up.

Sydney shared her autism diagnosis with her roommate and suitemates. She did not want them to think that some of her behaviors were because she hated them. "They deserved to know why I acted the way I did and that I had a hard time expressing my feelings. I thought it would help ease communication issues, and sometimes it did."

After the first day of class, she shared her diagnosis with every professor, mainly so they knew there would be times she would need extra assistance. She eventually shared her diagnosis with anyone she dated, though not right away. "I had to ease into that one. After my junior year, I was pretty open about my diagnosis and shared it with everyone: friends, church family, and social media."

Typically, her friends were supportive. They never took it personally if she felt overwhelmed and did not like hanging out. She eventually found good people. It just took a while to get there. Some friendships were made by extroverts adopting her into their circles. Others she sought out. "My main group of friends I actually initiated contact with through social media. I knew of them, and they were hosting a Bible study that they advertised on Instagram. I had a moment of courage and went spontaneously to their Bible study, and we have been friends ever since."

Sydney shares four tips for college students with autism:

- Stop hiding in the library or your dorm room and join a club. If you want friends, go out and make them. You cannot wait for extroverts to adopt you. Stop complaining that you are lonely, and go out there and meet people.
- Communication is essential for dorm success. Learn how to share space with someone and how to express what makes you feel safe, such as a heads-up if your roommate is bringing people into your shared space.
- Join clubs and organizations on campus. Being part of a larger community creates opportunities for fun adventures and to attend mixers, semiformals, formals, philanthropy occasions, and other events.
- Have fun and laugh. A small catastrophe, such as a bathroom flooding, might seem overwhelming at the time, but you'll see the amusement in it later. Try not to overreact but to find something in the situation to laugh about.

While transitioning to adulthood, Sydney learned valuable lessons, which include showing others you are not a stereotype, admitting when you're wrong, remembering to enjoy life beyond your education goals, and choosing a school that is a good fit—and find the disabilities office right away.

"I can control my career to some extent, finish my degree, find a job, and just do the best I can. I've come to understand that any social goals are more or less out of my control. I can't force people to be my friends or force a romantic relationship. I can only prepare myself to be the best version of myself when those opportunities arise."

Sydney has successfully defended her thesis and earned a master's degree in public history and a certificate in museum studies from the University of West Georgia. She works full-time in a museum helping children develop creative thinking, and she is creating new inclusive and sensory-awareness programs for the institution.

SYDNEY HOLMES'S BIOGRAPHY

Sydney Holmes is a proud Aspie and advocate for autism acceptance. Having navigated through homeschool, Christian school, public school, and college as a person on the autism spectrum, she loves to educate the educators on how to best include students on the autism spectrum in both education and the church setting. Sydney is available to speak at colleges and churches and to public school educators about autism acceptance and action for best inclusion practices, sharing her personal experiences of those who mentored and empowered her and the practices by well-intentioned professionals who were harmful and left a negative impact. She co-speaks with her mom, Dr. Stephanie Holmes, and serves on panels upon request.

REFLECT

1. Having a love for history, Sydney decided to pursue a history education major. What would you like to study in college or at a trade school, and why?

2. Sydney enjoyed her college experience more than her high school experience. Would you enjoy living in a dorm environment or an apartment more, and why? When considering attending a college or a trade school, what are some things you look forward to, and what are some fears you have? How can you overcome these fears and anxieties?

3. Of the four tips Sydney provides for college students with autism, which do you think would help you the most, and why?

Chapter 2

Living Healthy on the Spectrum

*A healthy life is one that is balanced
and living in the moment.*

—RON SANDISON

WHEN I WAS TWENTY YEARS old, I began a period of two decades without a doctor's appointment and six years without seeing a dentist. Fear kept me from scheduling these regular appointments. I was terrified of an abnormal lab result that would cause my primary physician to refer me to a specialist who would diagnose me with some rare, incurable disease or cancer. I was afraid that my dentist's intraoral X-ray would reveal thousands of cavities due to my binge candy-eating habits, which would deplete my savings.

My procrastination with health care and dental checkups ceased in September 2019 after I had my first colonoscopy at the age of forty-four. I learned the importance of annual checkups and eating healthy, balanced meals. In August 2019 I had been under extreme stress at work. I was constipated for two weeks and experienced pain in my stomach.

I googled my symptoms, and colon cancer was at the top of the list. I was terrified and contacted my primary doctor, and she referred me to a gastroenterologist, who ordered a colonoscopy. The GI doctor removed five polyps. For the next two weeks, I sweated and prayed, waiting for the lab results. I thank God that the polyps were noncancerous.

A few months after my colonoscopy, a close friend and autism advocate who was my same age was diagnosed with stage 3 colon cancer. For the next three years, he underwent more than forty chemotherapy treatments. Colon cancer is one of the most preventable forms of cancer, yet it is the third deadliest.[1] People with autism experience more digestive health issues, causing them to be at a higher risk for colon cancer, irritable bowel syndrome, and other illnesses.[2] Make sure you have a colonoscopy as scheduled, and, women—get mammograms as prescribed by your ob-gyn. This could save your life.

I learned a powerful lesson from my digestive pains, and this is a principle I live by: When you experience pain or symptoms, don't go to Google, but go to your doctor. Preventive health care with a healthy diet is the best way to stay healthy and enjoy life.

Don't allow fear or anxiety to keep you from your annual medical checkups. Common things happen commonly. Most medical conditions are easy to fix if a doctor is seen when a person is experiencing pain or symptoms. Those on the spectrum tend to think of the worst-case scenario when experiencing medical conditions that require lab tests or an appointment with a specialist. Don't become Dr. Wikipedia by googling your symptoms. This will only give you a list of the worst possible diagnoses—such as cancer or heart disease or kidney failure—and create fear and anxiety. Find a doctor and dentist who understands autism and with whom you feel comfortable.

When you experience a change in your health conditions, report it to a family member or a trusted friend and make sure to inform your doctor. Make it a rule that when you feel something unusual in your body, you tell somebody else immediately. They can help you determine the symptoms and let you know if they think your condition requires medical attention. People go to the doctor when they feel sick or when they experience pain from an injury, but some of us on the spectrum are hyposensitive to pain and discomfort, causing us to misinterpret our bodies' warning signals or fail to receive them.

My friend Angela Marquez shares, "People like my son, who are verbal but don't always know how to verbalize their physical feelings, need annual checkups. My son went with his grandpa to the dentist after telling me the night before that he had to go to the dentist. We got in quickly and discovered he had a terrible cavity on its way to infection."

Autism causes me to ignore pain and not respond to medical conditions as needed. I become hyperfocused on my special interests and can ignore severe pain. After a cross-country practice during my freshman year in college, I had extreme pain in my abdomen. I waited eight hours before telling my parents. By then the pain was unbearable. I was in the fetal position, unable to move. I was rushed to the emergency room, screaming in pain. When the ER doctor examined me, he discovered a testicular torsion requiring emergency surgery.[3]

The next day the surgeon came to my room and said, "Young man, I was baffled. Why would you wait eight hours to go to the ER when you were hurting so bad? Luckily, we were able to save your testicle. If you would've had the surgery any later, you would've lost it."

God was watching out for me. How do you know when to see your doctor immediately or to go to the emergency room?

When to see a doctor right away

- You have a fever of 102.5 or higher, or you have had a fever for more than a day or two and it is not going down.
- You feel so ill, weak, dizzy, or nauseous that you have difficulty getting out of bed.
- You are unable to eat or drink, or every time you do, you vomit.
- You have a common complaint, but it won't go away or takes a sudden turn. For example, you have a headache, but nothing

relieves it. Or you have acid indigestion even if you take antacid tablets and eat bland food.

- You have a common complaint to start, but it takes a sudden turn for the worse. For example, if you have a cold and suddenly your ear starts hurting, you may have an ear infection that needs medical attention.
- You fall down, bang your head, or crash into something and your body now hurts. If you are hyposensitive to pain, get an examination—even if you don't hurt or the pain is mild. You could have a serious injury you can't feel.
- You think some part of your body isn't working right or isn't working as well as it did. For example, you have heart pain or your heart races after taking your dog for a walk. Other examples include, but are not limited to, difficulty breathing, pain when urinating, or joint ailments.[4]

Three questions the doctor will probably ask you

1. What does your problem feel like?
2. How often do you have the problem?
3. Does anything help the problem or make the problem worse?

Answer your doctor's questions honestly, and don't be afraid or embarrassed to share the pain you're experiencing, even if it's in a private area. If you don't know the answer to a question, tell him, "I don't know" and "I'll get back to you with the answer." If you don't understand the question, tell your doctor, "I don't understand this question. Can you please explain it differently?" Don't be afraid to tell your doctor that you have autism and that it takes you longer to process information and answer questions. Also, if you have an appointment with a specialist, bring a family member or friend with you for support and to clarify your treatment plan.

Since most doctors only spend a few minutes with you, bring notes so you don't forget to share important information about your health and to remind you of questions to ask. If your physician warns you that your blood pressure or cholesterol is high, ask him for resources to help you with your health issues and how you should change your diet or lifestyle to improve your health.

Example of sharing about your abdominal pain with your primary physician

1. Describe symptoms: "I experience pain under my right rib and have gas and nausea."
2. Time: "I felt the pain and nausea late at night between 2:00 a.m. and 3:00 a.m."
3. Dates: "I felt the pain on December 9, 10, 12, and 14."
4. Describe the pain: "The pain felt dull. I also felt nauseated in the morning."
5. How the pain affected you: "The pain caused me to wake up and not be able to sleep."
6. Medical conditions: "I have acid reflux and high cholesterol."
7. Medication you take: "I take Simvastatin (high cholesterol) and Pepcid Complete (acid reflux)."
8. Question: "I typically lie on my right side. Can I do anything, such as prop myself up with a pillow or something, to help with the pain or nausea?"

By having a written description of my health concerns and questions related to my treatment, I receive the best care. This keeps me on track and prevents me from rambling on about my favorite topics that are not related to my symptoms.

Living Healthy

The most effective way to improve your health and well-being is by getting a proper amount of sleep, exercising daily, and sustaining a nutrient-rich diet. Where your mind goes, your body will follow. Our minds and bodies require eight to nine hours of sleep per night to function properly. Staying up late every night playing video games and watching movies will negatively affect our mental capacity and health. Tiredness will exacerbate our social difficulties with making friends or interacting with others and can make us more irritable, leading to a meltdown. Further, it contributes to psychiatric problems such as anxiety and depression.

Author Dr. Matthew Walker insightfully points out, "There is no major psychiatric condition in which sleep is normal. This is true of depression, anxiety, post-traumatic stress disorder (PTSD), schizophrenia, and bipolar disorder."[5]

Working in the mental health field, I have seen firsthand the ill effects of sleep deprivation. Lack of sleep can cause our minds to become delusional, create a loss of productivity, or make us hypomanic. After a few days of eight hours or more of sleep, many patients in the mental health ward for acute psychotic features or mania have been shown to have improved mental clarity and less disorientation. For these patients, sleep operated like a miracle drug.

Ten effects of sleep deprivation

Memory loss: Deep sleep converts short-term memory to long-term, and strengthens long-term memory. Sleep deprivation keeps this from happening and weakens our ability to remember.[6]

Inability to concentrate: Lack of sleep negatively affects our concentration and problem-solving skills, causing us to make unwise decisions and mistakes, while deep REM sleep enables us to make intelligent decisions by regulating our emotions and enabling us to focus on tasks.

Mood changes: People can see a difference in our moods and attitudes. When we are sleep-deprived, we are more easily agitated and moody, while a good night's sleep causes us to feel calmer and less anxious.

Accidents: Not getting enough sleep puts us at risk for car accidents. The risk is greatest for drivers who have slept fewer than four hours—they have 15.1 times the odds of being responsible for a car crash.[7] "Tragically, one person dies in a traffic accident every hour in the United States due to a fatigue-related error. . . . After being awake for nineteen hours, people who were sleep-deprived were as cognitively impaired as those who were legally drunk."[8]

Weakened immune system: Lack of sleep causes our immune system to be weakened in defense against viruses such as the flu or common cold, making us more vulnerable to sickness when exposed to germs.[9]

High blood pressure: "Sleep helps your blood regulate stress hormones and helps your nervous system remain healthy. Over time, a lack of sleep could hurt your body's ability to regulate stress hormones, leading to high blood pressure."[10]

Risks for diabetes: "Sleep deprivation sets the stage for diabetes by increasing the risk of resistance to insulin, a hormone that's essential for absorbing blood sugar and either converting it to energy or storing it. And insulin resistance is a precursor of diabetes."[11] Diabetes can take as much as ten years off an individual's life expectancy.[12]

Heart disease: Sleep deprivation may lead to heart disease through an increase in blood pressure and stress hormones linked to inflammation.[13] During sleep, one's "heart rate slows, blood pressure drops, and breathing stabilizes. These changes reduce stress on the heart, allowing it to recover from strain that occurs during waking hours."[14]

Weight gain: The chemical leptin tells our brains we have had enough to eat, and this prevents us from overindulging. Our bodies also produce the chemical ghrelin, which creates the hunger sensation. "Without enough sleep, your brain reduces leptin and raises ghrelin," making it more likely that you'll overeat when you're sleep-deprived.[15] New rule for grocery shopping: Don't go to the grocery store on an empty stomach or when you have had six or less hours of sleep.

Poor balance: Finally, lack of sleep affects our coordination and balance, making us more prone to falls and other physical accidents.

Four warnings signs of sleep deprivation

Four signs of sleep deprivation are chronic yawning, irritability, excessive sleepiness, and daytime fatigue. Caffeine and energy drinks can cause sleep deprivation to worsen by making it more difficult to fall asleep, so don't use them to cover your lack of sleep.

Dr. Matthew Walker recommends asking yourself two questions to see if you are getting enough sleep. First, when you wake up in the morning, could you easily fall asleep again within two hours? If the answer is yes, you probably are not getting sufficient sleep. Second, do you need a boost of caffeine before noon to function efficiently? If the answer is yes, you are probably using caffeine to cover your lack of sleep.[16]

Thirteen ways to improve sleep

1. Limit daytime naps and don't take a nap after 3:00 p.m.
2. Refrain from caffeine, coffee, and energy drinks.
3. Have a set bedtime each night.
4. The difference in bedtime on weeknights and weekends should be no more than one hour.
5. Wake up each day at the same time.
6. Don't use electronic devices with blue LED lights right before bedtime.
7. Exercise regularly but not right before bedtime.
8. Don't eat before bedtime; if you have acid reflux, refrain from foods that agitate it.
9. Refrain from studying or reading electronic books in your bed.
10. Do calming activities before bedtime such as taking a bath, listening to peaceful music, or using relaxation techniques.
11. Increase outside time during the day. Natural sunlight helps keep

your circadian rhythm in sync. This improves daytime energy as well as nighttime sleep quality and duration.

12. Put aside your worries.
13. Create a good sleep environment. Avoid using screens before bedtime. Keep your bedroom dark and use earplugs, a fan, or other devices to block out noises.

Daily Exercise

Autism causes me to love routines. My exercise routine consists of running, swimming, push-ups, and sit-ups. I try to do my exercises at the same time each day. In the summer I run and swim at 7:00 p.m. and do push-ups and sit-ups at 8:00 p.m. After a five-mile run, I feel re-energized, and my mind is fresh. Swimming takes away the tightness in my lower back and frees me from the stress of work. Regular exercise keeps my digestive system operating smoothly, prevents excessive weight gain, and enables my immune system to remain strong, preventing sickness. Many of us with autism are overweight or obese due to a lack of exercise, genetics, faulty digestive systems, and poor diets.

The prevalence of obesity in infants and children has more than tripled since the late 1970s in the United States.[17] "Children with ASD are more likely to be obese than children without autism, and obese children are disproportionately likely to have a neurodevelopmental disorder such as autism or attention deficit hyperactivity disorder (ADHD). . . . In addition, children with severe autism had a more than threefold greater odds of being obese compared to those with 'mild' ASD."[18]

Genetically, we tend to experience more health problems and have weaker immune systems. Exercise can enable us to live longer and have more satisfying lives. When I was eight years old, my family went on a vacation out west for three weeks. During this vacation, my parents discovered that if I did not eat protein every six hours, I would pass out and not wake up until the next morning. After returning home, the doctor ordered lab tests, and I was diagnosed with hypoglycemia (low blood sugar).

For the next five years, my parents used peanut butter to keep my blood sugar in balance. When I was thirteen years old, I participated in my middle school Olympic games and won a silver medal for the long jump. My new special interest and passion was track and field. I joined the track team and ran two miles each day. By eighth grade my hypoglycemia ceased, and I felt healthier and was no longer prone to sickness. My academics were also affected positively by athletics, and my anxiety and depression decreased.

Create an exercise routine

The American Heart Association recommends 150 to 300 minutes of moderate-intensity activity per week. Your exercise routine should include aerobic exercises—such as running, jogging, dancing, or swimming—which reduce the risk of cardiovascular disease, type 2 diabetes, and high blood pressure, and may even lower the risk of cancer.[19]

In addition to aerobic exercises, do flexibility stretches and strength training—such as squats, push-ups, crunches, and weight lifting (working your muscles by using resistance). Strength exercises increase lean muscle mass, which is important for weight loss because lean muscle burns more calories than other types of tissue.

Eric Chessen, director of Neuroadaptive Training and Innovation for Inclusive Fitness, and founder of Autism Fitness, says, "An effective fitness program is specialized for each individual and their physical needs, the same as it might for general populations. The exercise regimen should focus on strength, stability, and motor planning. It is important to focus on fundamental movement patterns; squatting, pushing, pulling, crawling, and carrying. The level of challenge will vary individually."[20] Eric Chessen's website, autismfitness.com, provides additional information on autism and fitness.

When you begin your weight training program, contact a fitness trainer and be sure to learn the proper form. "Start light with just one or two pounds. You should be able to lift the weights 10 times with ease. After a couple of weeks, increase that by a pound or two. If you can easily lift the weights through the entire range of motion more than 12 times, move up to a slightly heavier weight."[21]

Be sure your exercise routine includes stretching, which increases your flexibility and reduces risk of injury to your muscles.

An excellent way to get physically fit and make friends is by playing sports. Join a local softball or basketball team or join a gym that offers sports programs. Sports can boost your self-esteem and improve your hand-eye coordination. Playing baseball and running track and field helped me learn to control my sensory issues with sound and smell.

After you discover physical activities you enjoy, develop an exercise routine for each day and build upon it. Before you can race like a cheetah you have to be able to walk a mile or two without shortness of breath or fatigue. Begin by walking a mile or two on Mondays and Wednesdays. Write down the amount of time it takes you to complete the exercise activity, along with your goals. For example, say this past Monday you walked two miles in one hour. You hope in three months to walk three miles in an hour and fifteen minutes. Create a monthly calendar, marking how many miles you will walk or run each day with space to record your times. After a workout, provide yourself with a reward such as an energy bar, free time relaxing with a book, or some other activity you enjoy.

Eating a Nutritious and Balanced Diet

The best advice on nutrition and dieting is this: We are what we eat. This phrase is often attributed to the Greek physician Hippocrates, who is famous for coining the Hippocratic oath in the fifth century, which is still relevant. We cannot feast only on chicken nuggets, hot dogs, and pizza and expect to not feel sluggish or experience indigestion and heartburn.

The worst food for your body is processed food, which contains high amounts of sodium, potassium, and phosphorus. Processed food goes through fortification, preservation, or preparation that changes its nutritional composition when it gets canned, frozen, or packaged. Eating processed food can cause cardiovascular disease, kidney damage, and cancer.[22]

As a young adult, I loved eating spicy foods (such as Thai cuisine and jalapeños) and fatty foods. My motto was "The hotter the better," until acid reflux forced me to change my diet to bland, lean foods such as frozen vegetables and chicken. I learned to slow down when I eat and take smaller bites so my body can properly digest food. I quit drinking pop and energy drinks so I don't feel like a dragon blowing fire. I also take a multivitamin and vitamin C before work each morning to boost my immune system. However, don't use vitamins and supplements to replace a nutritious diet.

For a nutrient-rich diet, eat a variety of foods that provide the essential vitamins and minerals your body requires. Foods that are naturally rich in nutrients include fruits and vegetables, lean meats, fish, whole grains, dairy, legumes, nuts, and seeds. Focus on eating and drinking from the five food groups: fruits, vegetables, grains, proteins, and dairy.

Watch what you eat

If you have poor eating habits and a sweet tooth, consider talking with your primary care physician or a nutritionist and reading books on nutrition and fitness. Watch how much you eat and pay attention to your food selection. Don't be surprised that junk food produces unwanted weight.

It's easy to find yourself eating potato chips, ice cream, sugary cereal, and fatty foods, and quickly gaining ten extra pounds; and you will not stop there. After I got married, I went from 170 pounds—my ideal weight—to 195 in less than two years. This extra weight puts us at risk for high cholesterol, acid reflux, diabetes, and, later in life, heart disease. For me to lose those pounds, I had to exercise and change my eating habits.

One eating habit you can apply is to pay attention to your food portions. The secret to smaller portions is to eat slowly and to wait longer before getting seconds. You can often be as happy eating your four Oreos with milk as you would be eating ten in the same amount of time.

One final important food tip: Avoid eating too much red meat, which is rich in omega-6 fatty acids that can cause colon cancer.[23] Instead, eat more fish and shrimp, which are rich in omega-3 fatty acids that can help prevent cancer and heart disease.[24]

Closing Thoughts

Transitioning to adulthood requires us to take care of our health and well-being. No longer do we have our parents setting up doctor and dentist appointments, but we must take the initiative and do it ourselves. Healthy living is a result of maintaining a proper amount of sleep, getting daily exercise, and eating a nutritious diet. Exercise and diet will improve our mental health and increase our satisfaction with life.

REFLECT

1. Fear kept me from annual doctor appointments for more than twenty years. What are some fears you experience with doctor and dentist appointments? How can you have less anxiety visiting the doctor or dentist?

2. I enjoy running and swimming to stay physically fit. What are some exercises you can do to stay healthy? What are the best days and times for your weekly exercises?

3. We are what we eat. What are some foods you should eat in moderation? List foods that bother your digestive system or make you feel sluggish. How can you cut back on eating these foods?

FUN ACTIVITIES

Steve Smith, a nurse and my former co-worker, shares, "The body is a biological machine. Think of it like an automobile. You have a CPU. It's the brain. The brain has the coding that runs the rest of the body. You have an engine. That's the heart. There is a hydraulic system through veins and arteries. You have a built-in gyroscope for balance. Fat absorbs shock and insulates. We use fuel. Instead of gasoline we use food."

Since your body operates like a high-performance car, you should take care of it by eating healthy meals. This will help you to not feel sluggish or sick and hopefully live longer. For the next week, keep track of your eating habits. Record the four factors that affect your digestion, and share them with your group or a friend or family member.

Four factors that affect digestion

- When you eat: Record the time of day or night you eat.
- What you eat: Record everything you eat.
- How you eat: Record the amount of time it takes you to eat, fast or slow.
- Amount you eat: Record your portion size—small, medium, large, or supersized.

FURTHER READING

The Complete Guide to Autism & Healthcare: Advice for Medical Professionals and People on the Spectrum, by Anita Lesko

Why We Sleep: Unlocking the Power of Sleep and Dreams, by Matthew Walker

The Un-Prescription for Autism: A Natural Approach for a Calmer, Happier, and More Focused Child, by Janet Lintala, with Martha W. Murphy

Jackie Anne Blair's Story
Advocating and Serving in Health Care

*I'm often the first to hear alarms. I can differentiate sounds
quickly and more easily. My sensitivity to touch helps with
palpation during a nurse exam. I can feel if something is
different or off.*

—JACKIE ANNE BLAIR, RN

LIKE MANY WOMEN WITH ASPERGER'S, Jackie Anne Blair was diagnosed in early adulthood, at age nineteen. She was on her own in the middle of a huge transition, and the dorms were a bit of a sensory struggle. She would seclude herself when she became overwhelmed, but she had one meltdown in particular that made her go to the university's mental health office. After a few months working with the campus office, she was referred to a specialist who ultimately gave her a diagnosis.

Autism caused Jackie to have sensory issues and meltdowns. Her biggest sensory issues were touch and sound. She was not big into hugs or handshakes, and any surprise touches made her anxious. She also didn't particularly like loud noises—specific frequencies were a big issue. High-pitched noises and objects scraping against each other were the worst.

Jackie's greatest challenge was learning to socialize and adjust to college life. "Dealing with the change of location and support system while struggling to connect with my peers was overwhelming," Jackie says. Once she received her diagnosis, she was able to reach out online to other adults on the spectrum and build support. In the beginning, she wasn't open about her diagnosis with her family and college friends and spent a lot of time and energy masking. Masking became a way of life for her because hiding traits of her autism seemed easier at the time.

While dating, Jackie experienced socially awkward moments. On one particular date with a young man who asked her about her interests, she talked about her favorite football team. "He loved that I liked sports—until I word-vomited just about every statistic I knew about my favorite team." She eventually noticed his face—impressed and exhausted by her information.

"I laughed nervously. 'I'm guessing you didn't want to go on a date with a sports almanac.'" Luckily, that broke the tension, and he laughed back, but they never did make it further than friendship, and he continued to call her "Almanac" as a nickname.

Through trial and error, and the encouragement of close friends, Jackie learned to interpret social behaviors. "By upsetting a lot of people, I learned social clues." This used to be terrible for her. She knew she was saying things that bothered people, but throughout her teenage and early adulthood years, she couldn't grasp why it upset them. She couldn't understand why people asked questions but didn't really want the truth, or that there was more than one way to give truthful answers.

She became antisocial and introverted, because not having people around was easier than being around people who were angry with her or made fun of her. As she built a small group of solid friends, she was able to take notes on what was more appropriate. She then got a health care job in which part of the training was learning how to interact with people with developmental disabilities, including autism. Seeing the way neurotypical adults were trained to interact with the neurodivergent gave her some insight into the "appropriate" way to behave.

Working with individuals with disabilities inspired Jackie to study nursing. She worked for several years as an aide for the New York State Office for People with Developmental Disabilities in their long-term care facilities. Though being an aide was difficult in the beginning, she fell in love with health care, and she was good at it. An opportunity to go to nursing school through her union opened up, and she went for it, which was both exciting and terrifying. "Working in my current capacity in health care was already overwhelming for me. I wondered if I could overcome the added stresses and responsibilities of being a nurse. How was I going to handle life-and-death situations?"

Would she be able to quiet the constant noise inside her head or translate neurotypical behaviors quickly enough to function at the high-paced speed required by the profession? Despite all her insecurities, her work made her confident that she was a good caretaker.

Still, nursing school was extremely difficult for her. She had twenty students in her class and attended clinicals five days a week for seven hours a day. Jackie decided not to disclose her autism to her peers or instructors.

In nursing school, Jackie developed perseverance and compassion. The toughest part was her classmates. She was not well-liked. She used a lot of her social energy on her patients and even more energy masking her autism quirks while interacting with her classmates. "I was weird. I asked a lot of questions." It was hard for Jackie to be in a classroom of people who said they wanted to be compassionate caregivers but couldn't be nice to those learning alongside them.

Jackie's secret to interacting with co-workers is earning their respect through hard work and job performance. Interacting with peers had always been a big challenge for her. "I'm a little too blunt, or I'm too quiet, and I'm weird." She mostly focused on being good at her job and letting the rest fall into place. "Bullying is a huge problem within the nursing community. Neurodivergence adds another layer to that."

Working as a nurse required Jackie to adapt to sensory overload in the workplace. Her autism challenges her every day in her career. Certain noise frequencies make her anxious. When she first began a job outside of long-term care, she would listen to medical equipment sounds on a loop at home to get used to the stimulus.

Autism has provided Jackie with gifts as a nurse to serve patients and staff. She has an excellent memory. Her hearing is sensitive in a way that she can hear things others can't. She's often the first to hear alarms. Her sensitivity to touch helps with palpation during a nurse exam. She can feel if something is different or off. "I perseverate about my patient's issues. If something is off, or I just can't pinpoint a certain diagnosis or issue, I do everything I can to figure it out. I ask questions. I look things up. I defer to those above me. Whatever it takes."

She's also hyperaware of cross contamination and is obsessive about handwashing. She doesn't judge patients based on a diagnosis. "As your nurse, I understand that you are so very much more than the list of diseases, disabilities, and symptoms in your chart."

Jackie does not allow misconceptions about autism to hold her back but is an advocate for her patients and the autism community. She says that one of the main misconceptions about autism is a lack of empathy. "So many with autism are actually hyper-empathetic. I am so empathetic it's exhausting." She takes her empathy home. She worries about her patients around the clock. She visits former long-term care facilities and the patients there. "I build a bond that makes me an amazing caretaker. Yet so many in the medical field—aides, nurses, and even providers—can't get past this stereotype that those with autism lack empathy."

Jackie's son, who has characteristics of autism and ADHD, inspired her as an advocate. "By advocating, I demonstrate to my son that he, too, can accomplish his dreams by never allowing labels or misconceptions to hold him back."

As an advocate, Jackie would like the medical community to know that there needs to be more understanding in the ways that autism presents differently in females and males. Like many diagnoses, there is so much less research on female patients with autism. "Neurodivergence doesn't necessarily mean that a patient doesn't understand you. Speak to those with autism as you would any patient. Let us make decisions for ourselves, and trust that we know our bodies as well as neurotypical patients."

Jackie enjoys her work in health care and finds the medical field to be a fulfilling career. Her general demeanor, while straightforward, is calming. She's an excellent listener and de-escalator. She loves being able to connect with people in a way that makes them feel good about the care they are receiving.

Jackie shares some advice with young adults on the spectrum: "You don't have to know what you want or what you're good at right at eighteen years old. Try new things, learn as much as you can, and find what profession you see yourself in. It's okay to make mistakes and be bad at things in the beginning before you find what's worth the extra effort."

Jackie is currently taking classes to finish her prerequisites so she can attend graduate school, and she also enjoys spending time with her son.[25]

JACKIE ANNE BLAIR'S BIOGRAPHY

Jackie Anne Blair is a full-time mom and nurse in upstate New York. When not doing patient care or dealing with emergency boo-boos at home, she enjoys tabletop role-playing games, board games, Christmas movies, and writing responses to the crazy world around her.

REFLECT

1. What help did Jackie receive to pursue her passion to be a nurse? What are some ways your family and support team can empower you to accomplish your goals?
2. Jackie shared a socially awkward moment while dating. What

are some socially awkward moments you've experienced? How can friends help you feel more confident in social situations?

3. Jackie advocates to health care workers and doctors: "Let us make decisions for ourselves, and trust that we know our bodies as well as neurotypical patients." How can you be proactive in your health care treatment and make decisions for yourself? What are some ways you can share your health concerns with your primary doctor? Do you feel your primary doctor, or specialist, listens to your health concerns? Why or why not?

Chapter 5

Building and Maintaining Friendships

The most important ingredient in the formula of success is knowing how to get along with people.

—Often attributed to Theodore Roosevelt

The ability to delight makes friendships come naturally and produces an emotional connection. People love when we take an interest in the things they love and share in their passions. I was reminded of this principle by a message I received from a friend who has mastered the art of delight:

> Ron, I have enjoyed working with you over these past several years. Getting to know you and listening to you talk about all your passions like politics, your books, and even the honey badger on all his adventures will be something I miss as I leave for nursing school. I'll also miss being part of the "Dream Team." LOL. Keep up all the hard work, and one day when you run for Congress I'll make sure to vote for you—that way I can watch you take on all those people in

power for the little guy. You've been a true pleasure to work with and I hope you take good care. Happy holidays to you and your family.

Delight in communication can be as simple as sharing a picture of yourself with a college mascot when you just met someone who attended that university, or as complex as actively listening to a professor describe his latest invention and sharing in his interests.

Dr. Ami Klin, the Bernie Marcus Distinguished Chair in Autism at Emory University, in his lecture "Imagining a Better World for Children with Autism," noted on his screen, "Social Interaction Is the Platform for Brain Development."[1] The only problem is that those of us on the spectrum lack this innate ability to socialize, which most children master by age five or six. Communication can be learned, and those of us on the spectrum can create delight in conversation and build and maintain friendships, but it will require more work and practice for us. In this chapter, we'll learn effective communication skills and how to build and maintain friendships.

Four Steps to Creating Delight

When socializing, don't make it your goal to talk with every person in the room, but do connect with people who share your interests and values. Creating delight in these conversations can lead to friendships.

The first step to delight in communication is encouraging people to talk about themselves. People love to talk about themselves and share their stories. For this to occur, you need to create a common bond and break free from social scripts.

The typical questions of "What do you do?" and "Where are you from?" are so boring! It keeps people in their typical socially scripted answers. Instead, use more positive and exciting versions of these questions.

My favorites are "Work on anything exciting recently?" or "Any adventurous summer trips planned?" These always get great answers. Just make sure you have your own exciting answers ready to share. Asking these kinds of questions (along with a strong handshake and eye contact) will help you make a great first impression and spark interesting conversations.

Second, once you've created a spark, take time to listen before sharing your ideas. Slow down in conversation, as suggested by this African proverb: "If you want to go fast, go alone. If you want to go far, go together."

Once you're in a conversation, your goal is to have as many relatable moments as possible. These occur when you find a commonality. They create threads that tie you together and build loyalty. When you are listening, try to find and highlight these moments. Say, "Oh, I feel the same!" or "Me too!"

Third, make the person you're talking with feel important and valued. Good feelings make us remember the conversation and the person. Talking about themselves gives people pleasure. We can get people talking about themselves by highlighting their strengths and positive attributes.

Highlighting in conversations

- Listen with purpose; always search for good.
- Find something everyone loves to talk about and introduce it into the conversation.
- Be the high point of every interaction; give people a reason to remember you by making them feel good and want to be the best version of themselves.
- When you expect the worst, that's exactly what you get, so expect the best in people. Don't say "That idea is stupid" or "I hate cats." Instead, share things you have in common, such as "I also love dogs."

Finally, great conversations have spark. In the brain, sparks are marked by dopamine. Dopamine is a neurotransmitter that is released when we feel pleasure, and this greatly aids memory and information processing. When dopamine is released in our conversation, we remember both the conversation and the individual or persons with whom we were talking.

We can create spark in conversations by asking fresh questions and pushing hot buttons. These hot buttons are topics, hobbies, or activities that light up the person. You know you've hit a hot button when their eyebrows rise or they say, "Interesting!" Try to talk more about that. We are attracted to people who give us mental pleasure, push our hot buttons, keep us mentally alert, and learn our names. Again, avoid social scripts. If you keep using social scripts, you will be stuck in small talk forever.

For us to create delight in communication, we need to understand how people perceive us and redirect them to how they should see us. If you are shy, don't pretend to be outgoing. If you hate sports, don't act like a sports fanatic. Stay authentic. People can detect a fake. You can direct people as to how to perceive you by sparking an interest in conversations and sharing your passions and life. Self-confident people in social situations know their strengths and weaknesses and enrich others by their knowledge and gifts.

Don't become discouraged in learning social skills; it takes a lifetime and requires practice. As Dylan Volk, author of *Bad Choices Make Good Stories: My Life with Autism*, writes, "Having Asperger's, I wasn't born with the ability to read people. It's something I have to learn as I go. It never stops being something I need to work on. It's as if my whole life is like a school for social skills, but I'm never quite graduating."[2]

The Triple Threat

We decide if we like someone, if we trust someone, and if we want a relationship with someone within the first few seconds of meeting them. The power of our first impression lies not in what we say but in how we say it. The "Triple Threat," coined by Vanessa Van Edwards and explained to me when I interviewed her for my article "The Hidden Rules of Communication: How to Create a Lasting Impression,"[3] enables us to make a killer first impression by creating trust with our audience. Our hand gestures, posture, and eye contact create the Triple Threat. Our smile follows as the opening line.

First, using hand gestures in communication creates trust. The most popular TED Talkers used an average of 465 hand gestures in their presentations. Temple Grandin, Simon Sinek, and Jane McGonigal topped the hand gesture charts with more than six hundred gestures in their TED Talks.[4]

Researchers found that job candidates who use more hand gestures in their interviews are more likely to get hired.[5] Since hand gestures have such an impact on first impressions, keep your hands out of your pockets when you walk into a room or are waiting to meet someone. The easiest thing you can do to improve your first impression is to keep your hands visible.

Second, practice good body posture: straight back, visible hands, space between your arms and torso, and tilted-up head. When you have good posture, people view you as confident.

Third, make eye contact: Use eye contact to build trust. Eye contact is extremely difficult for those of us on the spectrum. I was unable to maintain eye contact until age thirty-four. It took me four years of hard work to master looking people in the eyes in conversation. Eye contact still does not come naturally for me.

Tips on maintaining eye contact
- Notice her eye color.
- Don't look over his head to scope out the scene.
- If eye contact feels unnatural or hurts, look at the person's forehead. Try not to look down at the floor.

Tactfulness

Proverbs 16:24 states, "Pleasant words are like a honeycomb, sweetness to the soul and health to the bones" (NKJV). Tactfulness and positive words will cause people to desire our friendship, while hurtful and unfiltered comments repel people. Nobody wants to be friends with someone who will embarrass them or act arrogantly.

Example of untactful behavior: While on an elevator, you ask each person their weight to figure out whether the combined body weight of the passengers exceeds the weight limit posted.

Three questions to ask to filter your comments and avoid embarrassment: Is it true? Is it kind? Is it necessary?

Is it true? Is what I am about to say based on facts or rumors, second-hand information, or opinions? A comment like "I think Bill stole the company computer because he's always on the internet at work" is based on opinion, not facts, and is a slanderous accusation against Bill's character and could get you fired.

Is it kind? Will what I'm about to say hurt someone's feelings? Don't tell a woman her new dress makes her look fat—even if she asks you. Instead, say, "The jeans look better on you than the short red dress." Temple Grandin says, "Where people are involved, err on the side of being too diplomatic, rather than too honest."[6]

Is it necessary? Is what I'm about to say economical with the truth and does it spare people the details? When people are gossiping to avoid offending others, don't join the conversation. Avoid sharing excessive details about your favorite topics or your personal life. Instead, give others a chance to share.

Those of us on the spectrum tend to miss abstract ideas and take everything literally. In a conversation, when you are unsure how to answer a question, take a second to ask yourself if a literal response matches the intent of the question. For example, someone might ask, "Do you know how to get to the library?" They are not looking for a yes or no answer, but for directions to the library. When in doubt, ask for clarification.

Becoming Socially Competent

Most people with autism have systemizing minds, which equips them to recognize patterns, such as bus schedules, and to engineer skyscrapers. But like the weather, most of our everyday behavior does not follow systemized patterns, and not having a highly developed empathy circuit makes social competency a challenge worth pursuing.

Becoming socially competent will empower you to be gainfully employed, experience independence, and enjoy meaningful relationships. People on the spectrum tend to learn social skills by watching others, modeling positive behaviors, interacting with family and friends, and reading books on relationships. Social competency requires self-awareness and understanding cultural norms. Think of the social world as a constantly moving river. It is never static. Just try to go with the flow.

Dr. Jed Baker, author of *Preparing for Life*, wrote:

> Most social skills rely on the ability to mentally adopt another person's perspective. For example, knowing why to say hello when you greet someone is based on understanding how others might think or feel if you ignore them rather than greet them. Knowing when to stop talking, take turns, respond to others' initiations, compromise, help others, or share, all come naturally when a person can easily take another's perspective. However, these social skills do not come naturally to autistic individuals, and must be taught explicitly if they are going to be mastered.[7]

Missing social clues can be embarrassing. Judy Endow shares her personal embarrassment of breaking a social rule:

> One day in the bakery department of my grocery store I saw a sign next to a plate of cookies that read "Free Cookies." I

thought it was a nice gesture on the part of the bakery department and promptly slid all the cookies off the plate into the plastic produce bag . . . in my shopping cart. A few moments later, the bakery lady chased me down shouting, "What is wrong with you?" She then proceeded to call me some derogatory names and said, "What kind of pig takes ALL the cookies?"

. . . Her shouting made me realize that even though the word "cookies" was plural on the sign, the plate of cookies was intended to follow the rules of grocery store samples: One Per Customer. . . . I switched grocery stores and never went back to that store due to my embarrassment.[8]

Becoming socially competent occurs by trial and error. When you make mistakes by doing something socially unacceptable, learn from them; don't view yourself as a failure or become isolated from society. Have friends and co-workers teach you social norms, and take notes. Always ask questions when in doubt, such as, *Why do people get offended when I tell them the truth? How do I rub people the wrong way by my actions or comments? What can I do to become less socially awkward?*

Qualities to Look for in a Friend

My dad is famous for saying, "You cannot hang around junkyard dogs and expect not to itch with fleas." He also says, "If you want to soar like an eagle, don't make friends with turkey vultures." Friends influence the course of our lives both positively and negatively. Therefore, we should be wise in the people we choose as our friends and acquaintances. I want my close friends to be honest, dependable, wise, ambitious, caring, nonjudgmental, good listeners, have positive attitudes, and find humor in life. Let's examine each of these qualities and how they impact friendship.

Honesty requires a friend to speak openly from the heart and not fear to speak the truth in love.

Dependability means keeping commitments and being on time. These friends don't leave you hanging when a better opportunity comes along.

Wise friends are those you go to when you are searching for practical advice or guidance, and they will keep you on track and help you make good decisions.

Ambitious friends have goals in life and don't play video games every night while feasting on potato chips and beer. They inspire and motivate you to reach your full potential, and they encourage you to take risks and try new activities.

Caring friends are sensitive to your needs—spiritual, physical, and emotional. When you make an unfiltered comment, experience a sensory overload, or melt down in public, these friends show compassion by helping you calm down, and they are not embarrassed by your autistic quirks.

Nonjudgmental friends accept you for who you are and don't judge others superficially by appearance, race, gender, or education. They try to understand people and see how differences make our world better.

Good-listener friends are generous enough to hear your stories and tolerate your autistic rants. They teach us to allow others to express their feelings and share their stories without interruption.

Positive-attitude friends view life's challenges as opportunities for growth. These friends achieve their goals and make a positive impact on your life.

Friends with good senses of humor make life more bearable and fun. Laughter defuses life's tensions; stimulates our hearts, lungs, and muscles; and increases endorphins, the feel-good hormone released by our brains. When we have friends like this, we experience less anxiety and become more creative and efficient in life.

Building Lasting Friendships

Daniel Tammet, an author and autistic savant, wrote, "I had eventually come to understand that friendship was a delicate, gradual process that mustn't be rushed or seized upon but allowed and encouraged to take its course over time. I pictured it as a butterfly, simultaneously beautiful and fragile, that once afloat belonged to the air and any attempt to grab at it would only destroy it."[9]

As a caterpillar metamorphosing into a majestic butterfly takes time, friendships also require time and work. In the 1980s, we had a perfect slogan from AT&T on how to maintain and build friendships: Reach out and touch someone. Today, text a friend. Give them a call. Meet up at a coffee shop. Invite them on activities. This will help you maintain friendships.

Lasting friendships are built around four simple rules.

Four rules of friendships

1. To have a friend, you need to be a friend. Don't do things that will annoy your new friend, like saying bad things about him behind his back or making plans to hang out and breaking those plans at the last moment.

2. Friends are loyal in good times and bad. Proverbs 17:17 says, "A friend loves at all times, and a brother is born for a time of adversity." When your friends are sick or in the hospital, visit them or give them a call or text to see how they are doing. If your friend needs a favor, offer a helping hand.

3. Friends keep secrets. Disclaimer: The only time you don't keep a secret is if your friend tells you that she is going to hurt herself or someone else or commit a crime. If a friend tells you any of these things, notify the proper authorities.

4. Friends show appreciation. When your friend helps, thank him and send a thank-you letter or give him a gift card to his favorite restaurant. Send Christmas cards to your friends, sharing how

much you appreciate their friendship. Occasionally email or text your friends with an encouraging word.

Four Types of Friendships

Friendships can be confusing. Sometimes people with autism will refer to a new acquaintance as a best friend or talk about their favorite celebrities as if they were close friends. Understanding the four types of friendships can help us to categorize our friends and the role they play. The four main types of friendships are acquaintance, friend, close friend, and best friend.

An acquaintance is someone you know casually but, unlike a friend, you don't go to movies or bowling together or talk on the phone. The maintenance man at my apartment is an acquaintance. When I see him working, I say hi and may have a short conversation, but we don't hang out or chat on the phone.

A friend is a co-worker, neighbor, member of your church, or someone you talk with on the phone from time to time and meet to go places. You share common interests with your friends and enjoy each other's company. When you have a problem or need someone to talk with, your friends are there for you. Just remember that the bigger the problem you need help with, the closer your friend should be.

A close friend provides emotional support and remains your friend during good and bad times, without exception. You talk with these friends regularly and, if they live nearby, go places together. My college friend Dave is a close friend. We talk regularly on the phone and send each other Facebook posts. Since he lives in Texas, we don't see each other often, but we stay in touch.

The difference between a friend and a close friend is that a close friend is someone you cherish, think of fondly, and no matter what you do or where you are in your life, you would drop everything to be at her side if she needed you. A friend can move to the category of close friend by any situation, including sharing life experiences, helping each other in times of hardship, working together for a long time, or staying friends for many years. Close friends feel like family to you.

Your best friend is the first person you call when you get good news or want to go out for a bite to eat. Many times with autism, our best friend is a family member who is a main part of our support team. A best friend will help carry your burdens and celebrate life with you. Your best friend knows every detail of your life, and you can finish each other's sentences. These friendships can be rough at times because you go through the bad as well as the good with each other, but it's all worth it because these experiences just make your friendship closer. It is common for people with autism to have their pet as their best friend. When I get home from working a double shift at the hospital, the only two waiting for me are my dog, Rudy, and my cat, Frishma.

Friends are even tied to longevity. Studies reveal that maintaining friendships, along with physical exercise, can add years to our lives.[10]

Closing Thoughts

The ability to delight in communication and the art of tactfulness can enable us to have confidence in social situations and make friends. We develop friendships by taking an interest in peoples' lives and hearing their stories. Listening is different from hearing. Listening is an active process of discovering common interests, building upon them, and creating a foundation of trust. We build and maintain friendships through communication, hard work, and trust. Friendships have a powerful impact on our health and quality of life.

REFLECT

1. How can you create delight in your conversations and not use scripted lines?

2. I mentioned the qualities I look for in friends. What are some characteristics you desire your friends to have?

3. What challenges do you experience in social settings, and how can you overcome them?

FUN ACTIVITIES

With friends, family, or in a group, role-play a conversation with someone you just met. Don't use scripted lines. Create delight in your conversation by asking exciting and new questions. Use active listening skills by reframing and repeating back what you hear. Look for common interests with the person you're talking with, and use the "Me too!" method to create a spark. Practice the Triple Threat of hand gestures, body posture, and eye contact. Debrief with the other participants how you can improve your conversations and make a lasting first impression.

FURTHER READING

What to Say Next: Successful Communication in Work, Life, and Love—with Autism Spectrum Disorder, by Sarah Nannery and Larry Nannery

Captivate: The Science of Succeeding with People, by Vanessa Van Edwards

Unwritten Rules of Social Relationships: Decoding Social Mysteries Through Autism's Unique Perspectives, by Temple Grandin and Sean Barron

Juliana Fetherman's Story
Making Authentic Friendships

Everyone deserves someone, and everyone deserves a friend.
—JULIANA FETHERMAN

JULIANA FETHERMAN IS THE CREATOR of Making Authentic Friendships (MAF), a mobile app that helps teenagers and adults with special needs to connect and make friends based on their age, diagnoses, common interests, and geographical location. Juliana's favorite function of her app is conversation prompting, which helps the user start and keep a conversation going by providing conversation tips. She was inspired to create the app by her younger brother, Michael.

Michael was diagnosed with ADHD at age two and autism at age eight. As the older sibling, Juliana was kept in the loop with Michael's therapy and the resources he needed. Helping Michael caused Juliana to develop compassion, patience, and understanding. These qualities prepared Juliana to create MAF.

Juliana shares, "Michael lacked the social skills to develop and maintain friendships. I felt bad doing things and going places without him. When I left Michael behind, I felt guilty because I felt like I was leaving him by himself. I desired to teach him skills to start conversations and keep them going."

Michael's family was actively involved in developing his individual education plan (IEP) and therapy, and provided him with love, acceptance, and support. In high school, Juliana started an anti-bullying club. As a cheerleader, she got the support of the cheerleading squad and football team to help students with autism feel included in school events. In college, Juliana was the president of the autism club and decided to dedicate her life to helping people with autism and disabilities.

Juliana and her parents encouraged Michael to socialize and make friends by leaving the comfort of his room and doing things other than watching Netflix or playing on his iPad. They encouraged him to go for walks for fresh air or to venture to the store to meet new people and learn social skills. The more Michael was in the community, the more his social skills developed.

Michael and Juliana share a close connection. "It's nice to have someone who is a built-in best friend. Michael and I have always been very close. Our sibling bond is different. Michael is a man of few words. I do a lot of talking, and he does a lot of listening. Through our app we have had fun traveling the country and doing TV interviews and attending promotional events."

Michael is an awesome younger brother to Juliana. He loves her so much and always gives her hugs and kisses. They love doing things together, such as going to the movies and bowling. Friendships and social interactions are hard for Michael. Juliana always had plans and friends to go places with on the weekend, and Michael never did. As Michael matured, he became more aware of his loneliness and desired to have friends.

After Juliana reflected on her middle school and high school years and remembered that many weekends she had plans with friends and her brother didn't, she created the Making Authentic Friendships app, or MAF, which also happens to be Michael's initials "because he is the inspiration for MAF," Juliana says.

Michael has difficulties making friends and feels lonely, and this app helps him and others build lasting friendships and have people to go places with. The app's catchphrase is "Everyone deserves someone, and everyone deserves a friend."

At only twenty-seven, Juliana has already achieved things she never thought possible. Creating MAF was only made possible by the support of her family and many people giving their time and resources. Juliana raised $25,000 through private investors and another $25,000 through charity golfing events. She implemented a plan to market her app through interviews and podcasts. She also learned to pitch her product to national TV shows and radio stations. "My 'why' is Michael and his community." In October 2020, Michael and Juliana were even guests on the *TODAY* show. "It was a humbling experience letting the whole nation know about MAF," Juliana says.

MAF is unique by focusing solely on friendships and not dating. The app works like a game, making it fun and interactive. Users create an avatar of themselves and can earn coins as rewards. The user picks the outfit, hair, and color of their avatar, matching their interests. Also, MAF has a web team in place to monitor the app, keep users safe, and prevent harassment. Any inappropriate language or content gets flagged, and the web team reviews it.

Juliana's app is already helping people with autism make friends. A boy living in the United Kingdom told Juliana that the app changed his life and gave him the chance to find someone who liked *Star Wars* just as much as he did. During the COVID-19 pandemic, the user base doubled.

The TV and radio interviews from MAF have helped Michael gain self-confidence. Because of MAF, Michael is video chatting, making lasting friendships, and feeling less alone. The more he uses the app, the more comfortable he is with it.

MAF is currently serving the special needs community in all fifty states, seventy-five countries, and five continents, and has more than eight thousand users. MAF also has more than twenty-eight thousand followers between Facebook and Instagram.

Juliana's goal is to bring awareness to the autism and disability community. She hopes to help people with disabilities gain employment and improve their quality of life by having authentic friendships.

JULIANA FETHERMAN'S BIOGRAPHY

Juliana Fetherman founded Making Authentic Friendships, an app that enables individuals with special needs to make friends. It was inspired by her brother Michael, who has autism. The app has thousands of users in all fifty states and seventy-five countries. It has been featured on Lifetime, *TODAY*, CNN, *Forbes*, and *Entrepreneur Magazine*.

MAF link: makingauthenticfriendships.com.

REFLECT

1. How has your family shown you love and support like Juliana did for her brother Michael?
2. Why do you think an online app would be a good way to meet friends, or do you not think it is a good way?
3. Share three tips your family has given you for making friends.

Chapter 4

Avoiding the Pitfalls of Dating

Dating is really hard because everyone puts on a front.
It's really difficult to see who is who, so it is
important to be yourself.
—BROOKE BURKE, an American actress and model

FOR ME, DATING WAS LIKE walking blindfolded through a minefield. One wrong comment or social mishap, and the relationship ended before it even had a chance to begin. Unsuccessful dating adventures taught me how to navigate through the pitfalls of romance. Dating is painful, and you will likely have your heart broken a few times before you meet the person you will marry or have a stable relationship with. When you decide to date, make sure you're emotionally and psychologically ready to get into a relationship.

Healthy relationships require us to know our expectations. What is our reason for dating? Is it to meet a spouse or to have a fun time meeting new people?

There is a difference between dating and a committed relationship. Dating is more casual and is centered on activities, while a relationship is more like sharing your life with someone. You no longer want to just date. You begin to care about your partner in a deeper way, desiring to help him or her in daily life and making plans for the future.

Meeting someone is easiest when you're not trying too hard. The important thing is to be involved in activities you enjoy. If you're enjoying yourself and you like your life, other people will take notice and respond to your positive energy. People are attracted to self-confidence. In dating, self-confidence comes from knowing your strengths and how to compensate for your weaknesses. Zosia Zaks, an author with autism, writes on relationships:

> Autistic partners can provide a stabilizing force in a relationship.
>
> We are adept at balancing emotional extremes with intellectual insight and objective analysis. When it seems as if the rest of the world is falling apart, we are plodding away, one task at a time, putting one foot in front of the other until we reach the goal.
>
> We value logic and can check overwhelming feelings with a rational approach. We can be wholly unaffected by chaos, concentrating instead with our gifts of intense focus on the main thing that has to happen next.[1]

One typical weakness is lacking the innate ability to decode body language or understand social norms. More than half of communication is nonverbal. Body language, unlike verbal communication, rarely lies. If a potential romantic partner is not interested in you, the actions will show it: folded arms, glancing around the room, checking the cell phone, or calling another friend over to create an easy exit route.

Literal thinking causes us to misinterpret dating lingo. For example, a guy you're interested in says, "You're a great girl, but I am currently focusing on academics and am busy with my job"; or if religious, "I am focusing on God right now"; or my favorite, "I am dating Jesus." These are all nice ways of saying, "I am not interested."

When you ask a girl out and she says, "Going out for coffee would be fun. If something comes up, you'll be the first to know," then she's turning you down nicely.

Those of us on the spectrum don't like to sugarcoat. We tend to say what we think—unfiltered. When I was a junior in high school, a girl I was not interested in from my church youth group called and asked me to the school dance. I told her, "I already asked a girl to the dance."

"What if that girl says no?"

"Then I would ask another girl to the dance. I have to go. I am playing *Super Mario*," I replied, and then hung up.

If I had the chance to go back to my college days at Oral Roberts University, where the ratio was five girls to every guy, the one thing I would've done differently is to realize that if a girl was not interested in me, she never would be. I would have shaken the dust off my feet and pursued another girl who was interested, instead of being hung up on one girl for the rest of the semester.

Obsessive passion isn't a healthy basis for a relationship. Autism can cause us to become depressed by being obsessed with one girl or guy. One of my friends said, "Women go to a bar knowing; guys go hoping." In other words, when a woman meets you, within the first three minutes she already knows if she would want to date you. God does not cause a person to love another person against his or her free will. If you can learn this, you will be ahead of the dating game.

A scene in *Dumb and Dumber* beautifully illustrates the principle that if the person you like is not interested in you now, they never will be. The problem is that many guys on the spectrum act like the character Lloyd Christmas.[2]

Lloyd Christmas: I want to ask you a question, straight out, flat out, and I want you to give me the honest answer. What do you think the chances are of a guy like me and a girl like you ending up together?

Mary Swanson: Well, Lloyd, that's difficult to say. We really don't—
Lloyd Christmas: Hit me with it! Just give it to me straight! I came a long way just to see you, Mary, just . . . The least you can do is level with me. What are my chances?
Mary Swanson: Not good.
Lloyd Christmas: You mean, not good like one out of a hundred?
Mary Swanson: I'd say more like one out of a million.
Lloyd Christmas: So you're telling me there's a chance. Yeah!

The concept of *matching hypothesis* says that people are more likely to form successful relationships with those they match in physical attractiveness, education, intelligence, and social desirability, among others.

Dr. Stephen Shore, a professor with autism, encourages young adults on the spectrum to meet people from a different country who also experience social awkwardness because of learning a new culture and social norms.[3] Dr. Shore's wife is from China. I had a friend who has Asperger's and would meet girls at the Polish culture club. He would say, "These beautiful women from Poland have no mode of transportation, and I have no date. It works perfectly."

Pitfalls

Nothing good in life comes easy. Dating can be difficult, but when you meet someone who loves you and shares your passions, you realize that it's well worth the work. Learn the seven pitfalls of dating.

1. Pitfall of emotional overdrive

Asking a girl out on a date caused me to be emotionally overwhelmed with fear of rejection. I stumbled over my words and forgot what to say. On a first date in high school, I was so nervous that I mistook the popcorn in my hand for my drink and spilled the popcorn all over myself as I attempted to gulp it down.

Dating requires taking risks and being vulnerable about our emotions. When you date, you take the risk of having your heart broken and experiencing emotions you don't know how to control or express. Those of us on the spectrum find it difficult to express our emotions verbally. Knowing what you feel and what to do when you feel that way will enable you to respond to the social world more quickly, more accurately, and with less confusion.

I experienced less emotional overdrive by asking girls on dates who were already my friends. When looking for someone to date, start with PAL: play it cool, ask, and let it be.

Play it cool by attending events that the person you like also attends, and talking to the person. Once you develop a connection and know his or her interests, think of a fun activity you're both interested in, such as bike riding, playing video games, or going to the art museum or zoo.

You can *ask* him or her out by saying, "Would you like to go to the zoo with me? They have a great new polar bear exhibit." If you ask someone out in person, make sure you do so in a way that is completely private, with no one overhearing.

Finally, *let it be.* Don't keep pushing the person to go out with you. If he says, "I am busy next week," give him a week and follow up. If he cancels again or shows signs of disinterest, such as not returning your phone calls or texts, let it be—and look for someone else to pursue.

Don't let your emotions control your relationships by overanalyzing every detail of the person you date. For example, "My date called me three times this week. He really has the hots for me," or "He forgot to call me after class, so he must not think I am attractive."

2. Pitfall of the spare-tire relationship

A spare tire is an additional tire carried in a motor vehicle as a replacement for one that needs replaced unexpectedly. Likewise, a replacement relationship that is not permanent is a spare tire. Autism makes you an easy target to be used like a spare tire by someone you have romantic feelings for. Some signs of being used as a spare tire: Your date only calls you when she needs a ride or has no other plans. She also quickly cancels her plans with you when she thinks a better opportunity presents itself. He does not introduce you to his friends or family. When he is with the popular crowd, he acts like he does not know you.

You can discern if the person you're dating is using you by considering these questions: Does this person show actual interest in you as a person, or does she always contact you to request that you do something for her? Do you hear from him only when he needs help of some kind? Does he show respect to you? Does she tell you she is your girlfriend and then says things behind your back? A spare-tire relationship will hinder you from meeting someone who will treat you with love and respect.

3. Pitfall of obsession

Our intense focus on details can help us be successful in a career or academics, but in dating it can lead to a restraining order. Dr. Lindsey Sterling explains that "even with the best of intentions, intense attention like repeated text messages can feel threatening to someone else. Make sure this attention is being reciprocated before making your next move."[4]

If you find yourself obsessing over someone, give him or her space. You don't want the person you like to feel uncomfortable when you're around or, worse, tell her friends you're a stalker. When dating, don't share your feelings too quickly. On a first date, don't tell your date, "You're the girl I waited my whole life to meet. I love you and want to spend the rest of my life with you." Instead, play it cool. Wait to give her flowers until your third date or to take her for a candlelit dinner until you've been dating for a few weeks or months.

Absence makes the heart grow fonder. Remember this: The busier you seem, the more desirable you become. People want what they cannot have; women and men love the challenge of the chase. Most women are turned off by a guy who constantly calls her and is insecure. When dating, at least once a month hang out with your friends. You can have a girls' shopping day or a guys' night out to watch a sporting event.

When thinking about getting closer to someone, maintain a comfortable level of physical and emotional closeness in your interactions. Never try to pressure your date to do anything he or she feels uncomfortable doing or believes should wait until marriage.

4. Pitfall of miscommunication

On a first date, two topics you should never discuss are religion and politics. Sharing your faith with a fellow believer is fine, but overwhelming your date with theological information can be a turnoff. In conversation, observe the body language and facial expressions of your date. If your date rolls her eyes when you are speaking, it likely means that she thinks something is not quite right with what you are talking about or how you are expressing yourself. It could mean that she thinks what you are saying is boring. If that happens, it's a good idea to finish your sentence and stop talking.

If you say something offensive, by all means apologize. "I'm so sorry—I really did not mean that the way it came out." Wait for her to respond, add a quick follow-up "Sorry" if necessary, and then change the subject. Whatever you do, don't try to justify or explain away what you just said because then you are holding everyone hostage in the offensive place you've created.

5. Pitfall of isolation

Dating requires you to be social and go out in public. You can't be like a prairie dog burrowing underground from society and expect your mate to find you. To be successful at dating, you have to leave your comfort zone. You can accomplish this by joining clubs on your college campus, attending social events, and dating online. Another great resource is Meetup, an online social network that facilitates group meetings in various localities around the world. Meetup allows members to join groups unified by a common interest such as politics, books, games, movies, sports, pets, careers, and hobbies.

6. Pitfall of discouragement

Don't allow discouragement to hinder you from dating. Remember— there are plenty of fish in the sea, and the secret to dating is perseverance. It can feel discouraging to meet someone only to have the date not develop into a second date or a relationship. There are also people who "breadcrumb date"—they lead you along with emails, texts, or calls while having no intention of a serious relationship or commitment. These people breadcrumb date because they enjoy the attention and pursuit. The only word to describe breadcrumb daters is *cruel*.

7. Pitfall of rejection

When you experience rejection in a romantic relationship, view it as a learning opportunity. When I was a sophomore in high school, I was on the phone with a senior girl I liked. I was about to ask her out on a date, when she said, "Why does your voice lack inflections? You sound like a Transformer." I thought I'd be cute, so I said, "I am more than meets the eye." But I still did not get a date with her.

Many of us know from personal experience that it feels like physical pain when we are rejected. The most painful rejection is when you're in a relationship, things are going great, you're ready to take it to the next level, and the person decides to break up with you.

Here are some classic breakup lines: "I just don't want to be in a relationship right now." "I just want to be friends." "I need some space." If the person you have been dating gives you any of these lines, it means he or she is not interested in you; don't wait for this person.

The best thing you can do is meet someone new who is interested in spending time with you. After a breakup, you should not reach out to the person. Don't call, text, or check their Facebook status updates.

After a breakup, if you find that you can't stop thinking about the person who broke your heart, if you're too depressed to resume your daily life or hang out with friends, if you can't concentrate at work or school, if you feel unlovable, or if you feel like giving up altogether, it's time to get help. Talk to somebody you trust or a professional counselor who can help you sort out and manage your confusing thoughts. A great book on breakups is *It's Called a Breakup Because It's Broken: The Smart Girl's Breakup Buddy*, by Greg Behrendt and Amiira Ruotola-Behrendt.

Success

After learning to avoid these land mines in dating, I discovered five ways to be successful in dating and romantic relationships.

1. Online dating enables you to communicate with a potential date before you meet in person, making you feel less social anxiety.

There are four important safety rules with online dating. When you meet someone in person, meet in a public location and don't go to their home after the first date. When you plan to meet someone, make sure that a family member or friend knows where you are meeting and what time you expect to be home. Don't give any personal or financial information online, such as your social security number or credit card information. Finally, even if your date tries to make you feel bad and tells you a sad story about why he really needs money, tell him, "Sorry. I don't have any spare cash," and don't plan a second date with that person.

Now the good news about online dating. There are millions of Americans using online dating websites and apps. I met my wife, Kristen, using an online dating site. After becoming discouraged trying to meet women at church and singles groups, my friend Matt persuaded me to create an online profile. Three years later I met Kristen, and after dating for a year and a half, we got married on December 7, 2012.

For successful online dating, you need a good profile and pictures. It's worth noting that "72% of women say it was very important to them that the profiles they looked at included the type of relationship the person was looking for, compared with about half of men (53%)."[5] You can improve your online profile by writing a positive, basic description of yourself, sharing what is unique and exciting about you. Some information to include in your profile should be your gender, age, height, religious background, interests, and what you're looking for in a relationship.

Online profile pictures should include one professional picture of yourself and at least three action photos. These action photos can show you playing sports or participating in an activity you enjoy, such as running or a chess club. You can include pictures with your friends, a pet, or a vacation, with a cool background of mountains or the ocean.

Don't put up a picture of yourself from five years ago, or a picture of you with a sad or disturbed face. And don't use a picture with your ex-girlfriend or ex-boyfriend cut out of it, or other cheesy photos.

Three tips for online dating: Be prepared with what to say in case the person who looked attractive in the pictures shows up looking unusually unattractive. Make sure you don't say something you will later regret; instead, always have an exit plan. My exit for this scenario was to have a friend call me twenty minutes into my date so if I was not feeling it, I had a reason to leave.

The more dates you go on, the better you become at judging your date's character and what you want in a relationship.

The first message can be a deal-breaker. Craft a message demonstrating your compatibility. If the person you're messaging has a picture of his or her pet cat, share an interesting cat story. Avoid copying and pasting generic messages. Make your messages personable and interesting. Also, have a friend read over your message before sending it, and always use spell-check.

2. Romance flourishes with communication.

People love talking about themselves and their interests. While on a date, make thoughtful observations and ask pertinent questions that spark conversation. Read chapter 3 for more details on this topic.

Ask good questions such as, "What was the last book you really got into?" or "Have you traveled to any cool places this year?" Make sure your questions are not too personal, such as "How many guys have you dated?" or "How much does your job pay?" Also, give your date time to answer your questions, and don't interrupt.

When in a group setting on a date, find something everyone in the group loves to talk about and introduce it somehow. For example, you could ask, "Have you tried the new Italian restaurant downtown?" or "Have you heard about the upcoming Vincent van Gogh exhibit at the art museum?" Be economical with the truth and spare people too many details.

3. Romance flourishes when you find a person who accepts your quirks and special interests.

I collect Calico Critters—three-inch-tall animal figurines dressed in handmade outfits. I had hundreds of unopened boxes lined up in perfect rows against my bedroom wall at my parents' house. My dad, with a concerned voice, said, "No woman will want a husband who collects children's toys and stuffed animals." Kristen proved him wrong by her unconditional love.

As a gift for the one-year anniversary of our first date, Kristen gave me the Calico Critters Meerkat Family. Two years later, we had Calico Critters on our wedding cake—the bride and groom were cats and the priest a beaver. During our honeymoon in the Windy City, as we walked from the train station to our hotel, an angry honey badger stuffed animal in a storefront display window caught my eye. My special interest took the best of me, and the honey badger found a new home.

4. Romance flourishes when you make your date feel important.

Always make your date feel like the most important person in the room. You can make your date feel important by listening to her and not talking about past relationships. Never talk about an ex-girlfriend on a first date, even if she talks about her ex-boyfriend. Remember this: How a woman talks about her ex is the same way she may talk about you someday.

A heartfelt compliment makes a date feel valued as long as the praise is genuine and personal, but be careful not to use flattery or be effusive.

Give compliments based on character and interests, such as "I love how last summer you traveled to Africa on a safari" or "It's cool how you and your dad go deer hunting every fall." Only give a compliment or mention that you're enjoying yourself if you mean it, because people can smell a fake. Don't overpraise or it will come across that you're working too hard. One or two compliments is plenty.

5. Romantic relationships require maintenance.

After a few months or years, when the newness and excitement wear off, you can begin to take your partner for granted. It evolves slowly: less romantic dinners, forgetting a card and chocolates on Valentine's Day, or worse, not remembering her birthday.

Remember, men—women desire to be pursued. Don't take your girlfriend for granted. Continue to do special things for her such as buying her flowers, taking her for a romantic dinner, or writing her a kind letter. Keep the pursuit alive. Women, your boyfriend loves praise for the things he does right. Growth in a relationship requires you to do things together that you genuinely enjoy. Try coming up with things that you enjoy doing together, and do more of those.

However, don't place all your hopes and dreams in your partner, or you'll be disappointed. Unrealistic expectations can be toxic to relationships, so leave space for imperfection.

Closing Thoughts

Relationships are challenging and confusing at times. View each date as an opportunity to grow and learn about yourself and the person you are interested in. Be aware of the pitfalls in dating. Always be yourself, enjoy life, and above all, stay safe. I want to leave you with this thought: The amount of energy it takes for you to date a girl or guy is the same amount of work it will take to maintain the relationship.

REFLECT

1. I described seven pitfalls I experienced when dating. What are some pitfalls you've experienced in dating? How can you conquer these pitfalls?
2. In dating, my greatest challenge was filtering my comments. What social mistakes have you made on dates? How did your date respond to your mishaps? Who are a few friends who can give you pointers on dating and romance?
3. Relationships require maintenance. What are some fun ways you can keep romance fresh and exciting? Where are some interesting places you could go on a date? Share three ways you can make your date or romantic partner feel important.

FUN ACTIVITIES

Write a positive description of yourself that you can use on a profile for online dating. In this profile, share what is unique and exciting about you. After you write the profile, have a few of your friends and your support team read it over and share their insights. Make a list of places you would enjoy taking someone on a date.

FURTHER READING

Love and Asperger's: Practical Strategies to Help Couples Understand Each Other and Strengthen Their Connection, by Kate McNulty

Love, Sex, and Lasting Relationships: God's Prescription for Enhancing Your Love Life, by Chip Ingram

Autistics' Guide to Dating: A Book by Autistics, for Autistics and Those Who Love Them or Who Are in Love with Them, by Emilia Murry Ramey and Jody John Ramey

Armando Bernal's Story
Romance and Love on the Spectrum

My fiancée loves me for me.
—Armando Bernal

When Armando Bernal was three and a half, he was diagnosed with autism and placed in a preschool program for children with disabilities in Houston, Texas. As a young child, Armando's special interest was the zoo.

Growing up, he believed he could talk to animals. When his family visited the zoo, he would rush to the meerkat exhibit and make funny sounds and noises at them. He pretended he could speak their language. His parents were embarrassed because he just kept chattering uncontrollably.

"Now," he says, "whenever my fiancée and I go to the zoo, the first animals we visit are the meerkats."

From an early age, Armando learned to mask his autism quirks from his peers. His biggest struggle was understanding how different his life was because of his autism and how that affected his relationships, both personal and professional. Throughout his life he learned to mask his behavior in order to fit in. Over time, it has just become a part of him, but every once in a while he still feels overstimulated or exhausted from his environment and sensory issues. When this occurs, he shuts down from everyone and everything.

Learning to control feelings and emotions was a challenge. Armando decided to acknowledge his feelings of frustration and stress in social situations and not allow his fears to hold him back from experiencing new things. He found support from family and friends to process his emotions and understand how these feelings influenced his decisions in life. Conversations helped him to analyze his fears and anxieties and overcome them. By acknowledging his emotions, Armando learned he could control them.

"Many young adults with autism avoid socializing due to fear and anxiety," Armando shares. "Social fears can result in anxiety attacks. It includes the fear of being judged or evaluated poorly by others or fear that you will do something humiliating or embarrassing in front of your peers or on a date. Social fears will result in a lack of self-esteem and self-efficacy, which are needed for dating."

Socializing was very difficult for Armando. He learned to understand acceptable behaviors by watching friends, family, and strangers. Filtering what to say and what not to say was also learned by observation. He'd play off his deficiency in social cues as part of his quirks and personality, causing most people not to question it. Thankfully, he is surrounded by people who accept him for who he is. "My fiancée loves me for me."

Family support and a military organization prepared Armando for college life and employment. His sister visited Texas A&M University with him and showed him where his classes were, and she taught him the social elements of college. Joining a military organization at the university was key to his academic success. The organization provided a schedule and structure.

Armando began his professional career as a special education teacher working with children in a life-skills program. Lacking experience in this field and desiring to help his students gain independence, Armando researched curriculum to teach basic skills and stumbled upon applied behavior analysis therapy, which led him to apply for a master's degree program in that field. Now that he has a degree, he serves as a board-certified behavior analyst. "I love giving hope to the parents of the children I work with."

The parents often come to him believing that an autism spectrum disorder diagnosis means that their child's life is over before it even begins. "However, nothing could be further from the truth," he says. Once they see their child going to the bathroom appropriately or beginning to communicate, they understand that the diagnosis is only the beginning of the incredible life the child will lead. "This field has let me assist so many children in gaining a level of independence their parents believed they would never achieve."

Armando met his fiancée on an internet dating app, and they had an incredible connection from the beginning. He couldn't wait to see her again after their first date, and he's looked forward to each and every one of their dates since then. "She has provided me with such incredible support for all of my goals and aspirations, and I have tried to do the same for her. We have certainly developed a partnership that I feel incredibly lucky to have."

Armando shares four tips on dating: First, find a partner who loves and respects you and is able to see your uniqueness. Second, never let the diagnosis of autism affect how you date. If you want to ask a specific individual on a date, go for it, because you never know what her answer will be. Third, give online dating a try. It's fun and may lead you to someone you will fall in love with. Fourth, don't be afraid to let your romantic partner know about your diagnosis. Answer questions openly and honestly.

The Museum of Science was the perfect place for Armando to propose to his fiancée. Familiarity and peace had always been at the center of their relationship, and it was something that drove him to propose.

The Museum of Science, where they spent so much of their time, became the setting for one of the best days of his life. "I arranged for Becca's engagement ring to be placed on the finger of a dinosaur found in the exhibit, without her having the slightest clue."

Armando's goal is to empower young adults with autism to thrive and gain independence. He hopes to develop a program promoting collaboration between schools and behavioral clinics that is focused on developing independence in each child. Autism enables him to see the world in a unique way. "I love working with individuals with autism and empowering them to gain independence and enjoy success in life."

ARMANDO BERNAL'S BIOGRAPHY

Armando Bernal is an experienced board-certified behavior analyst in Spring, Texas, who works primarily with children diagnosed with autism spectrum disorder. Armando is a proud graduate of Texas A&M University, where he earned his master's degree in special education in 2019. He is also the host of the podcast *A Different Path*, presented by Autism International, which presents the diverse stories of other individuals diagnosed with autism.

Armando enjoys traveling and physical activities, and he spends his free time experimenting with new cooking recipes and working out at the gym. He also enjoys walking his dog, Marshmallow.

REFLECT

1. Armando shares his social anxieties and how to overcome them by analyzing his fears and acknowledging his emotions. What are some social fears you experience on dates or in relationships? How can you feel more secure in social settings and confident while dating?

2. Ron met his wife, Kristen, online, and Armando met his fiancée on an online dating app. Do you think online dating is a good way to meet people? Why or why not? What are three advantages

and disadvantages to online dating? What are a few ways to stay safe if you choose to meet someone online?

3. Armando provides four dating tips. What tips do you think would be helpful to you, and why? Share three challenges you've experienced while dating or in a romantic relationship. What are some ways you can overcome these challenges?

Chapter 5

Overcoming a Hopeless Complex

Shoot for the moon. Even if you miss,
you'll land among the stars.
—Norman Vincent Peale, *The Power of Positive Thinking*

In interviewing hundreds of young adults with autism, I have discovered that the greatest hindrance to growth and transition is hopelessness and fear of the future. American psychologist Dr. Martin Seligman discovered the hopeless complex while researching learned helplessness in 1967 at the University of Pennsylvania. *Learned helplessness* is a behavior that occurs when individuals experience failure enough times that they believe they are incapable of success, causing them to stop trying.

Dr. Seligman and his partner, Dr. Maier, were conducting electric shock experiments on dogs, a highly controversial method by today's standards. The first group of dogs received a painful shock on the right side of the lab, learning quickly to move to the left side to avoid the shock again. The second group received shocks on the left side, so they learned to move to the right. However, the third group was shocked on both sides, so they remained in their spots, intelligent enough to realize that no matter where they moved, they would feel the shock. They learned helplessness.[1]

A hopeless complex can be the result of any mix of the following: past bullying, chronic illness, difficulty with communication, struggles in academics, a distorted perspective of all-or-nothing thinking, repeated sensory-issue overloads, emotional breakdowns, and failure with relationships or employment. The fruits of the hopeless complex are despair, lack of motivation, fear of trying new things, depression, anxiety, and other mental health issues.

Dylan Volk, author of *Bad Choices Make Good Stories*, describes the autism hopeless complex: "My life is such a minefield of failures, no matter how hard I try. And I try really hard. I can't keep a job, I can't keep a girl, I can't even keep track of belongings! . . . I feel like my optimistic nature is being slowly and painfully eroded by my increasingly soul-crushing life experiences."[2]

For years I experienced a hopeless complex. My hopeless complex was due to years of bullying and struggles with gainful employment and relationships. I felt hopelessness in my thirties as I received wedding invitations from my friends while I was single and living at my parents' house.

I was able to overcome my hopeless mindset by developing a healthy self-efficacy—the belief that when I set a goal or task, I had the power to accomplish it. This mindset motivated me to keep pushing forward, even when I experienced little success. Perseverance finally paid off, and now I see the fruits of my hard work—a family, career, and published books. Self-determination empowers us to be self-advocates and responsible to make our own choices in life.

Plan of Attack

Small steps in the right direction lead to a breakthrough. This requires a plan of attack and a kick in the butt to self-start. Both are extremely difficult for us on the spectrum. Every book I've written began with a thought, followed by an outline and scraps of paper with ideas. As I filled in the outlines of the chapters with details and stories, my book became a reality. It takes me about twelve hundred hours to write a book. My friend Jeff Snively once told me to always make the activity, not the reward, my goal.

Don't start when you feel motivated—just start. Motivation will follow. Actions produce results. Writing a book, getting a job, passing a driver's test, or moving out of your parents' home all begin with a plan, followed by actions. It may seem like an enormous task to undertake, but like eating an elephant, all it takes is one bite at a time.

For example, if your goal is to move to an apartment, this is what your plan of attack might look like:

1. Create a support team. These are friends and family members who motivate you and hold you accountable to reach your goals.
2. Have tasks you do daily. Spend an hour every day searching for jobs and emailing your résumé to at least five companies until employed. You will need employment to pay for rent on an apartment.
3. Once employed, save money for the apartment deposit.
4. Research the cost of apartments in the area and create a monthly budget.
5. Pick a few apartments to visit and compare, then choose one within your budget with the help of your support team.
6. Sign the lease and pay the deposit.
7. Purchase items you will need for your apartment.
8. Move to the apartment.
9. Host a housewarming party to celebrate your new independence.

Six Motivation Killers

Notice that a plan of attack requires actions. Without actions, a plan remains only an idea. A plan is an outline of steps you need to take to accomplish your goals. Motivation is the first step to overcoming a hopeless complex and achieving goals. Following are six things that can kill your motivation.

1. Distractions

I get distracted from writing in the summer by sunny days, and I find myself at the pool, swimming and suntanning with a good book. You may get sidetracked from your goals by binge-watching your favorite shows. Staying up late using social media can make you sluggish and lacking motivation the next day.

2. Perfectionism

Perfectionism destroys self-esteem by creating unrealistic expectations that can never be achieved, leading to loss of creativity. If you have a perfectionist personality, learn to analyze your all-or-nothing mindset and to verbalize obsessive thought patterns. Doing this enables you to see new opportunities for solving problems and boosts creativity in your brain. Life is not just black-and-white, but it is also gray.

For years I struggled with an all-or-nothing mindset. This mindset caused me to feel uptight and anxious and prevented me from celebrating my accomplishments, like when our 3,200-meter relay team set the school record, or when I graduated with a master of divinity degree with a perfect 4.0 GPA. When I accomplished a goal, I was always off to my next big thing and experienced fear that I would fail to complete the new task at hand.

Graduating from college was not enough for me. I had to have a perfect 4.0 GPA and a yellow ribbon on my robe as I walked across the stage. Looking back, I would've invested less time striving for perfection and more energy enjoying the moment with family and friends. My favorite memories of high school and college were not my academic success or track-and-field victories but the fun times I had with my friends, such as dorm movie nights with Jeff and Dave and my college missionary trips overseas to Cameroon, Bulgaria, and Madagascar.

In accomplishing my goals, I now don't seek perfection, but I break down larger tasks into manageable steps. I decide how much time to spend on each step, I give myself a deadline, and I reward myself for reaching each small goal. My personal reward for accomplishing a goal, such as writing a chapter in my book, is a good meal or a trip to my favorite store, Five Below.

You can accomplish your goals the same way, even if it's a smaller task, such as cleaning your room or completing a class assignment. The point is to finish the task, not to do it perfectly.

3. Depression

Anywhere from 54 to 94 percent of people with autism will experience mental health conditions, including depression and anxiety.[3] When you feel depressed, you lack motivation to leave your home and to take proper care of yourself, and you isolate from society. Depression makes our minds groggy with discouraging thoughts, low self-esteem, and a lack of motivation to hang out with friends, grab a coffee, or go to work. When we experience severe depression, we only want to sleep and forget our problems.

We experience depression for many reasons, such as the death of a loved one, guilt, loss of work, excessive stress, loneliness, criticism, bullying, weather conditions, or mental health issues. Depression can cause decision-making to become difficult, producing self-doubt and negativity. We feel unable to accomplish the simplest of tasks such as combing our hair or brushing our teeth.

Alix Generous, a mental health and autism advocate, describes her depression: "When you are depressed, you don't feel things as they are—you have a block. Depression causes some people to want to stay in bed all day and accomplish nothing, but I made a conscious decision based on who I wanted to be rather than what I felt like. I decided to arise from my bed and fulfill my dreams. This act of choice over feelings and emotions enabled me to discover the world around me."[4]

When I feel a lack of motivation because of depression, I take my dog, Rudy, for a walk or watch a comedy movie. Laughter lifts the cloud of depression. As Proverbs 17:22 says, "A cheerful heart is good medicine, but a crushed spirit dries up the bones."

Another great way to overcome depression is by helping others, often through volunteer work. As we help others, our bodies produce hormones that make us feel motivated and refreshed.

Persistent depression requires professional support and counseling. Some signs that you should seek professional help for depression include feelings of unrelenting hopelessness, an inability to make decisions or experience pleasure in activities you once enjoyed, unexplained aches and pains, an increased use of alcohol or abuse of legal or prescription drugs, changes in sleeping habits or appetite, a heightened irritability, agitation or moodiness, and thoughts of suicide or self-harm.

4. Lack of agency

When you fail to take proper care of yourself and to learn basic life skills—like driving a car, balancing your checkbook, and finding a job—others will make decisions for you. During a haircut at Great Clips, I saw this firsthand.

As my family and I were in the parking lot of Great Clips, I noticed a socially awkward young adult with autism. He was wearing a bright purple-striped polo with khaki pants, and had headphones connected to his iPhone. Entering Great Clips, he was tapping his two fingers against his left ear and failed to hold the door for us.

Tom Senior, his dad, was the polar opposite of Junior. Senior was wearing a college jersey and shorts, had an athletic build, and looked like a football coach.

As the two were getting their hair cut, the barber asked Junior, "Do you want me to cut the tail forming on your neck?"

In a soft robotic voice with a smirk, Junior replied, "Please keep it."

Senior quickly responded, "No son of mine is going to have a rattail. Cut that sucker off—I'm paying the bill!"

About ten minutes later, after cutting off the tail, the barber asked, "Do you want me to cut your hair shorter?"

Again, in a low voice, Junior replied, "No! If my hair is longer, it will be easier for my tail to grow back."

"Please cut his hair a little shorter!" Senior snapped back.

"Do you want your neckline to be square or round?" the barber asked.

"Square will work best for me to get my eighties tail back."

"Make it round. No son living under my roof will have a rattail," Senior barked back.

The inability to make choices as simple as hairstyle or clothes drains motivation. Choices create motivation and lead to action and hope. Our motivation does not lack in areas of special interests and passions.

Here are some ways to increase our ability to make decisions:

- Show yourself to be trustworthy. If you live at home and your parents tell you to be home by 10:30 p.m., be home on time. Then your parents will trust you with making other decisions. You can build bridges of trust by going beyond expectations. When you borrow a friend's car, return it with a full tank of gas. If your parents help you financially, pay them back when you are able to.
- Obey the rules of the land. People with autism have difficulty obeying rules they don't understand or that they think are illogical or unfair. Obey your college instructors by turning assignments in on time. When driving, don't speed and do obey the traffic laws. Breaking laws and probation will limit your ability to make choices in life.
- Devise a plan to make extra cash. Without finances, your decisions will be limited. You can earn extra hustle cash by walking

neighbors' dogs, performing handyman work and yard work, selling stuff on eBay or Craigslist, or starting a blog and website.

5. Past failures

This was the motivation killer I struggled with the most. Before I met my wife, I dated more than three hundred women and had many heartbreaks. In 2005, when I was laid off, I sent more than five hundred résumés and received hundreds of rejection letters. For the next three years, I was underemployed. I even worked for a moving company, hurting my back lifting heavy furniture. These experiences made me feel like an utter failure.

Dylan Volk describes the autism employment-failure cycle:

> Four weeks seemed to be the most common length of time before the axe falls. It would and still does usually go like this: During the first week, they couldn't fire me because they had just hired me—they think I'll be fine once I'm trained. The second week, I'm still pretty new to the job, so they want it to work out. The third week they're starting to think, "Uh-oh, is this guy going to make it?" It's also at about three weeks that they forget about my disability and start going by what they feel, and what they feel is that they're getting sick of me. By the fourth week, they've had it with me. They're done with the constant instructions that I need, they're annoyed by some of the decisions I've made or things I've said, so I get fired.[5]

The only way to overcome the relationship- and employment-failure complex is by refusing to give up. No matter how many times you experience rejection or are knocked down, refuse to allow it to define you as a person or cause you to lose hope. The best thing you can do is keep working until a better job comes along. In relationships, keep meeting new people and improving your social skills until you meet someone you click with.

After meeting his girlfriend, a young adult with autism shared with me, "If you're struggling to love yourself or to find love, it's truly not the end of the world. It's the effort that counts, and it's the fact you don't give up on yourself that matters most. After all, we only get so many laps around the sun. If you truly want to love and be loved, then go for it."

6. Criticism

The harshest form of this motivation killer comes from our own families, friends, and co-workers in the form of criticizing or labeling us as "too much," "overbearing," or "insecure," or with statements such as "You talk too much" or "You don't think before you speak." When we experience constant criticism, we freeze up and fear taking risks, such as applying for college, moving out of our parents' house, or pursuing relationships and a career. We fear rejection and criticism from our loved ones if we fail.

Before I became an author and autism advocate, I feared my dad's criticism and negative comments about how I did yard work or mowed our lawn. When I swept the berries from the sidewalk, my dad would complain about me not getting every single one. When I competed in the state final for track, I feared my dad's criticism, so I asked him not to attend. Seeing my dad in the stands would have made me feel anxious and would have affected my performance.

After I received my driver's permit, I would only drive with my mom and brothers because I feared my dad's backseat driving advice. After my dad read my books on autism, he better understood the challenges I experienced in life and became less critical.

There are four ways to handle criticism from loved ones and co-workers. First, speak up for yourself and let people know you will listen to their advice but not negative criticism. Take time with critical friends or family members to describe ways they can express an opinion that would be more helpful and less hurtful to you. For example, if your parents are always on your case about your low-paying job, tell them that it would be more productive if they forwarded job opportunities to you instead of criticizing your current employment situation.

Second, don't take criticism personally. Remember, everyone makes mistakes. If a friend or a co-worker constantly criticizes you, ask him to stop. If he doesn't stop, walk away when he is critical.

Third, stay calm as you evaluate the criticism. Don't allow a friend or co-worker's criticism to ruin your day. Take time to evaluate the comment and respond to the criticism in a positive way. For example, a co-worker criticizes you in front of your supervisor for forgetting to flush the toilet. After calming down, tell her, "I'm sorry for forgetting to flush the toilet. Sometimes I forget when I am busy. I'll make every effort in the future to remember. But if I should forget, can you kindly remind me privately? I felt embarrassed by you confronting me with the supervisor present. Thank you."

Fourth, if you are unsure if the criticism has any merit, ask a trusted friend or co-worker who will be honest with you. If the criticism is valid, ask your trusted friend for feedback on how you can improve in the area of the criticism.

We will encounter motivation killers in our efforts to accomplish our goals. Hope and perseverance will see us through.

Four Ways to Overcome a Hopeless Complex

Through my struggles with depression and anxiety, I learned four ways to overcome a hopeless complex and maintain motivation. King Solomon wrote, "Hope deferred makes the heart sick, but a longing fulfilled is a tree of life" (Proverbs 13:12). By applying these principles to your life, you can experience motivation and confidence to accomplish your goals.

1. A healthy self-esteem

People with high self-esteem feel confident to accomplish their goals and take responsibility for decisions. When we have a healthy self-esteem, we can accept rejection and criticism and don't blame others for our mistakes. Check below for the difference between high and low self-esteem, and circle your strengths and weaknesses.

People with high self-esteem

- have fairly stable moods,
- set realistic goals and achieve them,
- have self-motivation and stick-to-itiveness,
- can accept rejection or critical feedback,
- can say no to peers, and
- are realistically aware of their own strengths and weaknesses.

People with low self-esteem

- often blame others for their actions,
- need to be liked by everyone,
- see themselves as losers,
- are critical of others,
- get frustrated easily,
- have trouble accepting responsibility for their actions,
- make negative comments about themselves, and
- tend to be quitters.[4]

In order to maintain a healthy self-esteem, we cannot allow circumstances or feelings to dictate our self-perception and worth. A bad day of depression or losing a job or a breakup doesn't make us losers—it makes us human. We will have good days and bad, but we cannot allow our feelings to control and determine our future. Instead, we should move forward an inch of progress at a time, and sooner or later our feelings will catch up with our actions.

2. Self-awareness of strengths and weaknesses

Those of us on the spectrum tend to let others dictate our constraints, shackling us and preventing us from thinking beyond those constraints. Instead of focusing on our weaknesses, we should pursue opportunities in which we can enrich others with our unique gifts in the workplace and relationships.

My strengths in the workplace are humor, attention to detail, and faithful attendance. I never missed a day of work in sixteen years at the hospital. When my co-workers feel discouraged, I am able to make them laugh with witty psych stories.

I enjoy my career and using my gifts to help others. My talents in the workplace earn respect and praise. This motivates me to give 100 percent. When we work in a hostile workplace or a job unrelated to our strengths, we feel discouraged and exhausted.

One of my friends on the spectrum described the workplace environment: "Employment itself has many challenges, including doing things that you may not want to do, in a place not of your choosing, with people you may not get along with, in a way that you may not wish to."

Finding a career we enjoy requires self-awareness of our abilities, our likes and dislikes, our passions, and what our goals are in life. Sometimes family and friends see our potential for a job far clearer than we do. We should listen to their career advice. Internships and volunteer work can provide opportunities to discover our likes and dislikes and prepare us for the workplace. Doing something is better than doing nothing, as it gives us motivation to get up in the morning, prevents isolation, and provides a sense of achievement. Also, finding a job that plays to your abilities while cultivating a hobby can develop into a career.

3. Not taking things personally

Those of us on the spectrum tend to take things personally. When a co-worker cracks a joke about our clothes, we think the joke is based on truth, and we respond to it by never wearing that outfit again. If we call our friend and he does not call us back within twenty-four hours, we think that friend is mad at us, failing to realize that our friend may have worked an extra shift and was too tired to return a call. I still struggle with taking things personally. I am learning that life is busy, which causes friends to not respond to emails quickly or to cancel commitments.

Wendy Lawson, who has Asperger's, shares, "Until recently I always believed that if someone close to me was 'angry,' then it must be because of me. Now I am beginning to realize that people can be unhappy, or even angry, for many different reasons. In fact it may have nothing to do with me at all."[5]

I use the horse principle to assess whether to take a joke or comment personally and as something I need to change or adjust in my life. This is the horse principle: If one person calls you a horse, that person is crazy. If two or three people call you a horse, you have a conspiracy. If everyone calls you a horse, you better saddle up for the rodeo.

For example, your friend Bill says, "I hate your new hoodie. It makes you look like a thug." The girl you like says, "Your new hoodie looks great on you." Using the horse principle, I would determine: Wear the hoodie. Bill is only sharing his opinion.

Another example: You crack a joke in the conference room at work, and the room is so silent you could hear an ant sneeze. Five offended women inform you, "That's a sexist joke. Please don't repeat it." The horse principle assessment: Saddle up for the rodeo! Five women are not all wrong, so don't tell inappropriate jokes in the workplace. When it comes to offending, one offended person is too many.

While using the horse principle, ask yourself, *Does this person's opinion matter?* Personal things such as style do not matter as much as when you offended someone and could lose your job. When it comes to things we don't understand, such as someone's experiences or expertise, we should listen more carefully. Also, we should listen carefully to advice from a close friend or someone with a lot of experience on a subject.

4. Putting the past behind you and marching forward with confidence

Our hopeless complex was formed over years, and sometimes decades, of unresolved pain, abuse, and a sense of failure. A hopeless complex makes us feel defeated and causes us to perceive the world from a distorted perspective of failure. What if we can reverse this process and cultivate hope?

A man placed his wet clothes in the dryer and set the dial on maximum heat. Returning forty-five minutes later to check his clothes, he discovered that the clothes were still dripping wet. He touched the dryer, and it was cold. While exploring the electrical wires and the dryer's duct, he discovered a bird nest in the heating duct. This nest prevented the dryer from accomplishing its purpose of drying clothes. This nest had been formed one branch, patch of mud, leaf, and twig at a time.

Likewise, our hopeless complex was formed one branch of abuse, one patch of bullying mud, one twig of being fired from a job, and one leaf of a broken and unhealthy relationship at a time. Removing the hopeless nest from our lives will release the power of self-confidence to accomplish our goals. We can reverse the hopeless complex by cultivating hope and putting the past behind us. There are three ways to develop hope.

First, create hope with a support team to encourage you when you feel emotionally dead. Friends and family are often good at finding the silver lining of a situation. These friends can provide you with sound advice to accomplish your goals and the small steps you need to take.

Second, forgive yourself for past mistakes and don't allow them to haunt you. Think of each mistake as part of a learning process. Write the lessons you learned from them in a journal. Also use journaling time to make a list of the qualities you like about yourself, including your strengths and talents.

Third, make goals and the blueprints to accomplish them. Plans make the future look brighter. Have a plan of attack. Write down your goals on paper and the steps to accomplish them. A support team is important to keep you guided in the right direction. My goal is to be the first US congressman with autism.

Closing Thoughts

A hope complex empowers us to experience independence and accomplish our dreams. We cultivate a hope complex by overcoming the six motivation killers and forming a healthy self-efficacy. As we put our past behind us and march forward in hope, we will see new opportunities for employment and relationships and have the courage to take risks.

REFLECT

1. I described six motivation killers I experienced. What are some motivation killers you've experienced? How can you conquer them?
2. I shared that "small steps in the right direction lead to a breakthrough." What steps are you taking to accomplish your goals? What are some of your short- and long-term goals?
3. Self-awareness of our strengths and weaknesses equips us to achieve our goals. What are some of your strengths? How can you use these strengths to your advantage in relationships and employment?

FUN ACTIVITIES

With your group or a family member or friend, draw two mountains on poster board or two pieces of paper. Label the first mountain

"Hopeless" and the second mountain "Hope." On the "Hopeless" mountain, glue pictures of things or emotions that cause you fear and anxiety. On the "Hope" mountain, glue pictures of activities you enjoy, such as swimming or playing video games, and pictures of your goals, such as traveling, relationships, education, housing, and employment.

Now draw a path up the "Hopeless" mountain with a black marker. On the path, write three or four encouraging messages, such as "When unexpected things happen in life, I'll learn to adjust" or "If I experience sensory overload, I will take a break." Draw a path up the "Hope" mountain and write three or four steps to achieving your goals, such as "Sign up for classes online" or "Create a blog sharing my journey." Now place the mountains poster on your bedroom wall to remind you of the power of hope.

FURTHER READING

The Mental Toughness Handbook: A Step-By-Step Guide to Facing Life's Challenges, Managing Negative Emotions, and Overcoming Adversity with Courage and Poise, by Damon Zahariades

Exploring Depression, and Beating the Blues: A CBT Self-Help Guide to Understanding and Coping with Depression in Asperger's Syndrome, by Tony Attwood and Michelle Garnett

The Guide to Good Mental Health on the Autism Spectrum, by Jeanette Purkis, Emma Goodall, and Jane Nugent

Xavier DeGroat's Story
The First White House Intern Diagnosed with Autism

I'm a relentless guy who goes on and on.
—Xavier DeGroat

Xavier DeGroat is motivated, authentic, and relentless. These characteristics enabled him to build a strong résumé and a celebrity contact list equivalent to a Hollywood Walk of Fame. He has met Presidents Obama and Trump, Hall of Fame athletes such as Muhammad Ali and Dan Marino, famous scientist Stephen Hawking, and the Dalai Lama.

Xavier's formula for success is persistence: Never accept no for an answer. His story inspired civil rights icon John Lewis to create an autism awareness video. In March 2018 Xavier met for breakfast with former California governor Arnold Schwarzenegger. He was a guest on the *Huckabee* show and completed an internship at the White House. Xavier's friendship with former New York mayor Rudy Giuliani provided him with the opportunity for his internship. He met Giuliani after a keynote speech at the Els Center of Excellence in Jupiter, Florida. Xavier's most important achievement is establishing laws to empower and protect individuals with autism and other disabilities.

DeGroat experienced many challenges along the path to becoming an international advocate for autism and a force to be reckoned with.

He was diagnosed with autism at age four and experienced epilepsy, anxiety, and trouble communicating, especially with sarcasm or coping with any kind of nuances. "In my elementary years, I was chased in the hallways by bullies and labeled the r-word. My speech impediment made it difficult to share ideas in class. I felt misunderstood and like an outsider."

Xavier was born on October 17, 1990, in Colorado Springs. When he was a young child, his family relocated often because of his dad's job. Constant transition made it even more difficult for Xavier to develop and maintain friendships.

High school presented new challenges and learning experiences, and it was also where he faced his severest consequences—being disciplined often for many injustices. "The main injustice I experienced was bullies teasing me," he says, "and when I responded, the teacher would send me to the principal's office." He was treated as a troublemaker. This bullying caused his parents to homeschool him his junior year. Through homeschooling, he became more confident and learned to be an advocate by studying civil rights leaders.

Xavier took educational courses on leadership and was inspired by Mahatma Gandhi's principles of nonviolence and the "I Have a Dream" speech by Dr. Martin Luther King Jr. He studied subjects related to his interests of history and science, and he enjoyed reading books at the library and watching documentary films by his hero Ken Burns. Through studying, Xavier was motivated to be a civil rights and autism advocate.

The economic hardship and poverty Xavier observed as a child in Saginaw, Michigan, fueled a desire in him to make a positive impact on the urban community and to create programs and laws to help its citizens. Later, living in Lansing, Michigan's state capital, Xavier's interest in politics was sparked. With the injustice and discrimination he faced growing up, he became interested in the civil rights and human rights movements of the fifties, sixties, and seventies, which inspired him to do the same for autism rights. "I learned how politics can play a role in bringing social change, just as Susan B. Anthony did for the women's suffrage movement and helped bring about the women's voting rights act of 1920 and Dr. Martin Luther King Jr. did for the 1964 Civil Rights Act. I wanted to help lead and build a better environment and understanding of the mental health field and discrimination that exists."

Xavier's friendship with Republican State Senator Tom Barrett helped him learn the political culture and the importance of bipartisanship in establishing laws. In June 2020, Barrett helped shepherd a three-bill package into law that allows drivers with autism to indicate their communication difficulties on their license and vehicle registration. This information helps law enforcement during traffic stops to understand the behaviors of drivers with autism and not misinterpret their behavior as aggression.

The motivation for these laws came to Xavier after he was pulled over for speeding. The officer demanded that Xavier open his window and hand over his driver's license and registration. The officer and Xavier raised their voices and talked over each other. The stress combined with the bright lights caused Xavier to have a panic attack, and thoughts raced through his mind: *What am I doing wrong? Is the officer mad at me? Can you turn that light off behind me because it's making me worried that you're going to hurt me?* After this altercation, Xavier believed there must be a better way to alert police when they are dealing with an individual with autism or other conditions that make communication difficult.

Former Lansing mayor Virgil Bernero served as a mentor and motivator for Xavier. Virgil helped him develop confidence and gave him knowledge of how cities are structured economically, socially, and politically, which made Xavier later consider creating a foundation for those in his community facing challenges with autism.

In early 2018, Xavier founded the Xavier DeGroat Autism Foundation (XDAF), which provides autistic individuals and their families opportunities to become economically, socially, and politically successful. The foundation is dedicated to advocating on behalf of those with autism, which could mean pushing for equal treatment in employment and housing or combating injustices against those with the diagnosis.

Xavier then took autism awareness to Washington, DC, interning three months in the presidential correspondence office at the White House, responding to letters people wrote to the commander in chief. The internship provided Xavier more opportunities to serve as an autism ambassador and to network with politicians. "I bring nonpartisanship to DC and make politics nonpolarized because autism has no political boundaries. My desire is to help my community and bring awareness to their needs."

Xavier shared the humorous story of meeting President Donald Trump. In the middle of their conversation, Trump said to him, "If you hadn't told me, I wouldn't have known that you were autistic." Xavier responded, warning him, "If I started calling you, you would know I was autistic because I would just keep calling you."

Xavier's current goal is to advise future presidents on autism the way the late Rev. Billy Graham served as spiritual counsel to commanders in chief. "The White House, at this point, is going to be my permanent institution that I work with to make differences for people with autism. I know this may sound unusual or different, but I desire to be known as the evangelist for autism to presidents, just like Billy Graham."[8]

XAVIER DEGROAT'S BIOGRAPHY

Xavier DeGroat was the first intern at the White House diagnosed with autism. He is the founder of the Xavier DeGroat Autism Foundation. The mission of XDAF is to create and promote opportunities for people with autism through advocacy, education, economic opportunities, and humanitarian efforts. Xavier resides in Lansing, Michigan.

His website address is xdafoundation.org.

You can contact Xavier at info@xdafoundation.org.

REFLECT

1. How does Xavier model a hope complex?
2. What challenges have you, like Xavier, had to overcome?
3. Name a few people who demonstrate self-confidence and boldness like Xavier.

Chapter 6

Advocating for Your Accommodations

Advocacy requires the three C's of a cat: being cool,
calm, and collected.

—Ron Sandison

ADVOCATING FOR MY NEEDS STARTING at an early age enabled me to be successful in academics and in the workplace. When I was a freshman in high school, I advocated to my algebra teacher so I could eat a peanut butter sandwich each day in her class. The peanut butter sandwich provided me with the protein and energy I needed to stay focused and not be disruptive.

My senior year of high school, I was three months past the age requirement to compete in high school athletics in Michigan because I repeated kindergarten due to my learning disabilities. My mom and I advocated with an attorney for my right to compete in track and cross-country in the federal district courts. My case, *Sandison v. MHSAA*, became a precedent for the Americans with Disabilities Act (ADA) and helps others with disabilities be able to compete. By participating on the track and cross-country teams, I was able to receive an athletic scholarship to college.

During my junior year of college, my mom and I advocated to Michigan Rehabilitation Services (MRS) for them to supply me with a computer. MRS provided me with a new computer to help me with my academics. Twenty years later, I presented at MRS's National Disability Employment Awareness Month job fair, sharing my insight on disabilities and employment.

In this chapter I will teach you the art of advocating for your needs by using the three C's of a cat: remain cool, calm, and collected. When you feel that your rights are violated, it can be difficult for you to remain composed. A meltdown might hinder you from receiving accommodations and could get you fired or arrested. To stay calm, you may need a friend, co-worker, or family member to help you advocate. Depending on the accommodation you are requesting and the person, organization, or company from whom you're seeking an accommodation, it can be a laborious undertaking requiring patience and perseverance.

Advocating for Accommodations

When advocating, the three things you should share are your diagnosis, the accommodations you will need, and the benefits of those accommodations. During my master's degree program, I requested and received extended time for my biblical Greek tests. I shared with my Greek professor my diagnosis of autism, how autism affects me, and my need for extended time due to test anxiety and sensory issues. Here's an example of requesting accommodations for extended test time:

1. Diagnosis: "I have autism, which causes me to experience severe test anxiety. This leads to sensory overload, which causes my mind to go blank and forget the answers to the questions."

2. Reason: "Extended time on tests helps me stay calm and focused on the assignment and allows me to do my best. When I have a time restraint, I become anxious and hyperfocused on the sounds and sights around me."

3. How it will help: "When I have extended time, I perform my best on the test."

4. Benefits: "I'll need less help learning the material in the classroom."

Sharing Your Diagnosis for Accommodations

A formal autism diagnosis is important for accommodations in school and the workplace and to apply for Supplemental Security Income or Social Security Disability Insurance. Under the ADA, a diagnosis is required to request reasonable accommodations for employment.

A diagnosis can also help you understand how your brain processes information and the accommodations you need to reach your full potential. My diagnosis helped my family, friends, and co-workers understand my struggles in the workplace and the reasons for my unfiltered, inappropriate comments and jokes.

You can receive an autism diagnosis from any professional with the credentials to make diagnoses. Professionals qualified include master's level social workers, speech and language pathologists, autism specialists, and other mental health professionals.

When researching autism diagnostic testing, consider the cost. Some professionals and centers can be expensive. I recommend contacting local colleges and universities with programs for autism diagnostic testing. Many of these schools will do the testing at a reduced price or for free.

Once you receive your formal diagnosis, consider who you want to share this information with and why. If your supervisors are hostile toward people with disabilities or lack empathy, you might decide not to discuss your diagnosis with them. Also, if your disabilities do not affect your work performance and you don't need any accommodations, you may decide not to disclose your diagnosis. There are three questions you should ask yourself before disclosing your diagnosis: *Why should I share? What impact will sharing have? Do I need any accommodations?*

When disclosing, begin by explaining your strengths. For instance, autism helps me focus on tasks and pay close attention to details. Two of my weaknesses in the workplace are social awkwardness and difficulty understanding verbal instructions.

An advocacy letter I wrote to help my employer understand autism reads:

> Dear Employer, we with autism would love for you to understand that not all disabilities are visible. When we don't look you in the eye, it does not mean we are uninterested or not listening. If we fail to shake your hand or we say something inappropriate, it does not mean we are rude. When we need extra clarification to do the job, it does not mean we are slow or stupid. Due to autism, we process information differently, but we also have amazing gifts, like an attention to details and faithful work attendance.

Some people fear that disclosure will impact their employment. Haley Moss, an attorney with autism, suggests that if you don't have a formal diagnosis or don't want to disclose your diagnosis and you need accommodations, use the line "I work best when . . ."[1]

For example, you have sensory issues when co-workers talk in the office, so you might share this with your supervisor: "I work best with headphones on to block out the talking and background sounds." Or you're attending a science class and the bright lights in the lab cause you to have migraines, so you explain to your professor, "I work best when wearing sunglasses so the lighting does not give me migraines. May I please wear them?"

For self-advocating, use the acronym REACH: *receive* a formal diagnosis, *educate* yourself and others about autism, *acknowledge* the impact of autism on your life, *commit* to developing relationships and learning how to thrive with autism, and seek *help* when needed.

The Three C's of a Cat

When you feel your rights are violated or you're overwhelmed by a new company policy, staying cool, calm, and collected can be difficult. Even after years of self-advocating, I still lose my cool at times and become frustrated, like with a change in routine, a new company policy, a sensory overload, an unpredictable circumstance, a short notice for a deadline, or when a co-worker stabs me in the back and watches me bleed.

The first C of a cat is to remain cool. The key to remaining cool is negotiation. This enables me to stay in control of the situation and not become angry. When I need an accommodation, I negotiate to make it a win-win situation. During COVID-19, my company was mandating the nursing staff to work overtime. Being mandated by a supervisor can cause severe anxiety for an employee with autism. In response, I self-advocated by having an Oakland University autism research professor write a letter requesting accommodation for my autism under the ADA so I would not be mandated.[2] I also made it a win situation for my supervisors by agreeing to work extra hours each week when I was available.

Staying cool requires you to delay your gut reaction of frustration and pause to regain your composure before responding. Take three deep breaths before responding. Then ask for clarification to make sure you understand the information or task. You can say something like, "Do I understand you right, that the new policy is . . . ?" and repeat back the information you heard or read. Staying cool helps prevent a sensory overload leading to a meltdown.

The second C is to stay calm. When advocating, ask yourself, *Should*

I be worried and upset about this? How will this new policy or routine affect my life? Hating change, we often blow things out of proportion and think the worst. I have learned to stay calm by talking with my co-workers and family. My co-workers remind me that I was able to adjust to other changes in the workplace in the past, and I should go with the flow and remain calm.

If you respond with anger as you ask for an accommodation, the person will be less likely to grant your request. Instead, present your request politely, use words such as "please" and "thank you," and don't be rude.

I stay calm by writing down my needs for accommodations and having three people read my request before I submit it. I ask these three people to share their advice on how I should make the request, and I take their perspective into consideration. When you stay calm, you think clearly and you don't appear nervous. You have self-confidence, and people respond positively to confidence. If you believe in yourself, others will believe in your cause and provide you with support.

I experience extreme nervousness when waiting to board an airplane and fear the plane won't have room for my overhead bags. My social anxiety causes me pace back and forth at my gate. I bring a copy of my autism diagnosis and inform the flight attendants that I need to preboard due to autism and social anxiety. It is easier to remain calm when you know the circumstances that make you nervous and fearful and have a plan to receive accommodations.

The final C is to be collected. You can be collected by typing a letter, in business format, stating your need and sharing the four elements noted earlier: diagnosis, reason, how the accommodation will help, and benefits. Also, include positive words for the person or company from whom you're making the request. For example, if you're advocating to your company, state, "I really enjoy working here and am grateful for all the help you have provided me in the past."

Being collected in advocating helps you stay cool and calm. You have a plan and know how to request the accommodations you need to be successful. One of the main places you might need to advocate in is the workplace.

Advocating in the Workplace

The reason you should disclose your diagnosis in the workplace is so your supervisors and co-workers can understand and interpret your behavior positively—and so you can reach your potential and succeed in your position. Keep your discussion about autism related to how it impacts your work and the accommodations you need. Always present your autism in a positive way and your weaknesses as areas in which you need accommodations.

How you ask your supervisor for an accommodation is often more of a factor in whether or not you get it than why you're asking for it. Increase your chances of being heard by being tactful. Make your request in a positive way and not as a complaint. For example, maybe you have difficulty understanding your work assessments and feel your supervisor is unclear in his instructions. Ask this supervisor to be more direct in his instructions and requirements and not wrap up his message with extra words, but to keep his instructions brief and to the point. I request for my supervisors to give me clear written instruction and feedback. When my company develops a new policy, I request extra time to review and learn the new requirements for my job.

Advocating for an Emotional Support Pet

Some advocating requires advanced skills, such as advocating for an emotional support pet in an apartment building that does not allow dogs. In January 2018 I was experiencing severe anxiety and depression. I felt overwhelmed in the workplace and pressured to finish my third book, *Views from the Spectrum*, and was traveling and speaking at more than seventy events a year.

Working forty hours a week with acute and sometimes aggressive psychotic patients as a psychiatric care specialist (PCS) added to my worries and was draining my mental strength. This stress caused painful digestive issues, leading to my first visit to a gastroenterologist and a colonoscopy.

I adopted a puppy to help me cope with my depression and anxiety. My co-worker Brittany, the charge nurse of our unit, helped me search Petfinder. The moment we saw Rudy's picture online (a Jack Russell terrier and Pomeranian mix), I knew he was the perfect pup for my family.

Three days later my wife and my daughter, Makayla, and I met Rudy. We noticed Rudy's go-getter temperament. He had the personality of the Energizer Bunny intoxicated on Red Bull and the perseverance of a honey badger. It was love at first sight, and we brought him home.

A few days later, I returned to my apartment to find a note on the door from the apartment office: "Apartment Building #1 does not permit dogs." I advocated to the apartment office staff concerning my autism and need for Rudy to help me deal with anxiety and depression. The office management graciously gave me time to gather paperwork for Rudy to be an emotional support pet.

I set up an appointment with a psychiatrist to write a prescription for Rudy to be an emotional support pet. The doctor wrote an order. I also wrote a letter to the landlord advocating my need to have an emotional support pet. I collected letters from neighbors testifying that Rudy is a good fit for our building and does not bark loud.

After two months' waiting, the landlord approved Rudy to live in our apartment. He was now officially on duty. Rudy is the first emotional support pet who needs more emotional support than his autistic owner. Here's an example of requesting accommodations for an emotional support pet:

1. Diagnosis: "I have autism, which causes me to experience severe anxiety, depression, and sensory issues."

2. Reason: "My emotional support pet, Rudy, provides me with emotional support for depression, anxiety, and isolation."
3. How it will help: "Rudy enables me to handle sensory issues at home and in public."
4. Benefits: "My wife, Kristen, and I have lived in your apartment building for eight years, and we are faithful tenants and always pay our rent on time. The other tenants and children in the complex love Rudy. I have enclosed a letter from our neighbor, Dr. Fred, who lives in apartment 2, as a character witness for Rudy. Having Rudy as an emotional support pet means me and my family can continue to stay in our apartment."

Attributes of an Advocate

Areva Martin, who has a son with autism and is the author of *The Everyday Advocate*, developed seven principles of advocacy.

1. Take responsibility: Be a leader—speak up for your accommodations and the needs of others and be an agent of change.
2. Learn: Be an expert—learn as much as you can about autism and how it affects you. Read books and do your own research.
3. Think critically: Be discerning—evaluate information you read or hear about autism.
4. Speak with authority: Be proactive—demonstrate self-confidence when sharing about autism. Don't allow others to bully you.
5. Document: Be prepared—keep a diagnosis and medical records on hand and make an employment portfolio for interviews.
6. Collaborate: Be a team builder—make connections with others on the spectrum and in the autism community.
7. Educate: Be a voice in the autism community—write blogs or articles, host a podcast, attend conferences, and have a website.[3]

Building a Platform for Advocacy

Creating a social media platform can empower us to have influence in advocating for our needs and the needs of others in the autism community. In a noisy world with marketers, big corporations, and lobbyists, our voice might feel hoarse and we might feel like we have little ability to bring change. Building a social platform can enable us to have a voice in a noisy world and make it easier for requesting accommodations. Podcasts, speaking events, and blogs/articles are means that can be used to create an autism platform.

You can share your experience with autism and create your own podcast program by interviewing other adults on the spectrum and well-known autistic individuals. A podcast helps you develop social connections and friends in the autism community. Don't be combative when sharing your ideas on social media.

Speaking events can include autism conferences, companies, and religious services. At these events, make connections with other attendees and ask for their business cards. After a conference, email or call your contacts and share with them your autism advocacy and ask to speak to their company or organization on autism. Take notes, and write down the date you spoke with them and a date for a follow-up conversation within a month.

Create a speaking contact list. Include in this list the date of the event, place or name of the event, address, contact person, email, and topic of your message. Arrange the speaking contact list by dates of the events from last to first.

Date: 5/4/25
Location: First Baptist Church
Address: 110 Junction Avenue, Franklin, Tennessee
Contact person: Pastor John Jones
Email: pastorjohnjones@yahoo.com

Phone number: 555-111-3334

Notes: My message was "My Amazing Journey with Autism & Faith." Pastor Jones has a grown son who has Asperger's. He would love for me to speak again next year. Contact him in January 2026 to set up a speaking date.

Finally, after a speaking event, ask the host to write you an endorsement, and then send a thank-you card. Use these endorsements to promote your speaking events and help you receive more invitations to present.

Blogs and articles are great ways to share your journey with autism and help others on the spectrum by providing practical advice on relationships and employment. I write articles for the Art of Autism, *Autism Parenting Magazine*, the Mighty, and other sites. Each month I interview inspiring individuals with autism and their families. I also write articles on advocacy and topics related to living with autism.

I recommend creating a Facebook fan page and a website to share your articles so they get noticed. Develop social media partnerships with advocates in the autism community who share the same content on their Facebook and blog sites. These connections can help you receive more followers and reach a larger audience. Have these social connections share your articles and videos, and you in turn share theirs; this enables both of you to build a larger platform.

Podcasts, speaking events, and blogs/articles empower individuals with autism to be heard, to create an awareness of the needs in the community, and to find acceptance. Jenara Nerenberg, author of *Divergent Mind: Thriving in a World That Wasn't Designed for You*, shares, "Acceptance is at the core of what then enables people who feel marginalized to take risks, expand their sense of belonging, apply themselves in work and relationships, and thrive."[4]

Some good online advocacy resource groups are the international

People First movement, Self Advocates Becoming Empowered, and the Autistic Self Advocacy Network.

Closing Thoughts

Transitioning to adulthood requires you to learn to advocate for yourself. As you remain cool, calm, and collected, people and companies are more likely to grant your requests. When sharing your diagnosis, consider to whom you want to disclose and why. Have family members, friends, and co-workers evaluate your strengths and weaknesses and the accommodations they feel you need to succeed. Advocate by building social media and connections in the autism community.

REFLECT

1. I describe advocating for accommodations at work and for an emotional support pet. What are some accommodations you might need to advocate for?
2. Sharing my diagnosis helped me receive accommodations from supervisors and college professors. When have you needed to share your diagnosis and with whom?
3. I share how I built a social platform to advocate through speaking events and writing books and articles. How can you create a social platform, and what themes would you share in your messages?

FUN ACTIVITIES

Write a one page, double-spaced narrative describing your journey with autism. Share your strengths and weaknesses with autism, your passions, and your struggles, such as sensory overload, social anxiety, employment, relationships, or depression. Share your autism narrative in your group or with a family member or friend.

Next, write an accommodation you need. Use the four-things format: your diagnosis, the reason, how the accommodation will help, and the benefits of providing the accommodation. Role-play requesting the accommodation in your group or with a friend. Now change roles—you act the part of the person receiving the request and have your partner be the advocate. Receive feedback on your advocating.

FURTHER READING

NeuroTribes: The Legacy of Autism and the Future of Neurodiversity, by Steve Silberman

Getting a Life with Asperger's: Lessons Learned on the Bumpy Road to Adulthood, by Jesse A. Saperstein

Population One: Autism, Adversity, and the Will to Succeed, by Tyler McNamer

Amy Gaeta's Story
An Advocate for the Neurodivergent Community

By joining autism and neurodivergent communities, I've gained such a stronger and more confident sense of self!
—AMY GAETA, PHD IN ENGLISH

AMY GAETA HAD A PRETTY normal childhood and was unaware of her neurodivergency until reaching adulthood. She did well in school and was not shy, but she had trouble socially and enjoyed alone time, letting her mind wander in books and in writing. She was constantly rehearsing conversations in her mind and speaking aloud to herself.

Due to her neurodivergence, Amy had sensory limits with lighting and especially with sound. When she heard loud, unexpected noises, such as sirens, she felt pain. After a high-sensory environment, such as a concert, she would have to lie down in the dark for several hours until her senses felt less fragile.

School was always Amy's favorite place. She loved to learn and think out of the box. Amy knew that if she had a career working in a corporate office or as a tradesperson, she would be unhappy. "I need a space and community where I can dream up ideas that currently seem impossible," she says. "Probably due to my lifelong appreciation for fiction and poetry, my passion is creating things that are not yet real or realized."

Through academics, Amy discovered her passion in life for advocacy and teaching. For as long as she can remember, she wanted to somehow make the world a better, less hateful place. "My best skill is writing, and teaching brings me more joy than anything else." Although she loves academia, she has experienced how it can be extremely ableist in that most academic standards assume a normative, nondisabled body and mind. While there has been important progress thanks to disability rights activists, she notes there is a long way to go for teaching and learning practices to become truly accessible to everyone. "I teach because I want to be part of that change."

Amy's greatest challenge transitioning to adulthood was understanding herself. In her last years of high school, she developed a disordered relationship with food and her body, which she now knows was largely the result of being unsure of who she was and what she wanted to do with her life. Because she blamed all her social issues on herself, she was vulnerable to think that her body image defined her.

After high school, Amy attended the University of Massachusetts in Boston and received a BA in English literature and creative writing, but she struggled with socializing. "College is so big, so it is difficult to get to know people. Looking back, I wish I was more involved with student activism and the art students. At the end of the school day, I was socially drained, and my senses were at their limits, so I just wanted to go home, crawl into my bed, eat Goldfish, and watch *Buffy the Vampire Slayer* reruns." Still, college allowed her to flourish, and during her undergraduate years, she came into her own as a person and thinker.

Amy later attended the University of Wisconsin-Madison and earned an MA and PhD in English literary studies. Earning her PhD required perseverance. It took her two years to truly be able to manage the workload and meet deadlines without stressing out into burnout. It took a massive toll on her mental health. "With new, amazing friends and a fantastic medical team, I was able to come out of burnout and develop a healthier relationship to graduate life, setting many more limits for myself."

During her PhD studies, Amy discovered neurodivergency. In 2019, when she joined disability communities and devoted her research to disability studies, neurodivergency gave her a vocabulary through which she could finally understand her world and how her brain works within it.

Amy explains neurodivergency as a concept that acknowledges the vast biological diversity of the human mind and cognitive behaviors. It is used in contrast to neurotypical. While all human brains have differences, *neurodivergence* often refers to people with one or more cognitive, learning, or development disabilities, which includes mental illness. A common misconception is that neurodivergence is a synonym for autism, ADHD, schizophrenia, or any single experience. Neurodivergence is, she says, like autism—an infinite number of experiences that exist on a spectrum.

"Being neurodivergent means learning to be who you are with all your so-called mental imperfections and problems," Amy says. "It is embracing the beautiful but at times very difficult fact that I perceive the world differently than everyone else. In a society where we are expected to conform to the norm, neurodivergency is critical to respect."

Amy has the three C's of advocacy—cool, calm, and collected—and shares ways to advocate. Whenever she thinks about supporting a social issue, she asks herself, What skills and capacities do I have that I can best use to help this issue? "And for me, that is writing, teaching, and disclosing my experiences. I continue to take opportunities to write a personal essay and give talks about my experiences as a neurodivergent woman working in academia."

Her teaching is a central place where she advocates for neurodivergent people by experimenting with accessible design and trying new practices of communication, social interaction, and composition that welcome all different types of learners. In tandem, no matter the class, mental and physical health are central topics of discussion. Her students know from day one that she aspires to build an accessible community together and that their mental health and needs are more important than any class assignment.

By raising awareness, she believes we can also raise empathy and action toward accepting neurodivergent people in all their diversity.

Amy hopes to secure a university faculty job that allows her to teach and research topics about disability, gender, and how technology and society interact. She also plans to publish her poetry collection and turn her dissertation into a book manuscript to be published. Amy's long-term goal is to open a research center focused on creative approaches to technology and science at a university.

AMY GAETA'S BIOGRAPHY

Dr. Amy Gaeta earned her PhD in English and visual cultures at the University of Wisconsin-Madison. She takes a feminist disability approach to contemporary applications of science and technology, mainly human-robot interactions and digital surveillance. Amy's dissertation, "Drone Life: A Feminist Crip Analysis of the Human," asks how the category of the human changes amid the spread of drone technology in which passivity and interdependency are valued and accepted—a contradiction to the able-bodied individual liberal subject.

REFLECT

1. During her PhD studies, Amy Gaeta discovered that she was neurodivergent. How did you learn that you had autism and at what age? What impact has your diagnosis had on your life? Do you wish you'd known earlier that you're autistic? Why or why not?

2. Amy describes being neurodivergent as perceiving the world differently from everyone else. If someone asked you what autism is, how would you answer their question? Do you think you

perceive the world differently from people without autism? Why or why not?

3. Disability communities and research studies enabled Amy to understand neurodivergency and discover the unique way her brain processes information. Do you enjoy attending autism groups? What lessons have you learned from other people on the spectrum? Would you rather spend time with people who have autism or who don't have autism, and why?

Chapter 7

Learning the Ins and Outs
of the Workplace

*It is by developing our talents that we can step more easily
into the work world and find jobs that are a good fit for us.*
—TEMPLE GRANDIN

MY GREATEST STRUGGLE WITH AUTISM was not my speech delay, sensory processing issues, meltdowns, repetitive behaviors, learning difficulties, or even social interactions, though these were a challenge. My greatest struggle was employment. Studies and private estimates say that anywhere from 40 percent to 85 percent of adults with autism are unemployed.[1] I did not experience gainful employment until age thirty-two, even though I had two bachelor's degrees and a master's degree.

I have now been gainfully employed for sixteen years in the mental health field at Havenwyck Hospital and for twenty years part-time as a professor of theology at Destiny School of Ministry. I also speak at more than seventy events a year on autism, and I founded Spectrum Inclusion, which has a mission to empower young adults with autism and Asperger's for employment and independence.

The best description I heard for the challenges of having autism and being employed was when I worked at a center for juvenile offenders. A co-worker—I will call him Mr. Ellison—who had a master's degree in social work and was diagnosed as a teenager with Asperger's, told me this:

> People like me with Asperger's are the last to be hired and the first to be fired. I just lack the social skills to read people and the social graces to say things that don't offend. I have been fired from my share of jobs the past few years by saying the wrong thing to the wrong person at the wrong time! The only job I am able to maintain is a taxicab driver because clients are forced to listen to my stories since I am in the driver's seat.[2]

Mr. Ellison lasted only a few months at the center because of his inability to maintain control over a small group of juvenile offenders. A teenager kicked a soccer ball and hit Mr. Ellison square in the head. About thirty seconds later, as his group roared in laughter, Mr. Ellison responded, "Ah, was I just hit in the head with a soccer ball or something?"

The teens received rewards of pop and candy based on earning a certain number of points in their behavioral program. Mr. Ellison would open the office refrigerator and candy stash containing the children's rewards and say, as he ate a Kit Kat, "Ah, free prizes for everyone today! No points-checking on my watch." When confronted by a co-worker, he replied, "Ah, rookie mistake!" The last I heard, Mr. Ellison was driving for Uber.

Eighty-five percent of people on the autism spectrum with college degrees—including those in science, technology, engineering, and mathematics—are unemployed or significantly underemployed.[3] The underutilization of this population and lost productivity equates to more than $265 billion a year.[4] In this chapter I will share practical ways to change these statistics and show how autistic individuals can develop skills to be gainfully employed and to understand the workplace culture.

Strategies for Employment

The main benefits of employment are increases in self-esteem and independence. In order to move out of your parents' home or buy the things you desire, you need an income. When unemployed, we experience more depression, anxiety, and mental health issues. Employment requires us to have a plan to get hired and maintain employment.

Brian R. King, an author and social worker with autism, states, "Success in the workplace has little to do with your circumstances and everything to do with your strategies."[5] A work ethic and positive attitude are important for maintaining gainful employment. Try to get along with others, be aware of your actions and words, act respectful to authority, and communicate clearly.

Play to Your Strengths

Gainful employment requires us to have an awareness of our strengths and weaknesses in the workplace. My main weakness is with multitasking. I have difficulty transitioning from one assignment or task to another. I also struggle with unfiltered comments and jokes. Dr. Jackie Marquette, autism life coach and education consultant, wrote, "Strengths are anchors to one's contributions and work life. Strengths are the opened window to creating life satisfactions."[6]

As a psychiatric care specialist, my job plays to my strengths of routine, memorization, and speaking. Routines: I follow a set assignment sheet with times for my different tasks, such as patient rounds, groups, and charting. Memorization: I memorize the names of thirty-two patients each day—and their locations and behaviors. Speaking: I lead group discussions and teach on mental health issues, self-esteem, substance abuse, and setting goals.

It is always a good idea to discuss your strengths and weaknesses with your family, friends, and co-workers. Research careers online and at the library that are a good fit for your skills and abilities. Learn to use your strengths in employment by asking these seven questions based on your likes and dislikes:

1. What skills do I have?
2. What do I enjoy doing?
3. What are my special interests and passions?
4. What do I hate doing and why?
5. What do I have difficulty doing?
6. What challenges do I experience in the workplace?
7. What are my values?

Try different activities to discover what you enjoy and to develop social skills for the workplace. Angela Mahoney, a special education teacher, states, "When working on a plan for the future it is important to try a variety of activities or opportunities. This allows you to reflect and process if it was enjoyable or challenging, ultimately leading you to a narrower field for employment preferences. I recommend creating a personal portfolio to record each vocational activity."[7]

The skills you learn through volunteer work, education, and previous jobs prepare you for a career. Anita Lesko, a nurse anesthetist, shares:

> Being autistic and working a career-type job is like going to a foreign country, not speaking their language, and trying to survive. To this day, all these years later, I still feel like a foreigner in a strange land. Yet I've built enough experience and "learned the language" enough to stay employed and have a successful career. I know without a doubt in my mind that I would never have made it as an anesthetist if I hadn't had all my previous jobs.[8]

Jobs we hate prepare us for a career we love. The communication skills I acquired through telemarketing prepared me to write my first book, *A Parent's Guide to Autism*. In telemarketing, a large percentage of prospective buyers decline the service—but some respond positively. The trademark of a successful telemarketer is to never take rejection personally. This is hard with autism, but perseverance leads to sales.

While writing my first book, I interviewed over fifty of the top autism experts and over fifty parents who have a child or children with autism. I also had hundreds of experts and a few parents reject my cold calls and emails requesting an interview. Instead of taking these rejections personally and thinking that I was a failure, I shook the dust off my feet and sent another email or made another call. The next call or email often led to an interview or a speaking engagement. I have interviewed well over three hundred people and published more than two hundred articles. By building a platform and name in the autism community, I now receive few rejections for interviews.

Eight Tips for Employment

Twenty-six million Americans with disabilities are of working age. Every year, an additional fifty thousand young adults with autism diligently search and struggle for employment. Many of these young adults experience chronic underemployment and unemployment. After working for more than thirty years, I have learned eight valuable lessons for employment.[9]

1. Most people find employment through personal connections.

While working part-time for Comfort Keepers, I overheard one of the staff at the nursing home state, "I work at Havenwyck Hospital." I told this staff member, "I submitted my résumé to Havenwyck four months ago and never heard back!" She advised me, "Tomorrow, go and ask for my supervisor, and he will hire you. I'll call him tonight." The next day, I went to the hospital and asked to meet with her supervisor; he hired me.

2. Employment comes through experience.

I can guess what you're thinking: *How can I ever gain experience if no company will hire me?* Experience as a volunteer or an intern may open the door to entry-level employment within organizations or companies. I volunteered at Oakland Christian Church for a year before they hired me as a full-time employee. A recent job study found that 82 percent of people responsible for hiring workers are more likely to choose a candidate with volunteer experience on their résumé.[10]

3. An employer hires based on the company's needs.

In job interviews, focus on your strengths and gifts and how they relate to the company's needs. Some positive traits I share with prospective employers are honesty, perseverance, and attention to detail. Here are some positive traits individuals with autism bring to the workforce:

- Focus and diligence: When motivated and interested, people with autism work with full focus and don't quit until their task is complete.
- Pride in work: People with autism give 100 percent effort.
- A desire to please: people with autism often have a strong desire to be a part of a team and contribute.
- Independent, unique thinking: People with autism march to their own drum. We tend to spend a lot of time alone and develop our own unique thoughts as opposed to having a herd mentality.
- Visual, three-dimensional thinking: An example of this is Temple Grandin's design of the double-rail conveyor system to lead cattle calmly to the slaughterhouse; her design is used to handle half the cattle in the United States.
- Wordsmithery: Many people with Asperger's love words, and they also enjoy the study of the science of words. They are skilled

at work that involves the love and knowledge of words, such as writing and editing.

- Attention to detail: People with autism see small details others might miss and are quick to try to fix any problems.
- Loyal, honest, and punctual: The value of being able to say "the emperor isn't wearing clothes" should not be underestimated, even if it's not what people want to hear.
- Logic over emotions: Logic in the face of a problem can often be crucial when needing to find a solution in a timely manner.[11]

4. Employment comes to those who diligently seek it.

You can't wait around for opportunities to come your way. You must seek them out and make them happen. Do not become discouraged during your quest for employment. As my dad advises, "The only difference between a successful person and a failure is that a successful person rises one more time than he falls."

My final four points focus on helping you remain employed after you have a job.

5. Find a mentor in your workplace to help you learn your job.

A mentor can be a co-worker or supervisor who is willing to help teach you the job and offer you encouragement. Pick a mentor who is understanding of your disability, has been working at the company for at least a few years, and has patience. Watch and learn from that individual. Proverbs 27:17 says, "As iron sharpens iron, so one person sharpens another."

Your workplace mentor is the go-to person for questions related to work. Dr. Jackie Marquette shared the story of a young adult with autism who was bullied by a co-worker but wasn't aware that's what was happening. The co-worker informed the young adult that "the grocery store now requires we bring in at least four hundred shopping carts a day." The young adult became worried and told his parents, "I don't want to go back to work." After the mentor spoke to the young adult about his work anxiety due to misinformation from the co-worker and talked with the management team, the bullying ceased.[12]

6. Take advantage of every opportunity.

If your employer offers extra training classes or seminars, attend them. UHS, the corporation that Havenwyck Hospital belongs to, offered tuition reimbursement up to $1,000 a year. For four years I took $1,000 a year worth of psychology classes and other college courses, and was reimbursed by UHS. The psychology classes provided me with the degree and background for writing my books on autism. Proverbs 22:29 states, "Do you see a man skilled in his work? He will serve before kings. He won't serve before obscure men."[13]

7. Find a work environment where you feel comfortable and not stressed.

Ask yourself these three questions: *Do I work better with co-workers or alone? Do I like to make my own decisions or have an assignment from a supervisor? Do I work more efficiently with defined responsibilities and guidelines or with flexibility and spontaneity?*

8. Know your own limits at work.

Many individuals with autism experience sensory issues with touch, sound, taste, smell, or sight. If you have sensory issues, make sure you receive accommodations in those areas so they do not affect your job performance. Some questions to ask yourself about sensory issues in the workplace are:

- What environment or other conditions impact my sensory issues?
- What work conditions keep me calm or make me anxious? Do I work more efficiently in a factory, office, or outdoor environment?

- How can I adapt my sensory issues in the workplace?
- What accommodations will I need to perform my job?

Know your own limitations. The number one reason employees with disabilities are fired after they have been working at a company for five or more years is receiving a job promotion that they are not able to handle.[14]

A few years ago, my company was offering preceptor positions with a pay increase of two dollars an hour. I turned down the position because I knew my limitation and knew that I could not handle the extra stress of being a PCS supervisor and training new employees.

Your limitation could be socializing at work. A female with Asperger's shares, "Small talk is deadly for me. I am expected to talk with co-workers about babies, boyfriends, shopping, and gossip. I try, but then I become exhausted and resentful and can't keep up."[15]

Finally, your chances for success at work increase when you eat well, sleep enough, take care of your body, and have a relaxing home-life. I cover this in chapter 2, "Living Healthy on the Spectrum."

Difficulties in the Workplace

I will share a few difficulties I've experienced in the workplace, along with practical ways I have learned to adapt and be productive. My greatest fear in the workplace is new management. I have difficulty understanding supervisors' managing styles. When I get a new unit manager at the hospital, I introduce myself and learn about his interests and goals. I educate the new manager on autism and accommodations I need to perform my job effectively.

I have difficulty transitioning from one task to the next assignment. Switching tasks requires a few extra minutes to adjust and prepare my mind for the next assignment. I take a quick water break to relax my mind. Before work, I write down the tasks I need to accomplish, and I check them off my list after I complete them.

Early in my career in the mental health field, I had difficulty with prioritizing responsibilities and deadlines. I learned to prioritize my assignments according to the needs of my employer and clients and the immediacy of the deadline. I write my list from low-priority tasks to urgent must-dos. I then prioritize the items based on the importance, urgency, length, and reward of each task. I have learned to break down larger goals into smaller tasks, and I break down long-term goals into yearly, monthly, and weekly achievements. By doing this I almost never miss a deadline.

Prioritizing work commitments list

- Make a daily or weekly to-do list. Have a column marked A, one marked B, and one marked C.
- Place all the urgent projects in column A, those to be done next in column B, and things that can wait in column C.
- After defining the priorities with A, B, and C, break down each larger task into smaller tasks.
- After you finish your A tasks, begin B tasks. Move on to C tasks after the A and B projects are completed.
- Remember to check your to-do list daily, and mark on a calendar the date each task is to be completed.

I had difficulty balancing personal and work life. This required me to learn to say no to overtime. I don't allow work to burn me out. Working overtime can cause people with autism to become hypomanic or exhausted or to experience mental health issues. It's up to us to know our limits and inform our supervisors when we are feeling overwhelmed from working too many hours. Also, I plan at least one vacation a year to get my mind off work.

Trade School

Don't limit experience to only a college degree. While earning a college degree is one path to employment, we must remember there are many other paths. A trade school, which is hands-on training, is a great way to learn a specific job skill. These careers include electrician, plumber, HVACR and IT technicians, web developer, dental hygienist, legal assistant, licensed practical nurse, power utility technician, automotive mechanic, and others.

With the increased rate of autism, there is also a greater increase in technology, electronic gadgets, and scientific discoveries. For gainful employment, we on the spectrum need to take full advantage of specialization and technology careers.

Autism Specialization for the Job Market

I believe individuals with autism, with their intense focus and special interests, can create a symbiotic relationship in the job market. An example of symbiosis is the sea anemone and clown fish. The sea anemone provides the clown fish with nutrients and protection from predators. In return for a safe and protective home, the clown fish cleans the anemone, provides nutrients in the form of waste, and scares away predatory fish.

Likewise, employers can benefit from the unique talents individuals with autism provide in the workforce.

Mark Fleming, an autistic person, demonstrates the unique skill set autism supplies in the workplace. While working as a behavior analysis tech, Mark noticed that many children and young adults with autism were not physically active and were overweight. Mark shares, "Seeing the muscular weakness in the kids I worked with in ABA and the older adults I coached at Special Olympics made me realize that there is a physical activity gap that was not being filled. So I started an in-home training business that flourished to a full schedule in its first year and thus made me realize that to expand and grow to help more individuals, I would need to open my own gym. I founded Equally Fit in Tampa. This business helps individuals with autism become physically fit, healthy, and learn social skills."[16] Discovering his niche, Mark now has a successful business, Equally Fit, that empowers individuals with autism to stay healthy and in great physical shape. The skills needed to be a successful entrepreneur like Mark are passion, drive, and organization.

Networking Connection

The networking connections I gained through my nonprofit, Spectrum Inclusion, will enable me to transition smoothly into my next career. I already have more than forty thousand email addresses and more than five hundred churches on my contact list. I also have connections with every autism and ABA center throughout Michigan. It takes most people three to six months to get hired when unemployed. With my contact list, I could get hired quickly since I have a personal connection with the decision-makers in companies and churches. These decision-makers have seen my presentations or read my books and know the leadership skills and gifts I will bring to the workplace.

Closing Thoughts

Early in my working career, I often felt frustrated and disappointed. Learning my strengths and weaknesses and understanding the workplace culture has enabled me to thrive. A job coach and mentor can help you learn the ins and outs of the workplace. Have faith that the skills you are developing in your current job or volunteer work will prepare you for your career. Your work-experience dots will connect as you continue to persevere, mature, and keep a positive attitude.

REFLECT

1. I shared my strengths and weaknesses. What are some strengths and weaknesses you bring to the workplace? What type of career would your strengths be best suited for? What type of work would be a challenge for you?

2. I mentioned difficulties in the workplace. What are some difficulties you've experienced at work? How have you learned to overcome these challenges? Did you need any accommodations?
3. Share a time you offended a co-worker by not following the culture of the workplace. What lessons did you learn from this situation? Would you handle this situation differently now?

FUN ACTIVITIES

Create a personal vocational/job portfolio. Use a scrapbook, leather journal, or folder to create your vocational/job portfolio. Have four sections in the portfolio: Section 1: Volunteer Work/Jobs; Section 2: Skills I Learned on the Job; Section 3: Challenges I Experienced on the Job; and Section 4: Dream Career. In each section, include pictures with captions.

In section 1, share your volunteer work and jobs, dated and in chronological order. For each volunteer opportunity and work experience, have a picture of you in your work outfit and in front of the workplace building or with co-workers. Type up your duties for each job and volunteer work and tell what you liked best about this work experience. Place it in the scrapbook.

In section 2, have action pictures of you working. Type up the lessons you learned on the job and the skills you gained, and place it in the scrapbook.

For section 3, have pictures of the challenging work. For example, have before and after photos. Include a picture of you beginning a work project and a second photo of the finished product. Type up the challenges you experienced on the job and tell how you were able to overcome them. Place them in the scrapbook.

In section 4, have photos of your dream job and professionals who work in that career. Interview professionals in your dream career and type up the wisdom you gained from them and the skills required to be successful in that line of work, and place it in the scrapbook.

Finally, share your work at the end of the scrapbook. This can include artwork or articles you have published, pictures of you with famous people you've met, and letters of recommendation. Now share your portfolio with your family, friends, and people in your small group.

FURTHER READING

Asperger's on the Job: Must-Have Advice for People with Asperger's or High Functioning Autism and Their Employers, Educators, and Advocates, by Rudy Simone

Developing Talents: Careers for Individuals with Asperger Syndrome and High-Functioning Autism, by Temple Grandin and Kate Duffy

How to Find Work That Works for People with Asperger Syndrome: The Ultimate Guide for Getting People with Asperger Syndrome into the Workplace (And Keeping Them There!), by Gail Hawkins

Tiffany Fixter's Story
Brewability: The World's First Brewery Staffed with Adults with Disabilities

Society told my employees what they couldn't do;
I would show what they could.
—TIFFANY FIXTER

AS A CHILD, TIFFANY FIXTER gravitated toward helping those with special needs and hoped to be a teacher. After graduating from high school, Tiffany had difficulty choosing a major. She enjoyed studying business and loved teaching. Her mom encouraged her to follow her passions and be a special education teacher. She attended Northwest Missouri State University, earned a bachelor's degree in elementary education, and went on to get her master's degree in special education/ autism spectrum disorders from the University of Kansas.

For the next seven years, Tiffany taught students with learning disabilities and autism. She enjoyed discovering their unique interests, talents, and ability to absorb knowledge. Through teaching, Tiffany programed her mind to think outside the box. She began her career as a kindergarten teacher working in a lower-income school district in Kansas City, Missouri. While using picture education cards (PECs) to teach a kindergartner to speak, she quickly realized that this student was able to master most of the PECs but was unable to interpret the card of a bed. After numerous failed attempts to teach him with the card, Tiffany became frustrated. Knowing children with autism have difficulty with generalization, she decided to use a picture of his bed. Tiffany had the student's mom text her a photo, and to her amazement, his bed was a towel on the bedroom floor.

"This moment taught me that teachers need to think from the perspective of the child. Bed, to this child, was a towel on the floor. Special education teachers need to be creative and resourceful and empower their students to learn new ideas and have problem-solving skills," Tiffany says.

She became disheartened by the hardships her special education kindergartners experienced. These inner-city children faced extraordinary challenges that most could barely fathom, yet they survive.

She left teaching to be a day-program director for adults with disabilities. She was baffled and distraught that approximately eighty out of one hundred of her adult clients had learned basic reading, writing, and arithmetic skills yet could not use the restroom independently or cross the street, and they lacked other daily life skills vital for transitioning to adulthood. This inspired her to empower these individuals for independence and train them for employment.

"I wanted to do something that was cool and purposeful that gives people with disabilities an opportunity to show their ability. I hope to be an example for other businesses to think outside the box. That's when you really see what people are capable of and that we're all members of the community."

Teaching and directing the adult day program prepared Tiffany for her next adventure: Pizzability and the Brewability Lab—the world's first brewery to hire adults with developmental disabilities. Tiffany's hospitality-industry companies train people with disabilities to use their *abilities* for employment.

She had to learn, though, about the brutal life of entrepreneurship. As an entrepreneur, Tiffany's greatest challenge was finance. "Money!

Funding, financing, and balancing cash flow is extremely difficult."
She started small, applied for local grants, and worked her way into
proving her concept. Her only investors to this day are her parents.
As business owners themselves, they understand the difficulties. She
learned from them to persevere through hard work and be dedicated
to her customers and product.

Brewability Lab received both praise and persecution from the community of Englewood, Colorado. When she first put the idea of the
brewery out to the public, she received a ton of hateful emails and even
death threats. People were disturbed that individuals with disabilities
would be around alcohol.

Tiffany responded to the haters with, "We are brewing, not drinking. They are adults! It is precisely why I chose a brewery. It is an adult
industry. Infantilizing adults with intellectual and developmental disabilities must stop. When given a chance, people with disabilities can
do more than just work in the back monotonously rolling silverware
or asking customers, 'Do you want paper or plastic?' They can be a
contributing part of the community."

Tiffany learned dos and don'ts in entrepreneurship and developed
perseverance. Her first attempt was to partner with a preexisting business. She says it was like moving into someone else's home. "You're in
their house, which means you abide by their rules." She discovered a
few months in that this was not a viable business option. This business
did not pay Brewability Lab for the beer they brewed—only an hourly
minimum wage for the group. They would not allow the workers to be
visible among the customers or serve them beer.

She then purchased an affordable turnkey brewery in a rough part
of town, located three rows back in a business park. To make things
worse, signage was not permitted, making it impossible to attract customers to the remote location. She adapted to the environment by
hosting large gatherings in the parking lot on weekends and fundrais-
ers to attract crowds. She also had the menus translated into Spanish

because that was the primary language of the neighborhood. Brew-ability Lab survived there for two years.

Her third attempt was Pizzability, an affordable turnkey (but high rent) business in the prestigious neighborhood of Cherry Creek. She was confident the neighborhood would accept her and her staff because she was located near the Global Down Syndrome Association. She spent a year remodeling the restaurant to make it accessible. She had a sensory wall, adaptive utensils, and many other accommodations. "It was perfect. I built my dream restaurant, where staff and customers of all abilities felt comfortable. But my dream quickly turned into my worst nightmare."

It was a tumultuous year of ups and downs. The neighborhood did not embrace the business. They were continually verbally assaulted. People would walk by and state things like, "That's where the retards work" and "You would make more money if you would hire models and put your disabled people in the back." She left there crying every day, physically exhausted and an emotional mess. Considering the astronomical expenses of operating a restaurant in that area—more than $25,000 per month—she was forced to close shop.

This brought her to her fourth and final try. While googling, she found a turnkey brewery listed only five minutes from her house. Her parents encouraged her to find a building to buy "because when you lease, your future is uncertain."

The owner agreed to sell it. Her mother sold a bakery she owned to finance the purchase of the new building. She and her staff are thrilled with the current location. It is on a main street downtown, close to a school for the deaf and blind, a few blocks from a hospital, near low-income housing, and steps from public transit—which is extremely important for her staff. "We found our sweet spot! We are looking forward to making the neighborhood as accessible as possible, not only for people who use wheelchairs, but adding accommodations for everyone to feel safe and comfortable."

Brewability Lab focuses on an individual's abilities. The bartenders have various disabilities, such as autism, Down syndrome, and cerebral palsy. Some are blind, deaf, or have traumatic brain injuries. All staff members are expected to work with minimal hand-holding. If someone needs extra support, they receive it. If staff members come in upset, Tiffany processes through the situation with them and then they get back to work.

She tries to be consistent with scheduling and work tasks and provides modifications for learning disabilities, with color-coded beer taps and a visual menu—such as orange for amber ale and green for India pale ale—making it easier for employees who can't read. Braille was added to the taps. "The step-by-step brewing process appeals to those with autism who crave routine. The culture is *fun*—we are a bar, after all. The staff sing and dance while serving beer." Most importantly, her team is learning to socialize, and their self-confidence is skyrocketing.

Tiffany desires to change people's perspective of individuals with disabilities and empower them for employment. The current system, she says, heavily funds job placement but not job retention. She has seen how the system has been manipulated so that the job coach can maximize profits at the expense of the individual. "They will train someone to interview well, dress them up, then after they are placed in a job, there is little incentive for them to help them keep the job."

Tiffany encourages young adults with autism to learn practical skills related to daily living, safety, socializing, and work. This enables them to gain independence and be functioning members of society.[17]

TIFFANY FIXTER'S BIOGRAPHY

Tiffany Fixter has a master's degree in special education/autism spectrum disorders from the University of Kansas and a bachelor's degree in cross-categorical special education K–12 and general elementary education 1–6 from Northwest Missouri State University. Tiffany is the founder of Brewability Lab and Pizzability, which provide employment for adults with intellectual and developmental disabilities. She was awarded the 2024 Honey Badger Award from Spectrum Inclusion. Tiffany's story has been featured in *Forbes* and on *CBS News*.

Website: brew-ability.com

Facebook: facebook.com/brewability

REFLECT

1. Brewability is a bar that hires people with disabilities and autism. If you had an entrepreneur friend like Tiffany Fixter, what type of business would you want him or her to open? Why would you want to get hired in that type of work?

2. How do you feel employers and co-workers perceive people with autism and other disabilities? Do you think stereotypes of autism have hindered your employment? Why or why not?

3. Would you want to work in a place where most of the employees have autism? Why or why not? What advantages would this work environment provide? What disadvantages?

Chapter 8

Navigating the Social Nuances
of Interviewing

*People on the autism spectrum have to sell their skills, not
themselves, which is the opposite of the way most businesses
operate.*

—Temple Grandin

Learning to navigate the social nuances of the employment process will help relieve some of your job anxiety and fears. Tony Beshara, author of *Acing the Interview,* shares, "When people are emotionally stressed, they usually want to focus on their own needs, rather than on the needs of someone else. They often forget that, in order to get a job offer, they have to focus on how they can solve the hiring authority's problem—his or her needs, not those of the candidate."[1]

In 2005, when I was unemployed and searching for a job, I felt defeated. During this season, I emailed more than 350 churches that were hiring, only to experience further frustration. I traveled throughout Michigan, to Indiana, and to New York for pastoral candidate interviews. (I can't complain about the New York interview—I received an all-expense paid trip and visited Niagara Falls.)

While searching for stable employment with benefits, I experienced pressure from my dad as he cross-examined me with the question, "You have a master's degree, so why are you working only part-time at a skateboard shop for five dollars and fifty cents an hour?"

During interviews, I lacked social grace and was notorious for making a wrong comment to the hiring authority. I had a job interview for a director of youth-ministry position in a small Methodist church in Flint. As the interview drew to a close, the senior pastor smiled and asked, "Son, do you have any hands-on experience in urban ministry?"

Because I knew that the city of Flint had a high homicide and crime rate and because autism causes me to be brutally honest with my faulty filtering system, I joked, "Is urban ministry when you put on the full armor of God for spiritual protection and a bulletproof vest for physical protection?" Needless to say, the interview team never called me back.

Through my struggles and perseverance, I have learned to navigate the social nuances of interviewing and the importance of networking in finding gainful employment. The interview process begins by writing a cover letter and résumé that stand out from the competition, and then gathering references.

Writing a Cover Letter

The purpose of a cover letter is to introduce yourself to a potential employer. When you send out a résumé, you'll need to customize your cover letter. The quality and relevance of a cover letter could be the difference between an interview and a missed opportunity.

As you write a cover letter, consider the skills, personality traits, experiences, and accomplishments you want to share with the company. Mention how you heard about the position, such as through a personal contact, an employee, a co-worker, an advertisement, or online. If through an employee, mention his name and the department he works in. If you heard about the job through an advertisement, write down where and when you saw it and what in the ad caught your attention.

Note why you desire to work for the company. Maybe a friend is an employee, or you are impressed with their work environment or philosophy. This may require research online about the company.

The cover letter should be no more than one page, written in standard business letter format. Check out examples of cover letters online. A good format is four paragraphs.

In the first paragraph, note how you heard about the job. This is especially important if you've been referred by a friend who is employed there. You can begin this paragraph with something like, "I was excited when my friend Bill Smith informed me you had an opening in the IT department." Then share some strengths you provide for the position.

In the second paragraph, state your qualifications and education as they relate to the position. Reveal the top three skills that make you a good candidate, and how and why your talents and experience will benefit the company. The hirer is looking for a candidate who can produce results.

Tony Beshara recommends sharing your features, advantages, and benefits in this paragraph.[2] Your *feature* is what makes you unique and should include previous experience, special training, and qualities such as hardworking, attention to detail, or dedication. A feature demonstrates why you would be a good fit.

An *advantage* is what sets you apart from the other candidates. For example, "Through dedication and customer care [features], I was able to be promoted to the leadership training team" [advantage].

A *benefit* is something the company receives by hiring a candidate with your distinctive features and advantages. For example, "I have ten years of experience in computer software development [feature] and was promoted to supervisor of the software designer team with twenty-five designers under my care [advantage]. I work great under deadlines, and my leadership skills help our team finish assignments in a timely manner" [benefit].

In the third paragraph, describe how you're a good fit for the job. Mention the ways you connect with the company and their work environment. For example, "I have three friends who are employed with you" or "I've been using your software for the past five years." The hirer feels good when you have a personal connection and an understanding of the organization and its culture.

In the fourth paragraph, mention your résumé: "For my complete employment history and my skills and experience, please see the included résumé." Ask for an interview and for a time to meet in person, and thank the hiring manager for reviewing your résumé and cover letter. If you send your résumé by email, just type your name at the end. However, if you're mailing a hard copy, sign your cover letter.

Tips for writing a cover letter
1. Be yourself. Each letter should express your personality and enthusiasm. Take pride in who you are, what you've accomplished, and how you can benefit the company.
2. Write in the active tense. Action verbs are the key. Instead of saying, "My best attributes are leadership and knowledge in the software field," say, "I'm a faithful leader and motivator and have five years of experience in software development."
3. Customize your cover letter for each job opening. Don't use a generic cover letter: "Dear Hiring Manager, I am excited to apply to the open position at your company." Instead, use the first and last name of the hiring authority and share a few things you like about the company and why you're applying. Never use the generic "To Whom It May Concern."
4. Don't use a picture unless the job opening asks for it.
5. Share what you can do for the company, not what the company can do for you. The hiring authority wants to know what you will bring to the company. You do this by identifying the company's pain points—the problems they need the person they hire

to solve. Then emphasize the talents and experience you bring that make you the right person to solve them.

6. Don't include irrelevant information, such as sharing about your pet dog when the job has nothing to do with pets and canines.

7. Don't point out what you're missing or your weaknesses. If you lack a required degree, don't mention it. Instead, focus on the skills and experiences you can bring to the job, and explain how they make you a good candidate.

8. Explain why the job is cool and why you are passionate about this field of work.

9. Be confident but not boastful when noting your experience and achievements. Don't use words like "expert" or say, "I'm confident I'm the perfect person for the job." Instead, share a short story that demonstrates your experience and skills.

10. Read through your letter, looking for any typos and mistakes. Double-check that you have the correct company name, hiring manager's name, date, and position you're applying for in your heading. Have at least three people edit and proofread your cover letter before you send it out. Make sure to use spell-check.

Most hiring managers read your résumé first, then the cover letter. When writing your résumé, the same principles apply as for a cover letter. Your résumé presents your skills and work experience, while the cover letter showcases you and why you'd be a positive addition to the company.

Writing a Résumé

Before you create a résumé and cover letter, decide the type of work you enjoy that also matches your skills and personality. Discuss potential jobs with family, friends, educators, and co-workers based on the skills and passions you possess. To assess whether a job is a good fit for you, research it online and interview people who have a career in that field. Some jobs sound good when you read a description but may not work well for you based on your sensory issues, temperament, or the duties and training required.

As you create your résumé, develop a short elevator speech to describe your skills and abilities and the type of job you are seeking.

Be prepared to apply for numerous jobs, even as many as one hundred or more. "For an average online job posting, 1,000 individuals will see the job post, 200 will begin the application process, 100 will complete the application, 75 of those 100 resumes will be screened out by either the ATS [applicant tracking system] or a recruiter, and 25 resumes will be seen by the hiring manager."[3] The typical employer will interview four to six candidates for a job, and candidates will go through at least two rounds of interviews before receiving an offer.

Most companies scan the applicant's résumé for keywords relevant to the posted job description. Research online the appropriate buzzwords for the job you desire so you can sprinkle them into your résumé and cover letter.

> Every word on your resume counts. Be specific and concise, only using [words] that illuminate your point. Utilize keywords from the job description, but only where they're relevant. Avoid repetition, and only use words that you understand. . . . As you search for creative synonyms, it can be easy to reach for words you don't firmly grasp—and that can come across during your interview. And never forget to proofread your resume multiple times; recruiters and hiring managers overwhelmingly cite typos or bad grammar as an immediate deal breaker.[4]

The format should be single spaced, Times New Roman or Calibri, and size twelve font. Remember to customize your résumé for each job.

Six steps for writing a résumé

First, contact information: Your name, email address, physical address, and phone number. The top of your résumé should look like this:

Date _____

Name _____

Email _____

City _____

Phone Number _____

Second, education background: the colleges or trade schools you attended, and any special training or credits you received relevant to the job for which you are applying. Include the beginning date and the date of completion of each.

Third, career summary: an introductory paragraph packed with your skills, abilities, accomplishments, and attributes. Your career summary is key to getting noticed. In my career summary, I mention my duties with my current and previous employment and my work experience.

Fourth, professional experience: This section includes a list of your three previous employment or volunteer experiences. Begin with your most recent employment. Make sure to emphasize your job responsibilities as they relate to the position for which you are applying. Only include three or four previous employments.

Andrea Reger, a career counselor at Lehigh University, recommends "not to lump all job experience together but to break them into categories that relate to the job you're applying for."[5] For example, your categories could be teaching, journalism, and business.

Fifth, achievements and awards: This can include academic or athletic awards, scholarships, dean's list or honor roll, awards of excellence in voluntary activities, job-performance awards, publishing a book, and being an advisory board member. Along with mentioning your earned awards, give a quick explanation as to what each award means. Separate your professional awards from personal achievements, and don't include awards from too far in the past. For example, I won the Detroit Edison Poster Contest when I was in fourth grade. I would not include this because it was too far in the past to be relevant.

Sixth, be short and concise: Your résumé should be only two pages and to the point. Include only relevant information that demonstrates why you're qualified for the job and why you'd be a great employee.

The next step after finishing your résumé is to gather three or four solid references.

Selecting References

You have control over the quality of your cover letter, résumé, and portfolio, but you can't control what your references say about you. On the other hand, you can control whom you select as your references, so choose wisely. One wrong word from a less-than-enthusiastic reference can disqualify you, while a strong endorsement can convince an employer that you have the right skills and experience to excel in the job.

There are five types of people to consider for references. First, choose a previous supervisor or manager who knows your strengths and with whom you had a good rapport. This supervisor is able to share examples of your work ethic and skills and can share how you can benefit the company. The absence of a supervisor in your references can invite questions about your work performance. Don't use a previous supervisor you had an issue with or who disciplined you or gave you a warning. Be careful not to use your current boss (unless he or she knows you're searching for a new job). This could lead to termination from your employment.

Second, co-workers and colleagues make great references. They can attest to your qualifications and share personal examples. The more references you gather, the easier it is to choose references strategically based on the different requirements for each job opening.

Third, friends who are employed in the field to which you're applying provide a solid perspective. These friends can offer a character witness, and they understand the qualifications the hirer is seeking.

Fourth, consider a former professor. Use this reference only if you're a recent graduate. A professor can share your academic achievement and problem-solving abilities.

Fifth, internal references increase your chances of being hired. They are the best references because they are employed at the business where you're applying and may know the person involved in the hiring. A survey on the role of in-house recommendations finds human resource officials using employee recommendations for more than 40 percent of hires.[6] An internal reference holds higher credibility and understands what the hirers desire in a perspective employee. This type of reference is received by networking.

Nine reference tips

1. Before you use people as a reference, ask for their consent.
2. Ask your references to write you a recommendation that you can send with your cover letter and résumé. This will give you a clear sense of how they represent your background.
3. Have a friend or family member contact your references as a prospective employer would. Based on what the reference shares with your friend or family member posing as a hirer, you will know if they are a good reference or not.
4. Update your references periodically. When scrambling for a job, you don't want to take extra time gathering new references. Add new references and remove any who are less than enthusiastic or if a lot of time has passed since you've worked with them.
5. Choose references who are positive and whom you have known for at least a few years. Your best references will be able to describe your abilities, work ethic, and achievements on the job, in the classroom, or in your community.

6. Choose professional over personal references since you're applying for a professional position and not to be someone's friend.
7. Inform your references of the jobs for which you're applying. This will enable your references to tailor their responses to skills that apply to the particular position.
8. Ensure that the contact information is correct. If a potential employer calls the phone number of your reference and it has been disconnected, you probably won't get the job.
9. Thank your references. After you get hired, send your references a thank-you letter to let them know you appreciate them.

Now that you have written your cover letter and résumé and have gathered three or four references, you're ready for the next step: applying for jobs and preparing for interviews. I recommend marking the dates and times of your interviews on a calendar. This is a visual reminder that you're on the path to employment.

Preparing for the Interview

When you begin the job search, network by telling family, friends, and acquaintances that you're diligently searching for employment. Ask them if they know of any openings in the field you're pursuing. After networking, the best way to find a job is online. Four great sites are Indeed, CareerBuilder, LinkedIn Jobs, and Monster.com. When considering applying, keep in mind that a job description is a wish list. You don't have to meet every requirement.

Once you decide which jobs to apply for, research the companies to gain background information for the interviews. Check the company's website, mission statement, and staff. Read a few reviews from employees and former employees and from their clients.

When you receive a call or email for an interview, review on LinkedIn the profile of the person or persons who will interview you and, if possible, his or her Facebook page. (Don't send a friend request on Facebook to members of the hiring team.) This background check will let you know if you have common interests and connections with the interviewers.

An interview is a test of how well the hirer thinks you can do the job and how well you will fit in with the company. The hiring authority does not want to employ a person whom they view as a liability or risk. Some liabilities are job-hoppers (people who keep a job for less than a year), felons (people with a criminal record), and long commuters (people who live more than an hour and a half away from the company).

From the knowledge gained during research, prepare some positive things to say that show your enthusiasm about working for the company. Do not say anything negative about the job or the company, like, "I read online that you are being sued" or "I read an article that your former CEO was arrested for embezzlement."

Before the interview, prepare and memorize scripted responses to the most common interview questions and do a mock interview with a friend or family member. (In the next section, we will examine common interview questions and how to answer them.) Reread the job description and bring a copy of your cover letter and résumé to the interview. Be sure to prepare some questions to ask the interviewer. Avoid those that have yes or no answers, but rather choose questions that will elicit longer, more detailed responses.

Dress appropriately—professional attire—and keep your sensory issues in mind. Men, wear a suit and tie or polo shirt and khaki pants. Don't wear tight clothes or attire that itches, and wear a belt with your pants. Keep bright, flashy colors to a minimum. When wearing a tie, a traditional pattern with conservative colors—subdued stripes or tasteful paisley—makes the best impression.

Women can wear a dress or slacks and button-down shirt tucked in. Remember that the neckline should be modest, with no cleavage showing, and any skirt should be just above the knees or longer. If you use perfume or cologne, go light, as you never know if your interviewer might have an allergy or aversion to strong scents. If possible, talk to the company's employees and ask them how to dress for the interview. Remember—it's always better to overdress. Set out your clothes the night before, and get at least eight hours of sleep.

During the interview, practice good etiquette: firm handshake, back straight, and say please and thank you. Try to be a half hour early. When it's your turn to ask questions, select three or four of your prepared questions. Avoid any interview questions about money or compensation; this will turn the hirer off. Save these questions for when you're offered the job.

Here are a few good questions to ask at an interview: Can you tell me more about your team and the people I'll be working with? What are the company's upcoming plans, and how can I help you achieve them? How is success measured here?

With all the uncertainties, interviews can be scary. By practicing mock interviews, you can feel confident and prepared. Online virtual tools can help prepare you for interviews. You should view each interview as a learning experience and as one step closer to employment.

Common Interview Questions

Knowing what not to say and how to answer an interview question could be the deciding factor in getting hired. There are some things you should never say in an interview. Never answer a question by saying, "I don't know how to do that" or "I lack that kind of experience." This will disqualify you for the job. Instead, say, "I look forward to learning this, and I enjoy learning new skills. Let me share with you some work I have done similar to this."

If asked about your plans for the future, do not say that you plan to work there for only a few months, even if this is the case, as this is likely to lose you the job. Instead say, "I hope to work for your company for at least four or five years. I prefer not to change jobs, and as long as I'm experiencing growth, I'll stay committed."

Don't share your personal problems with the interviewer. For example, don't say, "My ex-girlfriend keeps texting me, and she is driving me nuts" or "I have digestive problems and take a lot of time off work because of these health issues." Instead, wait until you're hired to share any health concerns or family issues.

Sell your skills by sharing your features, advantages, and benefits. You need to efficiently "sell" to the hiring authority the benefit of hiring you and why you're the best candidate for the job. Here are eight common questions the interviewer could ask and how to answer them.

"Tell me about yourself." Answer this by detailing your professional experiences and how they relate to the job. Give three to five strong and relevant adjectives that describe you and your values; then give real examples of how you embody the adjectives. Avoid "I was born and raised . . ." The employer couldn't care less about your personal background unless it relates to the job. Only mention hobbies or interests that are relatable to the position. Also, if you know that the company has a culture for inclusion, you can share your autism diagnosis; otherwise you should wait until you're hired.

"What is the ideal job you're looking for?" You should have already done your research on the company. You can share why you applied. A good answer is, "After researching your company, I believe I would be a good fit in a way that would benefit this company, based on my experience and skills."

"What was the most difficult part of your previous job?" Don't say, "The manager or co-workers." The interviewer will always identify more with the supervisor than with you, so never bad-mouth your previous boss. Instead, mention a challenge you experienced and how you overcame it. Answer by sharing a short story or event and stating, "Even though this was a challenge, I learned valuable lessons and became a better person." Keep your answers positive.

"Why should I hire you?" Answer this using the feature, advantage, and benefit format.

"Why did you apply for this job opening?" Note how you are passionate for that field of work and the benefits you can provide based on your features and advantages.

"What gets you out of bed?" or **"What motivates you?"** This question is asked to determine your personal values, well-roundedness, and passions. You can answer this question by sharing your special interests or hobbies. Make sure your answer is short. Don't ramble on.

"What's your biggest strength? What's your biggest weakness?" These questions provide an opportunity to showcase how well you know yourself. If you know yourself well, you know when you're at your most productive, what sets you off, what motivates you, and what you really need to function at your highest level.

For weakness, don't answer, "I get fired easily" or "I lack motivation." When you mention your weakness, spin it into a positive trait. For example, "My weakness is hyperfocus and keeping at a project until it's complete. Over the past few years, I have learned to slow down and take breaks and strive for excellence rather than perfection."

"Why did you have so many different jobs over a short period of time?" Many people with autism struggle with maintaining employment and will have multiple jobs over a short stint. I suggest an answer like this: "Yes, I've had a few jobs I wish I hadn't taken. But I've learned to choose more carefully, and I hope you'll take my references into consideration." Don't try to justify why you had multiple jobs over a short period of time.

"What are some things we might not like about you if we knew them?" An interview team could ask an unusual question like this to check your reaction and response. One employer asked me that question. I answered this question with humor: "If you're a competitive runner and don't like to lose, you would not like to learn that I can run the mile in under five minutes. Every candidate has some quirks. My main quirk is an intense focus when I begin a project. I stay focused until the task is complete. I have learned during the last few years to slow down and take a break. This makes the task more enjoyable."

"Do you have any questions for me?" This is usually the final question. Ask two or three questions related to the position, and finish the interview strong with this question: "What more can I tell you about me and my skills to be seriously considered for this job?" You are either a candidate or not, and you need to know where you stand. Most people, afraid of rejection, finish the interview with the wimpy questions, "What is the next step?" or "When will I hear back from you?" Asking "What more can I tell you about me to be seriously considered for this job?" shows confidence and guts—desirable qualities. After the interview, within two or three days, send a thank-you letter.

Handling Rejection

On the average, job seekers receive twenty-four rejections during the hiring process.[7] Getting a job is a numbers game and takes three to six months. Therefore, numerous interviews are crucial to getting a job offer, so don't feel defeat on the journey to employment; instead, shake the dust off your keyboard and keep sending those résumés and cover letters.

Six ways to handle rejection

1. Don't take rejection personally, and don't allow rejection to make you feel hopeless. Your worth is not based on your employment but on you as a person.

2. Learn from each rejection. Call or email the interviewer and ask him or her how you could do better for the next interview. If the feedback feels superficial or generic, ask for a more detailed assessment. Take notes after each interview. Evaluate how you can improve your answers, and write down the questions the interviewer asked you.

3. Review and reflect by asking yourself, *What did I sense went well? What could I have done differently? Could I have worked harder to build rapport with the interviewer?*
4. Maintain your momentum. Continue to practice mock interviews with family and friends. Read books and articles on interviewing.
5. Follow up with the interviewer. Every three months, contact the employer who did not hire you and ask if they have any new openings in the company for your skills.
6. Pray and keep your faith high that a job is just around the corner.

The Job Offer

When you're offered a job, be sure to thank the interviewers, either verbally or by email. Ask for the job offer in writing, so you can review all your benefits before signing. These can include the health-care plan with copays and deductibles, vacation time, long- and short-term disability insurance, life insurance, and a retirement plan. Make sure you understand your benefit package and your start date.

Ask the interviewer for a few days to consider the offer. Talk to your family and friends about the position, and listen to their insight. In addition to the salary, consider the benefits, work hours, and growth opportunities. Ask yourself two questions: *Do I have an understanding of the work I'll be doing every day? Can I handle the responsibilities?*

According to the Pew Research Center, a large number of workers fail to negotiate for higher pay—about 60 percent—mainly because they were not comfortable asking for more money.[8] When deciding whether to negotiate, ask yourself if the salary is in line with comparable positions in your area, and if it works for your personal budget. You can find out how your salary compares in your field by researching on sites such as Salary.com and Payscale.com or by asking your friends and contacts for advice. If you negotiate, consider asking for 3 to 5 percent more in pay or additional vacation time.

Read every contract you sign for the job offer. Never assume the contract is worded properly. Pause and read it before you sign. Consider these questions before you sign: How will my success be measured? What are the specific goals and outcomes for my job, and how will I be evaluated? What are the business hours, and what schedule will I be expected to work? After all these questions are satisfactorily answered, you're ready to sign the job offer and begin work.

Finally, get your job description in writing, know what is required of you, and know who your boss will be.

Closing Thoughts

Searching for a job is stressful. A strong cover letter, résumé, and solid references are key to receiving job interviews. A support team of family and friends will prepare you for interviews and provide you with encouragement and confidence. In interviews, share your features, advantages, and benefits. Use these to focus on the company's needs and how you can help. Don't allow rejection letters to stop your momentum. On average, it takes three to six months and twenty-four interview rejections to receive a job offer. Once you get a job, make a network list to help you with future employment opportunities.

REFLECT

1. What fears do you experience when searching for a job? How can you feel more confident during the process? What are some ways your support team can encourage you during your job search?
2. I discuss the concept of features and advantages. What are three features and two advantages you can share in your cover letter and during interviews? How do these features and advantages make you a good candidate for the job?
3. In the past, what were some ways you handled job rejections? How can you motivate yourself after a rejection? Who are some friends, co-workers, or family members who can encourage you after a job rejection?

FUN ACTIVITIES

Discuss jobs you should apply for with family, friends, or members of your small group. Then pick one job that sparks your interest, and research it online. Make a short list of the job's requirements. Next, write a paragraph with your features, advantages, and benefits, applying them to the job. Do a mock interview with a family member or friend, and record it with a cell phone. In the mock interview, respond to the following:

- "Tell me about yourself."
- "What is the ideal job you're looking for?"
- "What was the most difficult part of your previous job?"
- "Why should I hire you?"
- "Why did you apply for this job opening?"
- "What gets you out of bed?" or "What motivates you?"
- "What's your biggest strength? What's your biggest weakness?"
- "What would your boss and co-workers say about you?"

After answering, have your partner answer the questions for a job for which he or she is interested in applying. Evaluate how you answered the questions, and ask for feedback on how to improve your interviewing skills. Review the mock interview video. Share it with your support team and have them evaluate it.

FURTHER READING

The Autism Job Club: The Neurodiverse Workforce in the New Normal of Employment, by Michael S. Bernick and Richard Holden

Highly Effective Networking: Meet the Right People and Get a Great Job, by Orville Pierson

Acing the Interview: How to Ask and Answer the Questions That Will Get You the Job!, by Tony Beshara

Father Matthew Schneider's Story
Navigating Life as a Priest on the Spectrum

*I have what's kind of a stereotypical autistic memory
for details and facts, which has been helpful in
different ways as a priest.*
—FATHER MATTHEW SCHNEIDER

FATHER MATTHEW P. SCHNEIDER HAS more than 81,400 followers between X (formerly Twitter) and Instagram. He is completing a doctorate in moral theology and is the author of *God Loves the Autistic Mind: Prayer Guide for Those on the Spectrum and Those Who Love Us*. Shortly after his ordination in his early thirties, Father Matthew was diagnosed with autism. This diagnosis gave him insight for his vocation in the priesthood.

Matthew was born in Calgary, Alberta, Canada, and was the only boy of four children. He grew up with a happy homelife and parents who were loving and accepting of all his quirks. He did well at school and was in the top five in academics. He didn't focus on friends as most kids did, but he didn't think of that as an issue at the time.

As a child, he had difficulty understanding his body in relation to other objects and people, and this caused him to appear clumsy and awkward—which led to some bullying, but his size (taller than the other children) protected him from physical abuse. Middle school years were an especially awkward period for him. He was a bit of an outcast and struggled to make friends. A new kid attended in his last year of middle school, and they clicked. They became best friends, and both enjoyed programming computers. "We were happy being nerds," he says, "knowing we'd never be the popular kids."

He attended a study-at-your-own-pace high school and did well, zooming through classes without getting bored. As for social relationships, he hung out with the computer nerds and magic-club members.

Matthew learned to socialize in high school through observation and analysis of proper behavior. He consciously examined social interactions and then imitated them. He enjoyed math, reading, and philosophy, and he used his mental capacity in these fields to compensate for the struggles he experienced with soft intelligence.

Father Matthew's family attended Mass every Sunday and occasionally prayed together. During his teenage years, he searched for answers to perennial questions such as, Why are we here? and What is the meaning of life? As he studied religion and philosophy, he discovered answers to his questions in Catholicism. "My final year of high school, I was one of the super-religious teens and took my faith seriously. During this time I thought about becoming a priest."

After high school, he pursued a computer engineering degree and stayed active in the Catholic group on campus. After two years, he left for the seminary upon hearing an inspiring message by Pope John Paul II. "I just knew God called me to be a priest and serve Him. My mom was supportive relatively quick after I said I'd join. Dad was a little more hesitant, but he always kept the attitude of he'd rather me be successful as a priest than be unsuccessful in a secular career."

During his first year of ministry as a priest, Father Matthew was assigned to be a school chaplain and youth-ministry leader for three years. He had difficulty relating to his students and the staff. At the end of the first year, things weren't working out for Matthew. The school administrators shared their concerns that he might have Asperger's and asked him to leave the school.

Father Matthew reflects back on the school experience as a blessing because it led to his diagnosis of autism and an understanding of himself and the ministries best suited for him. After failing as a school chaplain, he went to a psychologist and received a diagnosis of autism spectrum disorder.

At first he was devastated and not sure where to go, but as he read more and more, he realized this was who he was and that it was not just a slight personality variant but a whole different brain-structure way of seeing the world.

In a video released on April 2, 2019, World Autism Awareness Day, Father Matthew went public with his autism diagnosis. "I realize the need to evangelize this segment of the population. We're about 1.5 to 2 percent of the population. We have a much higher chance of being atheists, a much lower chance of attending religious services on a weekly basis. . . . We need someone to reach out to our community, to enculturate the gospel to the autistic mind."

Father Matthew decided to go public with his autism diagnosis for four reasons. First, he desired to help others on the spectrum with spiritual disciplines. He wrote his first book on autistic prayer, which Pauline Books and Media published.

Second, he wanted to create awareness in the Catholic community of autism. "Father Mark Nolette went public before me, but that was about the only one with a name you can find online. Having a few priests who are public about their diagnosis helps others see autism in a proper light."

Third, letting people know he is autistic allows for transparency to resolve any personal issues in the future. "If I meet someone and I come across as awkward or don't read their social cues right, knowing I'm autistic helps them realize I'm not being rude. It also helps me in that I don't need to mask as much."

Finally, being public allows him to better adapt the gospel to the autistic mind. "We autistics tend to think much more logically. So just simply a more logical explanation is more helpful so we understand why. We tend to be less easily satisfied with why answers. We don't have the social cues that a lot of people have, where after you've asked why three or four times, you kind of stop. We'll keep asking until we understand it, because that's kind of the more logical way our brain works in that regard."

Father Matthew did have a few fears in regard to disclosing his diagnosis. He worried that people would discount his other opinions, thinking that an autistic person was not intelligent despite proof to the contrary. He also worried about being pigeonholed or cut off from speaking about any topic other than autism in Catholic circles.

Autism has provided Father Matthew with some gifts. He has a strong memory and is able to connect many concepts together. Plus, he was able to take a more academic route beyond just a master of divinity degree, and this led to him writing a doctoral thesis, in which his autistic focus, memory, and data processing / pattern recognition proved helpful. His doctorate is about the right to privacy in Catholic moral theology. "Ultimately, I found a topic about which the church should speak but has not spoken much so far; thus my thesis can play a vital role in this important ethical discussion."

Father Matthew shares the faith challenges people with autism experience. He found that rational books teaching Catholicism were much more helpful than practical ministry books, as the autistic mind tends to look for rational explanations and is not satisfied with "because that's the way it is" as much as others.

His goals include finishing his doctoral degree, attaining a professorial position in a seminary, and writing on the topics of moral theology and inclusion in the church. He hopes to help parishes and dioceses establish ministries for autistics. Father Matthew's message is simple: "Jesus loves us and wants the best for us. As autistics, we have the opportunity to experience God's love in an autistic way. We don't have to conform our own experience of God, in prayer and in the liturgy, to how others think, but we can experience it our own way, which is 100 percent valid."

FATHER MATTHEW P. SCHNEIDER'S BIOGRAPHY

Father Matthew P. Schneider is an openly autistic Catholic priest. He's originally from Calgary, Alberta, Canada, but since joining the Legionaries of Christ, has done ministry across North America. He has written for many publications, including the *National Catholic Register, America, Crux,* and *Aleteia,* and is the author of *God Loves the Autistic Mind: Prayer Guide for Those on the Spectrum and Those Who Love Us.* You can find him on social media at @FrMatthewLC, @AutisticPriest, and FrMatthewLC.com. He currently lives in northern Virginia, where he is writing a doctoral thesis in moral theology.

REFLECT

1. Father Matthew P. Schneider shares his painful experience of being rejected from a school chaplain and youth-ministry leader position when his supervisor requested that he leave the school because he was unable to relate with his students and the staff. What are some painful experiences you have gone through in employment and when searching for a job? How do rejections impact your confidence in regard to job interviews and employment?

2. Reflecting back, Father Matthew saw the school rejection as a blessing in disguise because it led to his autism diagnosis. Share a few job rejections that, as you look back, were really blessings. What did you learn from these rejections? How have they helped focus your future job searches and employment?

3. Father Matthew noted four reasons he shares his autism diagnosis as a priest. Should you share your autism diagnosis with the interviewing team? Why or why not? What are some benefits of sharing your autism diagnosis, and what are some drawbacks of disclosing a diagnosis?

Chapter 9

Making Wise Decisions That Influence Your Life

You are always one decision away from a totally different life.
—Author Unknown

For us on the spectrum, decision-making is often exhausting, overwhelming, and anxiety provoking. Hating change in our routine and the fear it holds for our future, we may avoid making decisions by allowing others to make them for us. Transitioning to adulthood requires us to learn to make wise decisions for ourselves by evaluating the consequences of our choices. We should not fear making wrong decisions, but should instead have a desire to learn from our choices and see how we can improve our decision-making skills.

Most decisions have little impact on our daily life; these are based on preference. For breakfast, should I eat eggs or cereal? Do I want to purchase a red or silver Ford Focus? Other decisions require planning, research, and input from family and friends. Should I relocate twelve hundred miles away to Tampa, Florida, for a job? Should I attend college in state or out?

Success in life requires us to take proper risks at times, and learning to discern a minor decision from a crucial one is important. Lacking decision-making skills, some young adults with autism make unwise decisions in regard to their finances, friends, or living arrangements. This can have minor effects, such as loss of income and resources, or critical consequences, such as being arrested for drug possession when a friend transports drugs in your car or being fired for not following company policies or making inappropriate comments to a co-worker.

Decision-Making Support Team

Executive functioning in the frontal-lobe area of the brain enables us to make wise choices and get things done, allowing us to manage time, multitask, adjust to changes in our routines, avoid saying or doing inappropriate things, generalize concepts, and plan and organize for the future. The executive function is a key component for decision-making.

Dr. Lawrence R. Sutton shares, "Many people with autism that have an impaired executive-function system have difficulty understanding cause and effect. They do not recognize that something they do in one moment may have an impact on later events. This makes it very difficult for them to set goals or organize any kind of plan for the future."[1]

When our executive function is impaired by autism, our behavior is less controlled and we struggle with organizing and executing plans. A faulty executive-function ability can affect our work and school life, relationships, and independence.

The executive function serves two main purposes: organization (gathering information and structuring it for evaluation and decision-making) and regulation (taking an inventory of our surroundings and developing new behaviors and habits). Organization is implementing the steps needed to accomplish our goals and adapting to the challenges faced in accomplishing them. Regulation is putting off gratification for a greater reward. For example, you hope to lose ten pounds in the next month, so when you see your favorite chocolate ice cream in the freezer, you decide to put off eating it (gratification) for the reward of losing weight.

Difficulty with executive functioning requires us to build a strong support team to help us make important life decisions. I call this support team my "voice of reason." My support team consists of my wife, my parents, and my older brothers, Steve and Chuck. Your support team can include parents, siblings, friends, professors, and/or former teachers. Make sure the members of your support team are willing to mentor you and help you make sound decisions. Your support team members provide insights from their life experiences and knowledge in the areas in which you need advice.

During the 2008 real-estate market crash, my parents and brother Steve urged me to purchase a house or condominium. They informed me, "With the real-estate crash, prices will never be this low again." During the crisis, one could buy a $170,000 house for only $65,000. Fearing job loss, the economy, and taking a risk, I failed to heed their sound advice. Looking back now, I wish I would've purchased a home. For our support team to be effective, we need to heed their sound advice and learn from our mistakes. We should not fear failure but missed opportunities.

Seven Steps of the Decision-Making Process

The decision-making process enables us to be proactive in resolving issues by examining options and deciding on the best route to take. A step-by-step routine makes decision-making easier and more informative. Following are the seven steps of the decision-making process.

Identify the decision or goal. Ask yourself, *What is the problem I need to solve or the choice I need to make?* Write the decision as a question and as a goal. For example, you may desire to transition from your parents' home to an apartment to gain more freedom. The desire written as a question is, "How can I move from my parents' house into an apartment?" The decision written as a goal: "I desire to move into an apartment within the next three months." If you have fears or worries about the decision you are making, share these with your support team and write down their advice.

Gather information by research. Gather data by asking people who have recently made that decision, talking with professionals, and reading books and articles on the subject. Collect as much information as possible in order to make the best choice. Write down the information you gained from your research and share this with your support team.

For moving out of your parents' house, gather information on the different apartment complexes in the area and talk to the apartment office management to compare rent prices and necessary accommodations.

Identify alternative options. After you've gathered information, identify possible solutions to your problem or different ways to accomplish your goal. For example, I could save money for a deposit and first-month's rent (option one) or save money by having a roommate who helps pay the rent (option two). Write down your options and share them with your support team.

Weigh options. Once you have identified your options based on the information you gathered and your support team's insight, write a list of the pros and cons of the different options. Pros of moving out of the family home: more freedom and no curfew. Cons: cooking meals, washing laundry, and paying rent. Some could be both a pro and a con, depending on your goal.

Choose from among the options. You've gathered the information, discussed the options with your support team, and weighed the pros and cons. Now make your decision. For choosing the best option, ask yourself, *What's the worst that can happen?* and *What's the best that can happen?* This can help you understand the risk factors. Also, it can be helpful to lean on your support team for advice. They have wisdom from experience, they know what you need, and they can help you make a sound decision based on logic rather than fear.

The worst-case scenario when deciding to move into an apartment: You fail to pay your rent and get evicted from your apartment, which has a negative impact on your credit score. Factors that can cause this worst-case scenario include losing your job, a prolonged illness or serious injury, or forgetting to pay your rent on time. The odds of this happening: not very likely. Best-case scenario: You move from your parents' home and gain freedom. Positive effects: You make new friends, learn skills to take care of yourself, and gain more independence. The odds of this happening: highly likely.

Take action. Develop a plan and mark on a calendar the date you hope to reach your goal or solve the problem. Break your decision into small, attainable steps.

Each day, I write, in a pocket-size notebook, a list of the things I need to accomplish that day. I use my daily lists as a reminder, which helps me to remain focused on long-term goals and projects. My lists break large goals into attainable steps.

Steps for the goal to move from your parents' home: First, save money for a security deposit and the first-month's rent. Second, find a roommate. Third, purchase items needed to live by yourself. Fourth, take classes on preparing meals and read books/articles on life skills. Once you begin the steps and feel prepared, take the risk to accomplish your goal.

Evaluate your decision based on results and consequences. After you've taken action to reach your goal or solve a problem, wait a month and evaluate the consequences of your decision and then re-evaluate every six months. Examine the process you took to reach your decision. This will help you to further develop your decision-making skills for future dilemmas. Talk with your support team about the effects of your decision.

Analyze the positive and negative results. Ask questions such as, What other decision could I have made? How is my life better or worse by the decision I made? Did I have anything to fear by making this decision? The decision-making process enables you to prioritize your tasks by their level of urgency and importance and the severity of the consequences for not doing them.

Examples of the Decision-Making Process

Let's examine the seven-step decision-making process for choosing between a college and trade school and for deciding on a career. Keep in mind that the more choices we make, the easier the decision process will be. The following examples can help prepare you to make important decisions in your life.

Deciding what college or trade school to attend

1. Identify the decision. Written as a question: "Should I attend college or a trade school?" Written as a goal: "I desire to attend a college or trade school this coming fall."
2. Gather information by research and contacts. Check online college and trade school programs and degrees that relate to your skills and interests. Obtain information: cost of tuition, number of students, length of program, financial aid and loans available, distance from home, employment rate of graduates, and learning-support resource services. Write a list of questions, and meet with a few professors and staff members from the schools you're considering. Share your questions with alumni, listen to their advice, and write it down. Visit the college or trade school and arrange to attend a class in the program you're considering.
3. Identify alternate options: I could work part-time and save money for college (option one), try to receive an academic or athletic scholarship (option two), take student loans (option three), or find a job that will reimburse me for tuition for a trade school or college classes (option four).
4. Weigh your options by examining the pros and cons. Pros to attending a university: a chance to move away from home and

have a college experience of making friends in the dorm. Cons to a college education: owe thousands of dollars in student loans and have only a small increase in your chance of a job in the degree field. Pros to trade school: lower tuition cost, higher employment rate for graduates, and higher wages than a college graduate—plus, you can start your career faster, while a college degree requires four to six years. Also, trade schools provide more job security. Cons to trade school: rigorous schedule when attending, few school breaks, and potential difficulty in receiving financial aid.

5. Choose from among the options. Now that you have gathered information on colleges and trade schools and have had a chance to weigh your options, meet with your support team and make your decision.

6. Take action. You decide to attend a trade school based on higher wages, lower tuition costs, and hands-on experience. To take action, you enroll in the trade school and set up your class schedule.

7. Evaluate your decision. Three months after graduating from trade school, evaluate your decision based on results. Ask yourself, *How is my life better or worse by attending a trade school? Did I have anything to fear by attending a trade school?* Wait six to eight more months and ask yourself those same questions again.

Deciding what career to pursue

1. Identify the decision. Written as a question: "What career should I pursue based on my skills and experience?" Written as a goal: "I will pursue a career that complements my skills, personality, and interests."

2. Gather information by research and contacts. Meet with a career counselor at your school or a life coach or mentor and discuss career options. Check online for careers with high employment

rates and the education and skills required. Research jobs related to your skills and abilities. Make a list of those careers and share them with your support team.

3. Identify alternative options. Make a list of the jobs you would like to pursue based on your skills, experience, and interests. For example, you love working with animals and would enjoy working at PetSmart (option one) or as a veterinary tech (option two). You have a degree in psychology and enjoy learning how the mind works, and your background and experience match a career in the mental health field (option three) or employment in a group home (option four).

4. Weigh your options by examining the pros and cons. Pros of working for a pet store are that you get to work with animals and develop social skills through customer service. Cons are low pay, the odor of the store that could affect sensory issues, and little room for advancement. Veterinary tech pros would be learning about animals, which is emotionally rewarding. Cons are that it requires a two-year associate's degree and an ability to work as a team player (although you work better alone). Pros of working in the mental health field: follows a routine and offers job security, as the field is always hiring. Cons: stressful environment, risk of injury by an aggressive patient, and burnout from working long hours. Group home pros are that you can have a positive impact on people's lives and learn a variety of skills. Cons are low wages, requires flexibility to change, and multitasking.

5. Choose from among the options. Now that you have created a career-options list of pros and cons, meet with your support team and decide what career to pursue.

6. Take action. Create a résumé and cover letter, gather references, and apply for jobs related to the career you decided to pursue. Read the chapter "Navigating the Social Nuances of Interviewing" to help prepare you for your job search.

7. Evaluate your decision. After three months of working your new job, ask, *Do I enjoy my new job? Is this job what I was expecting? Can I experience growth in this career? Could I see myself in this career five years from now?* Wait six to eight months and ask yourself these questions again.

Three Decision-Making Hindrances

Three common hindrances of decision-making are fear and anxiety, a lack of ability to prioritize, and difficulty understanding consequences of actions. The first hindrance—fear and anxiety of the unknown— causes us to be indecisive. We experience fear and anxiety about making decisions due to a catastrophe mindset. We imagine the worst-case scenario, like jumping from an airplane and our parachute not opening or moving to Florida and our apartment being swept away by a hurricane.

A catastrophe mindset overgeneralizes the consequences of our decisions. When I was deciding and weighing the pros and cons of whether to move to Tampa, I had a few catastrophe thoughts, such as, *What if I take the job and three months later the company runs out of funds and I am unable to find another job?* and *What if I agree to take the job but am unable to find a moving company or housing in Tampa?*

A catastrophe mindset causes you to fear making decisions. You can take this mindset captive by asking yourself the following questions: *One hundred years from now, will anyone remember or care about the decision I am making? How will this decision impact my life five years from now? What happened to other people who made this same decision?*

Another way to take captive this mindset is by calculating the odds of your fear occurring versus the odds of a good outcome. The odds of losing the new job in three to six months were only about 10 percent compared to odds of enjoying the new job at 90 percent. Not finding an apartment in Tampa had odds of only about 15 percent compared to finding a nice place to live, with odds of about 85 percent. Rating the risks can help bring relief from the catastrophe outlook and create a positive mindset.

Finally, we can overcome the catastrophe mindset by thinking about positive outcomes. For example, consider enjoying the sunny weather in Tampa while your family and friends in Michigan endure an ice storm. The positive mindset is optimistic and can see a silver lining in challenging circumstances.

The second common hindrance in decision-making is an inability to prioritize the sequence order to execute an action. Once we make a decision, like moving into an apartment or to Tampa, we may have difficulty prioritizing the steps we should take to accomplish the decision. We may not understand how to execute the actions required because we don't know what we should do first and the order of the other steps. For example, when moving out of our parents' house, we may sign a lease on an apartment before we have money to pay the rent, or we may sign a contract with the landlord without finding out if they allow pets. Our support team can help us outline the steps needed to reach our goal.

We can learn to prioritize by making a list of the tasks and numbering them from most important to least.

Task list for moving into an apartment
1. Find a job to pay for rent.
2. Save money for first-month's rent and security deposit.
3. Find a roommate to help pay rent.
4. Search for an apartment within budget.
5. Find friends or family members to help move into the apartment.
6. Sign lease.
7. Move into the apartment.
8. Have a housewarming party to celebrate the new freedom.

The third hindrance of decision-making is difficulty understanding consequences—the cause and effect—of our actions. This inability makes many autistic children an easy target for bullies. Anthony Ianni, the first NCAA Division One basketball player diagnosed with autism as a child, was tricked by a bully to stick his tongue to an icy metal pole. He failed to understand the consequence of his action, that he would be stuck to a pole, and he experienced severe pain when he tried to pry his tongue free.[2]

I had a similar bullying experience my freshman year of high school. A muscular jock stole a tarantula at a track meet. He placed the tarantula in a plastic bag and left it on the bleachers. Some fellow runners double-dog dared me to smash the dead tarantula and brew up tarantula soup. Not thinking about the consequences of my actions, I smashed the jock's stolen prize. After he saw me holding up the plastic bag filled with tarantula guts, he hit me in the eye and gave me a shiner.

As an adult, not understanding the consequences can lead to dangerous situations. For example, on a dating website you message back and forth with a woman and decide to invite her to your apartment. The dangerous consequence could be that the person you're meeting is not a nice woman but a criminal planning to steal your money and hurt you.

We on the spectrum sometimes fail to understand consequences because we overestimate or underestimate our abilities. At work, we may overestimate our leadership ability after being offered a supervisor position, and after taking the promotion, realize that we hate it. We may underestimate our skills and stay in the same job for years, afraid of failure with more responsibilities or a change in routine.

Our lack of ability to generalize can cause us to fail to understand the consequences of our actions. Thus, we keep making the same mistakes. For example, we offend a co-worker by discussing politics, so we quit talking about politics in the workplace—but we fail to apply this rule to our dating life and continue to offend dates by talking about politics. Our support team can help us evaluate the results of our decisions and properly estimate our strengths and weaknesses.

Autopilot Decision-Making Style

Developing good habits enables us to conserve energy in the decision-making process. When we develop healthy eating habits, we no longer have to decide whether to eat a candy bar or an apple. Our good habits, created by our routines, kick in, and by autopilot we subconsciously decide to eat the apple. I have many habits that I do on autopilot, such as driving to work, performing my memory work, eating healthy, taking daily vitamins, and doing thirty push-ups a night.

Habits are rooted in routine and become harder to break the longer we do them. A routine that is done for about ninety days becomes a habit and part of our daily life. The speed of the formation of the habit can be quicker or slower depending on the strength of the emotion you feel toward it. Habits save us time and energy because we do them automatically and don't have to think about each step.

As we saw earlier, we on the spectrum have difficulty remembering the steps necessary to accomplish an action, and our habits formed by routine can make our action automatic. Habits are composed of the *cue*, the *behavior*, and the *reward*.[2]

First, the cue—the reminder to do the activity or behavior.

A habit is triggered by a cue. This can be just about anything the mind associates with the behavior or actions based on the data stored in the brain. A cue for you could be seeing McDonald's golden arches, causing you to crave chicken nuggets. For me, the cue to do my memory work is 3:45 p.m., the time I do my memory work each day, or 8:00 p.m. for my push-ups. With driving home from work, the cue is seeing the roads and landmarks I recognize. This causes my mind to go into autopilot and accomplish the behavior of driving home. I don't have to consciously think each day about how I will get home from work (unless construction work forces me to change my route). This frees my mind to think about my speaking events or books I am writing.

There are five main categories of cues that stimulate behavior: cues that result from location (driving home), cues associated with time of day (memory work and push-ups), cues generated by people (social etiquette), cues created by a particular emotional state (happy when you see a puppy or sad when you see a friend bullied), and cues that result from an immediate response (stopping at a red light). Cues remind us of things to do and produce a predictable behavior.[3]

Second, the behavior—the action we take in response to the cue.

When stopped at a traffic light and the light turns green, you instinctively look both ways, put your foot to the gas pedal, and go. The cue is the light turning green, and the automatic behavior is looking both ways and pushing on the gas pedal. Before you begin work, you proceed to the time clock to check in for work. The cue is the time, and the behavior is clocking in for work. Most things we do are based on habits. Some good habits are exercise and self-care, like showering and brushing our teeth. After we make self-care a habit, we no longer have to decide whether to skip brushing our teeth to finish watching the movie. A scheduled time can be the cue for doing the behavior. Motivation is what gets you started; a habit keeps you going.

Third, the behavior leads to the reward.

The reward for brushing your teeth is fresh breath (and the long-term reward is not having cavities). For exercise, it's a sense of elation or euphoria (long-term reward is feeling healthy). For eating chocolate, it's the sweet taste. The reward is the reason the brain chooses to remember the cue and the actions leading to the behavior. The brain remembers the cue and sequence to the behavior because the reward makes us feel great. The reason we repeat a habit, both good and bad, is because every habit produces some kind of positive feeling, or physical or psychological incentive, that keeps the process going.

By developing good habits, we can replace the bad ones. Make a list of a few new habits you'd like to do each day. Some good habits are taking a daily walk, eating vegetables rather than candy for a snack, performing a set number of push-ups for physical strength, or reading books. Start small and build on the habit to make it stronger and create cues to remind you, like posting sticky notes around the house. Have a set time for the new habit—maybe a half-mile walk each morning or ten push-ups after lunch or a chapter of a book before bedtime.

These new habits can uproot the bad ones, such as watching TV three hours a night, mindlessly scrolling through your phone, or feasting on ice cream. Habits can help you take responsibility for your life and transition to adulthood—habits like paying your bills on time, eating healthy meals, and faithfully going to work each day. Over time, family and friends will see your good habits and trust you with more responsibilities.

Closing Thoughts

The seven-step process of decision-making can enable us to resolve issues with less anxiety and provide self-confidence to make sound choices. A positive mindset helps us see the silver lining in challenges. When making an important decision, consult your support team for advice. Don't be afraid of failure or a catastrophe due to your decision, but learn from your mistakes and adjust. Habits keep us on track to make right decisions, such as eating healthy meals, exercising daily, or reading more books while spending less time isolated with electronics.

REFLECT

1. I share some of my fears and catastrophe thoughts. What are some fears you experience when making decisions? How do you handle those fears?

2. Share a decision you recently made and the steps you took to

make that decision. What steps did you use from the seven steps of the decision-making process?

3. I describe the three hindrances to decision-making. What are some difficulties you have when making a decision? Who are some people you seek advice from when making an important decision?

FUN ACTIVITIES

The purpose of this activity is to develop a positive mindset and get you out of the house. This week, choose to do one of the following activities: Order a different meal at your favorite restaurant or visit a place you have not been before, such as the zoo, a nature center, a park, or a museum. Take a walk downtown or attend a social event (perhaps a sporting activity, religious service, or concert), or meet up with a group of friends or co-workers for food.

On a piece of poster board, write on the top the caption "Positive Mindset" and on the bottom the caption "Best-Case Scenario." Then go online and print out pictures of good things that remind you of the place you're going. In the middle left side, paste pictures of the good things you expect by trying something new.

For example, if you decide to order a different meal from your favorite restaurant, go online and choose the new meal you will try and paste a picture of the meal and pictures of the good emotions you will feel when you taste the meal. Find pictures of the restaurant and things that remind you of the experience of eating there. If you decide to visit the zoo or a nature center, paste pictures of the place and the things you look forward to seeing there, like animals or a lake. For a social event, paste pictures of the place you're going to and the fun things you plan to do.

While doing the fun activity, take photos, and then paste the photos on the poster board on the right side, with the caption "As Good As It Gets." This exercise encourages a positive mindset in decision-making.

FURTHER READING

Make That, Break That: How to Break Bad Habits and Make New Ones That Lead to Success, by Dave Martin

Thinking, Fast and Slow, by Daniel Kahneman

How We Decide, by Jonah Lehrer

Cody McLain's Story
Achieving Success One Decision at a Time

I was the outcast in school who had to figure life out on my own. I went from self-loathing to realizing we're truly capable of anything we set our minds to.
—CODY MCLAIN

CODY MCLAIN IS THE FOUNDER of three multimillion-dollar companies and managed a support company that employed over five hundred people and served some of the biggest names in Silicon Valley. The companies he founded have served over thirty thousand customers and businesses in over one hundred countries.

In middle school Cody struggled with social awkwardness. He had friends but always felt like something was off or different about him, though he didn't know why. He started his first business while still in middle school, so he had even more of an inability to connect with others based on commonalities.

Becoming a successful entrepreneur with Asperger's required Cody to learn decision-making skills by trial and error, perseverance, and a balance between personal development, work, and occasional time off.

When Cody was in high school, his dad passed away and he was placed in the foster care system for a short time. "I was forced at an early age to be ambitious and do what many considered impossible," Cody says.

He discovered inspiration in books and from Tim Ferris, an entrepreneur, investor, author, podcaster, and lifestyle guru. Books were Cody's guides from an early age, and his grandfather and a local judge taught him about life.

At age fifteen Cody started his first business to earn money to buy an Xbox. "I was a poor kid who went to a rich high school, and I was made fun of for not only being weird but also poor." His rich friend got into an argument with his mom, and she decided she would not buy him an Xbox, so his friend tried to devise a business plan to purchase an Xbox. Cody shut down all his ideas for being so ridiculous—until his friend proposed selling web hosting.

Less than a week later, their partnership disintegrated, but for the first time in Cody's life, he felt a connection to something, and that connection was the thing that carried him through all his family tragedies, including the death of his parents. "The business I created was truly my first mentor, teaching me marketing, sales, managing, and customer relations. It also provided me with comfort and hope."

By the time he was eighteen, his businesses were generating almost a million dollars in annual revenue. Then he was defrauded and lost everything. It was one of those times when he didn't listen to his gut feeling.

Cody learned three lessons as an entrepreneur: First, when making a business deal, always get the contract in writing—especially if it's a friend, lover, or family member. "I would not have been defrauded and lost everything if I had all the details of the contract in writing."

Second, if you plan on hiring a friend, you must ask yourself a question: *Am I willing to throw away the friendship no matter the state of the relationship?* "Money changes people in ways you can't imagine, until you experience it firsthand."

Third, find something you're passionate about. For example, if you're considering quitting school, only entertain that possibility if you have a business that generates cash flow and has a high potential for increasing profit margins that you can live off for at least six months. "If it's not, you should be absolutely obsessed with the business, day and night—as if it's a game you can't stop playing until you beat the last level."

Cody offers advice to young adults with autism who experience difficulty making decisions and taking risks: "Be introspective about your life and where you are, not ruminating on the negatives. Realize that we are often our own worst critics, and if we can't love ourselves, how can others love us? We must learn to find awareness and embrace our feelings toward ourselves. A good therapist can help you with that. You have to get over the internal voice—see it as a friend and validate your own emotions instead of numbing yourself to it."

Cody is learning to enjoy life. He had been working twelve-hour days for weeks and months on end, rarely giving himself a break. His dedication to success had blinded him to the reality of his very existence. His concern wasn't so much with the number of hours he was working but with his efficiency during those hours. Using a system of delegation and checklists, he figured he could go on to do bigger and better things, so he learned more about productivity, health, and mindfulness.

He read articles and books on personal development, including *Getting Things Done* by David Allen and *Meditations* by Marcus Aurelius. He also pushed himself outside his comfort zone to do things he never thought he could do, such as travel the world and take photographs, and even fly airplanes. He decided to maintain a relentless drive not only to create more successful ventures but also to expand his own awareness by constantly optimizing his routines and business systems.

Cody is currently working on a few start-up ideas and expanding his *MindHack* podcast. *MindHack* seeks to break down the routines, habits, mindsets, and ideologies of successful people, scientific studies, and popular books. It's a self-help podcast dedicated to finding out the keys to success, happiness, and limitless productivity.

After he sold his business, Cody's goal was to share his unique set of knowledge, experiences, and habits, ultimately to lead people to live more successful and purpose-driven lives.

CODY MCLAIN'S BIOGRAPHY

Cody McLain is the founder of SupportNinja.com and author of *From Foster Care to Millionaire: A Young Entrepreneur's Journey of Tragedy and Triumph*. He is featured in several online publications, including *Forbes*, *Mashable*, and *Entrepreneur*. Cody is the host of *MindHack* podcast, and his website is codymclain.com.

REFLECT

1. What are some risks Cody McLain had to take to create successful businesses? What are some risks you fear when making a decision? Do you feel afraid to take risks? Why or why not?

2. Cody shares a painful experience of being defrauded in a business deal, causing him to lose everything because he didn't listen to his gut feeling. Have you ever made a poor decision by failing to listen to your gut feeling that something was not right? If so, share the incident and what you learned from it.

3. What are some good habits Cody demonstrates by his business decisions and choices in life? What are two habits you would like to change in your life? Name three good habits you have and explain how these qualities can help you as an adult with autism.

Chapter 10

Managing Emotions and Sensory Issues

Most people's emotions and sensory issues are like bottled water; when shaken up they feel a little anxiety—not much else is happening. I am carbonated like Mountain Dew—I get stirred up, KABOOM!!! Anyone want to do the Dew?

—RON SANDISON

MOST OF MY PEERS AND family pay little attention to their sensory processing. When they feel cold, they put on a sweater. When music is too loud, they turn down the volume. For me and many other people with autism, our senses provide unreliable information, causing great discomfort and anxiety. You may also experience sensory issues with touch, sound, taste, smell, or sight.

I have struggled with managing my emotions and sensory issues my whole life. This makes it hard to adapt to my environment or transition from one activity to another. When I was in school, it affected my ability to socialize with my peers and stay focused on assignments.

When I was five, I saw my first movie in a theater with my family. During the previews, a glove grew gigantic and popped like a balloon.

The sound of the explosion overwhelmed my senses, and I experienced a severe meltdown and ran around the theater screaming. It took my mom an hour to calm me down. I refer to my meltdowns as my "honey-badger moments."

My favorite honey-badger moment happened when I was in third grade. I was at a Cub Scouts Halloween event with Bozo the Clown and more than two hundred people to witness my stellar performance. My mom had me sit front and center with the other Cub Scouts for the main event: a clown—complete with a red nose, white makeup, red fluffy side hair, and a lamb sock puppet.

The poor clown knew nothing about autism and thought it would be comical to take my baseball cap, place it on another kid's head, and then place it back on my head. When the clown attempted to place the cap back on my head, I grabbed the lamb sock puppet and proceeded to repeatedly beat the clown with it. By the time I was finished, that poor clown's red nose and hair were on the floor and her makeup was smeared across her face.

Needless to say, I never earned my Bobcat Badge. Instead, the next day the leaders of the Cub Scouts informed my parents, "Your son is banned from any future events. If he did that to a clown, imagine what he might do to one of our children."

My current sensory-processing issues, or "kryptonite," are sound (bass music and electric power tools) and odor (bleach, nail polish, and fish). I can smell bleach a week after it has been applied, and the odor of fish or nail polish gives me a migraine. The more anxious and tired I feel, the worse my sensory processing operates. I can tolerate more noise and odors I dislike when I am calm and alone, but less when stressed and in a crowd.

Exposure to different environments and social situations has enabled me to adapt and manage my emotions and sensory issues. Meltdowns still occur, but much less frequently. This enables me to work full-time, travel, and enjoy trying new things.

Emotional-Stress Level

Emotions motivate us to take action and engage in life, but when our emotions take over, the thinking part of our brain shuts down. It is essential to learn how to calm ourselves down when emotions run high. Managing our emotions requires us to understand our emotional-stress arousal level.

Many people with autism have trouble rating their emotional-stress levels—whether we are upset or not. What causes high anxiety for you may cause no stress for someone else. Each of us is wired differently. I experience no anxiety when speaking to audiences of five thousand people but extreme anxiety when I have a doctor's appointment or when I am waiting for a car repair. What makes you upset may not bother your friends. Working in the mental health field, I am not bothered if a patient makes a derogatory comment toward me, but I get upset when I have problems with my computer or when I am trying to figure out electronic devices or directions to a speaking engagement. Rating my emotional-stress level helps me stay calm and put things in perspective.

Rating your emotional-stress level

1. I feel fine—nothing is bothering me.
2. I feel a little agitated—I can still handle myself and my feelings.
3. I feel nervous / on edge—my mind is racing with worries.
4. I feel upset and anxious—I am losing control of my emotions.
5. I feel overwhelmed—I am experiencing a meltdown and cannot control my emotions, thoughts, or body.

A rating of 1 could be a relaxed day off work or going to the zoo with friends. Level 2 could be when your friend cancels plans to the zoo at the last moment or a waiter at a restaurant brings you the wrong meal. Level 3 might be when one of your parents is in the hospital for tests or surgery. Level 4 could be when a girlfriend or boyfriend breaks up with you. Level 5 might occur when you are fired from the job where you had been employed for over a year, or you are in a car accident and your vehicle is totaled. The emotion/stress rating helps us evaluate our emotions and put them in perspective.

Learning to Express Emotions

Processing issues can cause our emotional level to go from zero to sixty quicker than a Lamborghini, leading to a meltdown. Our emotional arousal is often like an on/off light switch rather than a dryer with a knob to gradually increase. We will efficiently manage our emotions by understanding how emotions affect us and learning healthy ways to communicate them. Our ability to control emotions is affected by our environment, fears, and physiology. Stimuli in our environment, such as odors we hate, flickering lights, or exhaustion or hunger, can cause us to have less control and may trigger emotional or sensory overload.

Make a list of your emotional and sensory triggers and know your limits. Ask yourself, *What causes me to feel emotionally drained or results in a sensory overload?* When attending a social event or a concert, know the level of stimuli you can handle. This can include people talking, loud music, or anything that arouses your sensory level. Once you've reached the max amount of stimuli, have an exit plan.

Phobias can also be emotional triggers. The National Institute of Mental Health says phobias affect about 10 percent of all adults.[1] A phobia is an extreme and irrational fear. The American Psychiatric Association identifies three main types of phobias: social phobia, agoraphobia, and specific phobia.[2]

Social phobia is extreme anxiety in social situations and fear of being scrutinized or judged negatively by others. *Agoraphobia* is the fear of leaving your home or of being in situations in which escape is difficult. *Specific phobia* is fear of an object or thing, such as snakes or heights. My favorite phobia, although not an official diagnosis, is coulrophobia—the fear of creepy clowns.

From age six to twelve, I had a phobia of bare feet. On a family vacation when I was six years old, I saw an elderly woman's rotten yellow toenails in the shape of fusilli pasta. I was instantly terrified of bare feet, and just the sight of them would result in a meltdown. I was unable to go to the beach or anywhere I might see bare feet. My dad helped me overcome this phobia by rewards and exposure. If your phobia continues and hinders you from social activities, seek professional counseling.

The summer or winter seasons and temperatures can impact our emotions. When I feel anxious or depressed, I like to take my dog for a walk or go for a swim. I use natural light as a natural antidepressant. Natural light improves our mood, raises our energy, and meets our need to connect with nature. Our body uses light as a nutrient— natural light stimulates essential biological functions in the brain.

Knowing what you feel and what to do when you feel that way will enable you to respond to the social world quicker, more accurately, and with less confusion. For example, when you feel anxiety or depression, what can you do for relief? What routines can you do daily to limit your stress arousal?

Three positive ways we can express our emotions are by visual metaphors, drama and role-playing, and stating emotions as verbs. For *visual metaphors*, we create artwork that expresses our emotions and feelings. Use different shades of colors to categorize emotions. For example, use brick red for anger, iris blue for depression, shocking pink for excitement, sunset yellow for joy, and pale plum for mellow. We can also write poetry and journal to share our emotions.

When we feel emotionally overwhelmed and need time to decompress, we can use visual cards to express our emotions to our family, friends, or roommates. For example, if you feel rushed when communicating with friends and loved ones, you may use a red flashcard that declares, "Overload—Need Time to Process." This informs your family or roommate that you need time to decompress and gather yourself before answering their questions.

Drama and *role-playing* with family and friends can teach us to express the emotion of empathy. Improvising different situations or acting out the role of someone else can help us understand how others feel and how to express those feelings. Swapping roles will give us a different perspective.[3] When we learn to role-play feelings, we will be able to manage those feelings.

Regulate emotions by stating feelings as action verbs instead of as a state of being. Our behavior is composed of our daily actions, and we can monitor our behavior through self-awareness. If you feel sad because you are alone on a Friday night, you can express your feeling by stating, "I am crying because I wish my friends would hang out with me." When we express our emotions through words, we can evaluate them and discern why we feel that way and how we can change those negative feelings with our actions.

We can change a state of being into a verb by adding "ing" to the word. For example, you feel depressed because you received a low grade on a test. You can state your emotions as a verb by saying, "I am depressing because I received a poor grade on the test." Adding "ing" to some feeling words is poor English but good therapy. Feelings stated as verbs can empower us to control our emotions and actions.

Health Issues and Emotions

Health issues can cause stress and emotional disturbance. A 2014 study by epidemiologist Lisa Croen of Kaiser Permanente compared 2,108 adults with autism to 21,080 non-autistic adults.[4] The results revealed that adults with autism have a significantly higher rate of medical conditions than their peers:

- 24 percent higher rate of gastrointestinal disorders
- 42 percent higher rate of hypertension
- 50 percent higher rate of diabetes
- 69 percent higher rate of obesity
- 90 percent higher rate of sleep disorders

The adults with autism also had a notably higher rate of mental health issues than peers, such as:

- 117 percent higher rate of anxiety
- 123 percent higher rate of depression
- 433 percent higher rate of suicide attempts

If these medical and psychiatric health conditions are left untreated, they will negatively impact our quality of life and lead to a shortened life expectancy. Emotional instability from health issues can lead to isolation and sleep deprivation and interfere with good nutrition, diet, and exercise. Too much caffeine can put our emotions on edge and make us feel jittery. Chronic stress, which is common with autism, causes our bodies to produce the hormone cortisol, which can lead to excessive weight gain and deplete the body of certain proteins and minerals required for healthy bone growth. Cortisol in large amounts weakens our immune system, making us more prone to sickness.[5]

Eating fruits, vegetables, and salmon, and drinking plenty of water, can help our emotions to stay calm. Regular doctor checkups, exercise, and diet can help us manage our physical and mental health, and this preventive care keeps our emotions stable. In chapter 2, "Living Healthy on the Spectrum," I examine this topic in depth.

Expressing Emotion with Logic

Understanding emotions is often a struggle for us. A friend is grieving the loss of a family member, and our emotions overwhelm us. We feel awkward or frightened, not knowing what to say or how to comfort our friend. I express my emotions not by feelings but by actions of love. When a friend who is a co-worker was diagnosed with cancer, I got him a card and had the hospital staff write him encouraging words. Actions produce empathy, which I have difficulty understanding.

Jory Fleming, author of *How to Be Human: An Autistic Man's Guide to Life*, wrote, "I think there is logical empathy, . . . an empathy that's not based on an emotion but is based on thinking. I may not be able to fully understand someone else's situation emotionally, but I still can reason through and think about it in depth and in a detailed way. . . . If anything, I also think that's more permanent as well. If it's emotional, it kind of burns brightly but then it fades away. But if you think about something, it sticks with you."[6]

Logic can help us evaluate our emotion of fear. We often experience irrational worries about life. We may fear traveling or our annual doctors' appointments or a social event. I deal with fear by writing down my fear and, with courage, doing the thing that is causing me anxiety. After I take action by doing what I fear, I record the results in a journal. When I read the journal, I usually realize I had nothing to fear.

Evaluating emotions

1. What is causing me anxiety and stress?
2. Is this feeling based on logic or emotion?
3. Why do I fear that this will happen to me?
4. What actions can I take to prevent it from occurring?
5. Write down the anxiety and pick a color to represent your emotional state.
6. Rate your stress level using the five emotional-stress levels.
7. Share with your support team the thing causing you stress.

Evaluating our emotions will keep our stress level down and improve our quality of life. Our high level of emotion could be caused by a change in routine, sensory-processing issues, lack of sleep, hunger, physical pain, or persistent discomfort. Learning to handle our emotional level with coping skills can help us relax for social interactions and keep our stress down.

Coping with Emotions

We cannot choose to numb emotions to manage them, because if we numb our painful emotions, we also numb our pleasurable emotions. Instead of hiding from emotions, we can use coping skills and sensory soothing to live with them. Coping skills can help us adapt to our sensory issues and social environment. When we experience emotional overload, having a safe place to decompress can provide comfort. My safe spots are my living room with my reclining chair and my Man Cave with my five thousand books at my parents' house. I feel comfortable and restful in these places.

Our minds and bodies are closely connected. Just as our brains can trigger our bodies to be anxious by thinking worrisome thoughts, so our bodies can trigger our brains to calm down through sensory soothing. After a stressful day of working with aggressive patients and feeling exhausted, I unwind by reading a book or watching a comedy on Netflix.

Your sensory soothing could be a hot bath, allowing your muscles and your mind to relax. The hot water triggers your mind and body to calm down. Sights, sounds, touches, tastes, smells, and body movements can activate the calming part of our nervous system and soothe our brains. These are examples of sensory soothing, and we can use them as a form of coping skills to manage our emotions.

We can use different sensory soothing for each type of sensory issue. For example, for sound, your sensory soothing could be soft background music or listening to running water on your iPhone or iPad. For smell, use scents of lavender or peppermint. Lavender can help calm the mind and body almost instantly and can be used for sleep issues. Studies have found that peppermint improves our ability to concentrate.[7] Aromas create nostalgic memories that put our minds to rest and bring relief from stress and headaches. Unlike touch or taste, scents are directly correlated with our past experiences.

For touch, lying on a heating pad or petting your cat or dog can trigger your body and mind to relax. At work you can soothe yourself by keeping a soft-textured piece of carpet in your pocket and gently rubbing your fingers against it. Before bed I splash cold water on my face, which helps me to relax and quickly fall asleep. For sight, watching a lava lamp or looking at pictures on your phone can soothe your mind.

For taste, try eating your favorite treat slowly or drinking a hot cup of tea. Body-movement soothing can occur by going for a walk outside or swinging on a swing set. Breathing exercises can help lower blood pressure and reduce chronic pain. Do breathing exercises in a quiet place with few distractions. One breathing technique is to inhale slowly through your nose while keeping your shoulders relaxed, and then exhale slowly through your mouth. You can repeat this exercise a few times until your body relaxes. After the exercise, re-evaluate the level of your anxiety.

Coping skills for handling stress can include an activity we do, a place we go, a devoted friend we share our feelings with, or an object that brings comfort. We can channel our emotions and anxiety by having a daily routine or activity that helps us decompress. This could be going for a mile run, taking a walk after work, or setting aside time to create art or play a musical instrument. My routine for stress release is my two hours of Bible memory work each day after work. As I repeat the verses, I feel a sense of peace, and my concentration improves.

Your coping activity does not have to be a daily routine but can be something you do when you feel stressed. It can be a breathing exercise, a silent prayer, a peaceful place you go, or a quote you repeat a few times to make your mind relax and your body less tense. Many individuals with autism use stimming to manage emotions and cope with overwhelming situations—they go to a place by themselves and flap their hands or twirl in a circle until their sensory issues calm down.

Coping skills and sensory soothing can help you manage emotions and adapt to your environment, even at an event like the Super Bowl. You can evaluate the effectiveness of your coping methods and soothing techniques by asking these four questions: What is my body feeling? How is my breathing—is it slowing down or remaining the same? What is my emotional level now? What is happening with my thoughts?

A Sensory Soothing Kit

A sensory soothing kit can help you stay grounded when you begin to feel anxious or upset. You can create a soothing kit by placing items that calm your sensory issues into a backpack, purse, or box. Decorate your sensory soothing kit with positive and inspiring messages or patches. Keep your kit in a place where you can easily access it. To prevent an overload, use the items to soothe yourself throughout the day or when your emotional level rises.

Example of a sensory soothing kit

- Sound—earplugs or music player for auditory sensitivities
- Sight—sunglasses or a brimmed hat to shade your eyes from bright lights; pictures and postcards for visual stimulation that keep you relaxed
- Hunger—snacks you like with textures that feel good to you, such as gummy or crunchy snacks (like fruit snacks or pretzels)
- Taste—gum, candy, or mouthwash to eliminate unpleasant aftertaste from unfamiliar food
- Touch—clothing to help with temperature sensitivities or to replace a piece of clothing that is creating discomfort
- Smell—personal filtration mask to filter out smells, or aroma oils of some of your favorite scents that bring back pleasant memories
- Body movement—objects you can use to calm yourself and that may make stimming less obvious, such as a spinning ring, a piece of ribbon to stroke, or a squishy stress ball to squeeze
- Soothing objects—items you can use to keep yourself occupied when you are in a line or have to wait, such as handheld video games, toys, stuffed animals, or books

Closing Thoughts

Managing our emotions and sensory issues can be challenging. Rating our emotional-stress level can prevent a sensory overload. By learning to express our emotions and regulate sensory issues, we can adapt to social environments and reduce anxiety. Excessive stress affects both our physical and mental health. Coping skills and sensory soothing provide relief from emotional overload and improve our quality of life. A sensory soothing kit is a tool that we can use to keep us grounded at work, in social settings, and when we are on the go.

REFLECT

1. I share things that cause my emotional-stress level to increase. What are three things that arouse your emotional-stress level?
2. What are some sensory soothing or coping skills you can use to help manage your emotional and sensory issues?
3. What items will you keep in your sensory soothing kit and why did you choose them? How can these items help you manage your emotions and handle sensory issues?

FUN ACTIVITIES

The purpose of this activity is to help you evaluate your emotional-stress arousal level, recognize things that increase your emotional-stress level, and learn sensory soothing / coping skills to manage your emotions and handle sensory issues. This will enable you to adapt to your environment and reduce stress.

Rating emotional-stress level

Level 1: I feel fine—nothing is bothering me.

Level 2: I feel a little agitated—I can still handle myself and my feelings.

Level 3: I feel nervous / on edge—my mind is racing with thoughts and worries.

Level 4: I feel really upset and anxious—I am losing control of my emotions.

Level 5: I feel overwhelmed—I am experiencing a meltdown and cannot control my emotions, thoughts, or body.

List on poster board or a piece of paper: Level 1, Level 2, Level 3, Level 4, Level 5. On the top of the poster board or paper, write "My Emotional-Stress Level." For the next two weeks, record your emotional-stress level each day and keep track of the things that make your emotional-stress level increase. Rate each event from level 1 to 5.

Next to each level, write the things that preceded the arousal. After you finish the chart, discuss with a friend or a support-team member the sensory soothing and coping skills you can use for each situation. Next to each level, write the sensory soothing and coping skills you can apply in that situation so you can manage your emotions and handle sensory issues.

FURTHER READING

Cognitive-Behavioral Therapy for Adults with Autism Spectrum Disorder, second edition, by Valerie L. Gaus

Sensory Issues for Adults with Autism Spectrum Disorder, by Diarmuid Heffernan

Temple Talks about Autism and Sensory Issues: The World's Leading Expert on Autism Shares Her Advice and Experiences, by Temple Grandin

Tal Anderson's Story
Costar of Season Three of Atypical

A career in acting is not something that happens quickly;
it requires work and passion.

—TAL ANDERSON

IN 2019, TAL ANDERSON MADE her debut as Sid on Netflix's hit show *Atypical*, a comedy-drama series about a teenager's life with Asperger's. This was the perfect role for Tal, who, like Sid, has a strong work ethic and determination. Tal enjoys portraying Sid, who is sassy and has a no-nonsense approach to life, always speaking her mind. Unlike Sid, though, Tal is careful not to offend others and has learned to control her comments and emotions.

Tal was born in New Orleans and raised in Cape Coral, Florida. When Tal was a year old, she was diagnosed with a developmental disability, and she was diagnosed with autism in preschool. Tal's parents had her attend private schools with a higher teacher-to-student ratio to help her academically. They also provided her with therapists for language and social development.

From an early age, Tal's dream was to be an actress. Tal's journey to Hollywood required perseverance and overcoming her difficulties in social situations. As a child, she had few friends and felt misunderstood because of her sensory issues and hyperfocus. Life began to make sense for Tal when she was fifteen years old and her parents told her about her autism diagnosis. For Tal, transitioning to adulthood required learning to adjust to life's challenges. "My family is very supportive," she says, "and I was fortunate to have a lot of resources, love, and education available to me."

In elementary school, Tal spent most of her time working with teachers and therapists. Her parents and two other families started a school because they felt she wasn't learning in the public school environment. Tal's parents supported and fostered her unique abilities. "I was fascinated with movies from a young age, and my parents encouraged my interests. As a young child, I loved Disney films, but not just the stories. I knew every actor and singing voice of every character, as well as who the animator was for each character. My fascination with the entertainment industry just grew from there."

Tal found solace in movies and television. As a child she acted out Disney movie scenes with her two younger brothers and would write her own scripts, which included her favorite characters from different movies. She also loved to watch shows like *Kim Possible*, *The Proud Family*, and *American Dragon: Jake Long*. Tal was fascinated with classic films, silent films, and 1980s movies, like *The Princess Bride*, *The Goonies*, and *Sixteen Candles*.

She later became obsessed with horror movies and is a huge fan of the *Nightmare on Elm Street* franchise. Currently she enjoys horror and psychological thrillers, like *Get Out*, *A Quiet Place*, and *Us*.

This early love for film sparked Tal's passion for acting and filmmaking. "I have always been a storyteller, creating ways to express myself, writing scripts and making videos, though I didn't necessarily dream about being an actor, so my love of acting didn't come until I was about to enter high school."

Her parents wanted her to work on socialization more, so her mom hired an acting coach to come to the house to work on improvising everyday teen situations, and in the process, she learned how to actually do those things. After a few months, she felt more confident and took more social risks. Then at age fifteen, she started studying acting techniques, and she fell in love with acting and the process of analyzing characters and scenes.

Acting provided Tal with confidence on the stage and helped her to interact socially. Tal pursued her dream of acting by making the most of every opportunity and taking classes on improvisational acting, stage acting, stage combat, and character analysis. "I did a few plays while I was still in high school, and then I worked as background on a couple of independent films. This is when I really knew that I wanted to work toward a film and TV career versus a stage career."

After high school, Tal wanted to go straight to LA to pursue an acting career, but her parents persuaded her to go to college first. She moved from Cape Coral to Orlando to attend Full Sail University, where she majored in film with a concentration in postproduction.

After graduating from film school, Tal moved to Los Angeles. In Hollywood, Tal quickly learned that acting is a business. "I just wanted to act and be on television, but the reality is that it is very hard to do, and you have to do all of the right things. I am lucky because my mom, who is my manager, is very good at these kinds of things, and she takes care of all of the business stuff. Together we make a really good team."

Autism has provided Tal with gifts for acting and film productions. "I believe the biggest advantage is that I tend to be hyperfocused and very persistent. Once I am given a role to work on, I continue to work on it until I feel I understand the character. Also, I am not emotionally attached to opportunities. I just enjoy the process and keep learning and moving forward."

Still, even with all her college and acting roles, transitioning to adulthood has been a challenge for Tal. "I am still transitioning to adulthood and independence, and I have no idea if I will ever be comfortable with it. I struggle with anxiety and still have difficulty at times with doing new things, but I continue to work on these things and try to find ways that can help me."

For stress relief and relaxation, Tal finds comfort with her cats. "I have a cat here in Los Angeles named Winifred, and she's the coolest cat ever. She will fetch her toys like a dog and bring them to me and drop them into my hand. Honestly, Winifred is my best friend and keeps me sane, entertained, and happy."

Acting has enabled Tal to be an advocate in the autism community. Being atypical has made her more visible. For the first time, people other than her family are interested in what she has to say. "I am grateful to be able to advocate for inclusion and representation just by doing my job. I can speak for myself and for others who don't yet have a voice. I'm very grateful for *Atypical* giving me the opportunity to represent others in the autism community as Sid."

As Tal transitions into adulthood and pursues her acting career, her goals include playing a role in a major motion picture—a Marvel or horror film—and to be a series regular on a television show. She also desires to use her platform to help others with autism achieve their dreams.[8]

TAL ANDERSON'S BIOGRAPHY

Tal Anderson is an accomplished Los Angeles–based film and television actor, currently appearing in the Netflix original series *Atypical* as Sidney and seen in Times Square as part of a 2019 campaign and PSA for *Delivering Jobs*, directed by Jason Zada. Tal is also a working and award-winning film editor, certified in AVID Media Composer and experienced in the use of Adobe Premiere Pro and Davinci Resolve systems. She received her BS in film from Full Sail University, has experience editing a variety of short and feature-length content, and has written, directed, and edited several of her own films. Her first film, *Joy*, was selected for six film festivals, including a nomination for Best Super Short Film and a win for Direction of an Experimental Short

Film. Tal can be contacted through her agent at KMR & Associates in Los Angeles or by visiting instagram.com/theTalAnderson or her website, theTALanderson.com.

REFLECT

1. Tal Anderson found solace in movies and television. List three things that bring you solace when your emotion level is aroused. How do these three things help you to relax and feel calmer?

2. Tal shares that she created ways to express herself through storytelling, writing scripts, and making videos. What are some creative ways you can express yourself and become in tune with your emotions? If you would create a short film that reflects your emotions, what would the title of the video be and why?

3. Tal learned to identify "characters" in her life, such as "social Tal," "school Tal," and "just Tal." She would role-play these characters to develop new social skills. What are some characters you could develop for your life and what special skills would each of them teach you? How would these characters express their emotions differently? Which created character would be your favorite and why?

Chapter 11

Managing the Mind for Organization and Executive Functioning

> *For people with autism spectrum disorder, executive function can be a big challenge. They may find it hard to manage their time, keep things organized, switch between activities, and interact with others.*
> —LAURA NG, certified behavior analyst

MY EXECUTIVE FUNCTIONING CAUSES ME to experience challenges in education and employment. Because of autism, my executive function causes me to have a great long-term memory. I can quote more than fifteen thousand Bible verses and five thousand other quotes, but I have a horrible short-term memory. I don't often wear a coat in the winter because I often forget where I put it, and when I go to the mall, I never remember where I park my car, like the title of the movie *Dude, Where's My Car?*

I also struggle with organization, transition, prioritization, and planning for the future. When my Geo Prizm had 250,000 miles and I needed a new vehicle, it took me two years to decide to purchase a Saturn Ion. Decision-making often overwhelms me and requires longer processing time than my brothers and peers need. As I mature, I continue to learn new ways to adapt and process information more effectively. In life there's usually not just one correct answer for any situation but many, and some are better than others. Through practice, my executive-function ability has drastically improved, and so can yours.

One morning as I started my Saturn Ion, I heard a loud rattling, and I knew something was wrong with the exhaust system. My executive-functioning system informed me, *You have three options: Ignore the problem, which will cost you more money in the future; take your car to an auto repair shop; or—best choice—take your car to a muffler shop that specializes in exhaust systems.* Two of these three options are both right. In the past I would have chosen the wrong option of procrastination, but having learned to adapt to circumstances, I was able to pick the best option—I took my car to a muffler shop and saved money on the repairs. This choice required my brain to plan and generalize the information.

Living on our own requires us to prioritize the things we need to do and organize. If we continually forget to pay our rent, the landlord will evict us. If we cannot keep track of our bills, we will pay late fees and have a lower credit score. Attending college requires us to turn our assignments and projects in on time, and steady employment requires us to show up on time and be ready to work. Prioritizing is part of becoming a responsible adult.

Prioritizing Time

If we fail to prioritize, we risk spending valuable time on things that are not aligned with our life goals, like moving out of our parents' house or attaining gainful employment. We may waste our time playing video games instead of studying for college classes. When you prioritize your goals, you are generally better prepared to pursue your passions in a more controlled environment, and this leads to less anxiety.

I write a book every two years, and this requires over twelve hundred hours of writing, interviewing professionals, and researching. I am only able to do this because I prioritize my time. I know that the four days I have off each week are devoted to speaking events and writing, so I rise early and spend six to ten hours writing. I only check my emails once each hour, and I don't allow social media, like Facebook or X, to distract me. This creates a controlled environment free from distractions.

To prioritize, you need to record how you spend your time each day. In a notebook or on a piece of poster board, keep track of the activities you do each day for a week, as well as how much time they take. Write on the top of the paper or poster board a horizontal column with the days of the week, Monday through Sunday, and a vertical column with the times of the day from when you wake up until you go to sleep. Now make columns down and across to break up each day into square hours.

Each hour of the day, record how you spend your time. For example, on Monday I studied for a history test for an hour and twenty minutes—from 7:00 p.m. until 8:20 p.m. On your time graph, pay attention to how much free time you have each day and the number of hours you worked or studied or attended classes.

At the end of the week, record how much time you spent in these four categories: personal (fun and interests), work/school, health (exercise/sports), and family and relationships. With your free time, you can plan activities related to your goals and values. If your desire is to have friendships, set aside two hours on a Friday night to attend a social group at your church.

Use your time graph to create a schedule to manage your time. Include allocated time slots for breaks. Separate your schedule into a daily to-do list to work through. Also note weekly and monthly goals. I have a calendar to help me keep track of my appointments and speaking events. I also learned five ways to prioritize my time:

1. Plan your time with values in mind—things you hope to achieve and enjoy doing. Your values can consist of time you spend with family and friends, attending college, or volunteer work. I schedule time for writing books, speaking engagements, and family interests—playing games, movie nights, and a camping trip each year. Also include things you want to accomplish, like academic or career goals.

2. Distinguish between things that are urgent versus things that are important—urgent means there's a deadline and you need to do it as soon as possible. When something is urgent, such as a problem with my car, I take care of it immediately. If I have a deadline for an assignment at work, that takes priority over everything else on my agenda. Situations often become urgent because we procrastinate and do them at the last moment. Something important could be an event, like a friend's wedding or requesting time off work for your vacation. When something is important, you need to get it done but have time to plan it out.

3. Prioritize what you need to do each day and month by level of importance. For example, taking your dog outside to use the restroom when you get home is more urgent than washing the dishes right away. Washing the dishes each night is more important than watching your favorite TV show. Mailing out your rent payment that is due is more urgent than getting your car washed. Making a priority list allows you to feel less stress.

4. Schedule self-care time to prevent burnout. This is time you set aside to do things you enjoy, like playing video games or going for a run. Self-care time causes you to stay fresh and experience health and well-being.

5. Set a visual reminder to prioritize your time. This can be a wall planner, a calendar, an app, or a journal.

Managing Executive Function

In chapter 9, "Making Wise Decisions That Influence Your Life," we examined ways to break our decisions into smaller steps to make it easier to accomplish them. Smaller steps enable our executive functions to process information quicker and help us stay calm. Managing our executive function also requires us to understand our weaknesses and have a step-by-step plan to overcome those challenges.

I have difficulty transitioning from one activity to another and understanding verbal instructions. Knowing my weakness with transition, I adapt by having a written schedule and taking a five-minute break when switching from one assignment to the next.

I adapt to verbal challenges by writing out instructions. I still experience difficulty when working with new co-workers because I cannot decode their body language or anticipate how they will respond to my usual behavior and psych stories. In areas I don't understand, I have learned to proceed with caution. For example, with a new co-worker, I hold back telling my stories and sharing too much personal information until I get to know them. I tell the person that I have autism and explain how it affects my behavior and ability to filter comments.

I find it easier for my executive function to make a decision if I evaluate my options on paper. When I have the options on a list in front of me, I feel calm and in control, knowing that I can change the situation by my actions. After my blood lab for A1C, I found out I was prediabetes at a 5.7 level. I wrote down my options: (1) Ignore it. (2) Immediately quit eating foods with sugar and high carbohydrates. (3) Research the foods I should avoid and pace myself as I change my diet and exercise regularly.

The first option of ignoring my high blood-sugar level could lead to diabetes and an early death. Quitting cold turkey would probably only last a few weeks before I went on a food binge and returned to my old eating habits. Researching the foods I should avoid, changing my diet, and exercising regularly was the best choice because I could pace myself as I ate healthier and worked out. Pacing my new eating habits and regular exercise would enable me to develop a new routine slowly, resulting in less anxiety and lower blood-sugar levels.

I accomplished the third option by tracking the foods I ate for two weeks and researching which of these foods I should eliminate from my diet. As I recorded the foods, I noticed I was eating too much candy at work and while watching TV in the evening. Instead of quitting candy cold turkey, I picked two set times during the day and evening when I could eat a piece of candy, thus creating a new routine. I also cut back on the amount of sugar and carbohydrates, began eating a salad for lunch, and started exercising in the evening.

External and Internal Factors

External and internal factors play a role in our executive function's ability to operate efficiently. Our environment and schedule are external factors. For example, I have less brain power to make a decision in a noisy conference room or in the evening when I am exhausted from working all day. When I feel burnout from working too many hours or from researching for hours with no rest, I lose my ability to concentrate. I have learned to overcome burnout and fatigue by pacing myself and breaking up assignments over a few days.

Internal factors that affect my executive function are tiredness, blood-sugar level, emotional arousal, and feeling fear and anxiety. When I am well rested, my emotions are in check and I am eating a healthy diet. My mind processes information more efficiently and I make better choices.

Optimizing Executive Function

I have learned four ways to strengthen my executive-function ability so I struggle less with transition, generalization, and short-term memory. These methods empower my executive function to operate quicker and process information efficiently. When my executive functioning is optimized, I feel confident, less anxious, and experience a decrease in sensory-processing issues.

1. Begin each day with at least one small goal that relates to your interests.

Before work, I spend twenty minutes memorizing new Bible verses in my car. After I finish, I declare to myself, "I got at least one thing done today." When I finish leading a mental health group, I repeat to myself, "I got at least one thing done today." Later in the day, after I read a chapter from a book, I again exclaim, "I got at least one thing done today." I also use this affirmation after each chapter I write.

Completing small goals daily causes our executive function to feel confident to accomplish bigger goals, like finishing college or moving out of our parents' house. These small daily chores of life develop our self-efficacy—the belief that when we begin a goal, we can accomplish it.

For your daily assignments, use this equation: Purpose + Goals = Results. Consider your interests and how they can empower you to reach your goals. Small assignments can be simple, like reading a chapter of a book, washing dishes, or mowing the lawn. After you finish a task, declare to yourself, "I got at least one thing done today." This affirmation will encourage you to keep pressing forward and to expect results.

2. Create a visual reminder of your accomplishments and goals.

One of the best ways we can strengthen our executive function is by visual stimuli that produce growth. Prepare a portfolio of your work and achievements. During a season of disappointment or an employment drought, your portfolio can produce hope and is a reminder of the growth you've experienced.

After publishing an article for the Art of Autism or *Autism Parenting Magazine*, I make a copy and place it in a three-ring binder. I keep a running list of every book I read and every conference, workshop, and church at which I speak. These lists are a visual reminder of the things I have accomplished. Neurotypical people also use visual encouragement reminders by placing vacation and family photos on their office desks or posting videos on Facebook and Instagram.

As mentioned earlier, get organized by relying on visual aids such as a calendar to remind you of appointments and when your bills or class assignments are due. Visual reminders can help you remember where you parked your car. When you go to the mall, take a photo of the section number or letter where your car is parked. Make a schedule on paper, and look at it several times a day. On the schedule, have a checklist and estimate how long each task will take. Keep the schedule in your pocket. This will make transitions easier as you see the chronological order of events for the day and the times, but remain flexible to unexpected changes in plans.

Here is a sample schedule:

1. Wake up at 7:00 a.m.
2. Take a shower, eat breakfast, and drink coffee.
3. Drive to work at 8:00 a.m.
4. Begin work at 8:30 a.m.
5. Lunch break at noon.
6. Finish work and drive home at 4:00 p.m.
7. Do homework for classes from 4:30–5:30 p.m.
8. Eat dinner at 6:00 p.m.
9. Do chores from 6:30–7:30 p.m.
10. Free time from 7:30–9:00 p.m.—watch a movie.
11. Get ready for bed at 9:30 p.m.
12. Bedtime at 10:00 p.m. Set alarm for 7:00 a.m.

3. Be prepared for the unexpected.

Plans in life change and our routines will be broken. When a five-year-old has a meltdown because the bank ran out of her favorite blue suckers, people are more understanding than when a forty-year-old autistic person has a meltdown over suckers. Participating in life activities enables our executive functions to adapt to transitions and to generalize concepts. As we interact socially, we are able to generalize concepts we have previously learned. For example, if our relatives are offended by a sexist joke, our co-workers will also be offended by the joke. By watching people interact, we learn new social etiquette and are able to model appropriate behavior. You see someone say "Excuse me" when she sneezes, so you say the same thing the next time you sneeze. You see men wear suits and ties to a wedding, so you model their style and wear the same.

We become prepared for the unexpected by breaking our routines. After planning all week to write a chapter in my book on Saturday, my wife informed me, "This Saturday is the birthday party for Makayla's friend Billy." The birthday party had a reptile show with a boa constrictor and monitor lizards. As the snakes slithered across the carpet, some of the mothers experienced a sensory overload of fear. My executive function had difficulty adjusting to the sounds of popping balloons and thirty-plus kindergartners screaming and laughing. This was a small expense compared to the joy of seeing my daughter dancing and enjoying herself at the party.

The unexpected prepares us for transition. The more times we transition, the easier it becomes to adapt to our environment. The more exposure we have to different environments, the easier it becomes to adapt. The moms at the party were forced to adapt to their fear of snakes, and I had to adapt to the loud sounds of children. When you attend a new event, bring your sensory soothing kit and have an escape plan.

You can feel comfortable with the unexpected moments of life by writing down the positive results. When you have an unexpected moment, draw three lines on a piece of paper. On the first line write "Unexpected Event," on the second line write "Feelings/Emotions," and on the third line write "Result." Keep the paper in your pocket until the event is over.

Unexpected event results

Unexpected Event: Attending a birthday party.

Feelings/Emotions: Anxiety from kids running around and unexpected noises, like popping balloons and laughing.

Results: I enjoyed seeing my daughter dancing and having fun with the other kids. Good food, such as cake and pizza. A cool reptile show with a boa constrictor, baby alligator, and different lizards.

4. Direct your attention to positive thoughts and ideas that promote growth and maturity.

Positive thoughts produce a healthy self-esteem, while negativity can lead to fear and anxiety of the future. I keep my thoughts positive by reading the Bible and taking captive thoughts that lead to anxiety and fear—thoughts such as, *Working at a hospital—you're going to get COVID and die* or *You will have a stroke and not be able to talk to your wife and daughter.* Instead, I replace them with positive thoughts: *When Makayla gets married, I will walk her down the aisle* or *When I speak, my message will bring people hope.*

The apostle Paul wrote, "For though we live in the world, we do not wage war as the world does. The weapons we fight with are not the weapons of the world. On the contrary, they have divine power to demolish strongholds. We demolish arguments and every pretension that sets itself up against the knowledge of God, and we take captive every thought to make it obedient to Christ" (2 Corinthians 10:3–5).

We cannot stop negative thoughts from popping into our minds, but we don't have to dwell on them. During COVID-19, I quit watching and reading social media news because I found myself angry and depressed. Instead, I focused my attention on writing books. I realized I couldn't change the government COVID policies, but I could do something positive with my time.

When evaluating a thought or idea, I use the STOPP method, which is the acronym for stop, think, observe, plan, and proceed.

When to take a thought captive

1. Is this thought based on truth or a lie? If the thought is false, take it captive.
2. Does this thought reflect growth and maturity—the belief that *I can* do something rather than *I cannot*? If not, take it captive.
3. What are the fruits of this thought—peace and joy or fear and anxiety? If negative fruit, take it captive.
4. Does the thought produce faith, hope, and love, or does it produce jealousy, lust, or bitterness? If the latter, take it captive.
5. Would I want others to know I am thinking this thought? If not, take it captive.
6. Does the thought pass the Philippians 4:8 test of "whatever is true, whatever is noble, whatever is right, whatever is pure, whatever is lovely, whatever is admirable—if anything is excellent or praiseworthy—think about such things"? If not, take it captive.
7. Does the thought bring glory to God and promote life? If not, take it captive.

Safety and Executive Function

Our executive function is prone to safety issues when it overestimates our abilities and underestimates the risk factors. This is the reason I don't drink alcohol or swim in the Great Lakes and oceans.

Many individuals with autism have difficulty gauging the amount of alcohol they consume. This can cause unsafe behavior since alcohol can impair judgment and reaction time by slowing down the functions of the central nervous system. It is a depressant, and continuous use can cause severe depression and memory loss. Studies have found that individuals with autism spectrum disorder are more vulnerable to becoming dependent on substances such as alcohol and drugs. This is most likely due to the intense anxiety and sensory problems caused by autism.[1]

I choose not to drink because I don't want my judgment impaired and I experience difficulty monitoring the amount I consume. When I drank in high school, I would engage in risky behavior like jumping off a roof at a party to show off to the cheerleaders or making an inappropriate comment that could get me beat up by their jock boyfriends.

My executive function causes me to overestimate my abilities. I was swimming in the Atlantic Ocean at New Smyrna Beach, and I overestimated my swimming ability—and a kind lifeguard led me back to the shore. My difficulty with generalization caused me to repeat this folly while swimming in Lake Michigan at Traverse City, when the water temperature was only sixty degrees. I swam so far out in freezing water that I barely had enough strength to make it back to shore.

There are three ways to keep safe and compensate for executive function challenges. First, rate the danger of the activity or choice on a scale of 1 to 5. Level 1 is no danger—a child could do this activity. Level 5 is super dangerous and foolish and could result in a permanent injury or death. If you're unsure about what the level of danger is for an activity or a choice, contact your support team or a trusted friend. When in doubt with safety, it is better to err on the side of caution. You can think of the safety rating as traffic lights. Green: super safe, and you can go. This is level 1 and 2. Yellow: proceed with caution and possibly contact your support team. This is level 3 and 4. Red: stop and contact your support team immediately. This is level 5.

Second, learn to evaluate inappropriate versus appropriate behavior on a scale of 1 to 4. Category 1, "Good—Mature Adult Behavior," demonstrates maturity and is appreciated by others. This will make people want to be your friend and invite you to social activities. This includes appropriate behavior like flushing the toilet, being honest but tactful, asking first (before you do something, get permission), integrity (what you say is what you do), proper hygiene (using deodorant, brushing your teeth, and showering each morning), being responsible (cleaning your room or being home on time), having common courtesy (apologize when you do something wrong, or not interrupting when someone is having a conversation), being polite (using words like *please* and *thank you* and holding the door open for others), giving (being generous with your time and resources), showing kindness (helping those in need), and other behavior that displays maturity.

Two questions for this type of behavior: *How can I behave in this way more often so I can make friends and demonstrate maturity? Who are some people I know who have these qualities and would be good friends?*

Category 2, "Things People Consider Gross," is behavior in public that is rude or disgusting. This behavior is legal but socially unacceptable and will cause your peers to not invite you to social gatherings. This includes inappropriate behavior like burping, farting, having lack of attention to personal hygiene, picking your nose, scratching or touching your private parts, not covering your mouth when you cough, swearing or making rude comments, spitting in public, displaying bad social etiquette (chewing food loudly at the dinner table or bumping into someone and not saying "Excuse me"), and any other action society regards as impolite or distasteful.

For this behavior, ask yourself these two questions: *Would this behavior be appropriate in front of a large audience or at a wedding? If I do this behavior, will I offend someone?*

Category 3, "Very Bad and Not Acceptable," is behavior that makes people not want to be your friend or hang around you. This includes inappropriate behavior like cheating (dating more than one person at a time and not letting them know), lying (falsifying information about yourself or not being truthful), aggressive communications (verbal or written threats), disclosing too much personal information (sharing your medical history or love life with someone you just met), selfishness (putting your own interests ahead of others), having a bad attitude (negative view on life), violating trust (a friend shares a secret and you tell others), and anything else you would not want others to do to you.

Two questions to ask yourself concerning this behavior: *Would I want to be friends with someone who does this? How would I feel if someone did this to me?*

Category 4, "Absolutely Not Allowed," is behavior not accepted by society and will lead to jail or get you fired from a job. This includes inappropriate behavior like stealing, touching someone inappropriately (forcing someone to kiss you or a touch that makes someone feel uncomfortable, such as a pat on the butt), stalking (following someone or constantly checking their social media), sexual harassment (unwanted sexual advances or comments), urinating in public, fighting (verbal threats or physically assaulting someone), bullying (physical or emotional abuse toward someone), and anything else against the law or behavior that makes others feel uncomfortable and/or in danger.

For this type of behavior, ask yourself these two questions: *Is this activity or behavior against the law or will it make others feel unsafe? Is this behavior dangerous or could it lead to death or an injury?*

By evaluating inappropriate versus appropriate behavior, we can change our actions to attract friends, avoid offending others, and develop character that causes us to stand out as a good job candidate by our kindness, maturity, and polite manners.

Third, after solving a problem, evaluate the lessons learned and consider how to apply that knowledge to the next challenge—this produces the ability to generalize ideas. When the low-tire-pressure light went on in my car, I had three options: (1) Ignore the light and keep driving until the tire or tires were completely flat. (2) Drive to the nearest gas station and put air in the tires. (3) Check the tire pressure, and if the pressure in one or more tires is low, drive to the nearest gas station and put air in those tires.

I chose option 3 and checked the air pressure in my tires, which were low, and then I drove to the nearest gas station. The only problem was that the air pump was out of order, so I drove to the next gas station—and that air pump was also out of order. Finally, the third gas station had a working air pump, so I filled my tires. I learned from this experience that simple things like putting air in your tires can be a challenge, and that achieving a goal requires following steps.

Strengthening your executive-functioning ability will cause you to develop situational awareness, make fewer mistakes due to absent-mindedness, learn to generalize ideas for problem-solving, and—most importantly—live safer by discerning risky behavior.

Closing Thoughts

Optimizing our executive function will improve our short-term memory and empower us for transitioning, planning, and generalizing. By regularly performing the activities explained in this chapter, you will strengthen your executive-functioning ability and enhance your life with confidence, less anxiety, and a decrease in sensory-processing issues. And significantly, you will learn to make wiser and safer decisions and gain more independence.

REFLECT

1. I describe factors that can impact our executive functioning. Which ones on the list do you struggle with and what are some ways you can accommodate for them?
2. Name two inappropriate behaviors and three appropriate behaviors you do. What are some new appropriate behaviors you can begin doing? Who are some family or friends who model these

good behaviors? What impact would developing these good behaviors have on your ability to socialize and make friends?

3. I share how to apply lessons you learned from solving a problem
to improve your ability to generalize. What is a problem you
recently had to solve or a challenge you overcame, and what lessons did you learn? How can you apply these lessons to future
problems or challenges?

FUN ACTIVITIES

On poster board or a piece of paper with your group or a friend, write
on the top *Purpose + Goals = Results*. Below this phrase, write what
your purpose is, what your goal is, and what results you desire. For
example, mine are these: (Purpose) Speaking and Writing on Autism
and Faith + (Goal) Create an Awareness of Autism in the Faith Community = (Result) Churches and Religious Organizations Becoming
Autistic Friendly, Resulting in More Families with Autistic Children
Attending Religious Services.

Your *purpose* is to reach your full potential and maximize your ability to gain independence. Your *goal* could be attending college or a
trade school, moving out of your parents' house, employment related
to your passions, traveling, or anything you hope to accomplish. The
result could be graduating from college or finishing trade school, employment in your dream career, traveling to all fifty states, moving into
your own apartment, or anything related to your passion.

Underneath your purpose, goal, and results, write down your schedule for the week and track your free time. Record each hour of the day
and how you spend your time, and break this down into these four
categories: personal (fun and interests), work/school, health (exercise/
sports), and family and relationships. Using this schedule, record your
free time for the week and figure out the amount of time you will
spend doing things that will help you accomplish your goal.

Discuss with your support team, group, or a friend your purpose, passion, and goal, and share how you hope to accomplish this. Create a schedule based on your free time to work toward the goal each day. Record the times you have set aside to reach your goal. Break your goal into days, weeks, and months. Set a timeline for when you hope to achieve milestones. Have your support team, group, or a friend provide accountability to keep you on track to reach your goal.

FURTHER READING

Brain Hacks: Life-Changing Strategies to Improve Executive Functioning,
   by Lara Honos-Webb
Autism and Everyday Executive Function: A Strengths-Based Approach
   for Improving Attention, Memory, Organization, and Flexibility,
   by Paula Moraine
The Autistic Brain: Helping Different Kinds of Minds Succeed, by Temple Grandin and Richard Panek

Elisabeth Wiklander's Story
Cellist in the London Philharmonic Orchestra,
Diagnosed with Asperger's

No diagnostic manual can truly explain the multifaceted
experience of autism.
—Elisabeth Wiklander

Elisabeth Wiklander was raised in a musically talented family. Her dad is a pianist, organist, and composer, and her mom is a conductor, singer, and clarinetist. When Elisabeth was a newborn, her parents played Bach's Brandenburg Concerto No. 5 from a tape recorder in the delivery room. She learned to play the cello, using the Suzuki method, at age three. Even at such a young age, Elisabeth was inspired by her dad's concerts with the principal cellist of the Gothenburg Symphony Orchestra.

"I'd sit with two sticks on the steps to our house, pretending to play cello, and when the principal cellist saw it, he enrolled me in lessons," Elisabeth says. "Dad and I played our first concert when I was five, and we still perform to this day."

Elisabeth's parents continued to encourage her passion for music. Her dad performed many big concerts when she was young, and her mom and dad also performed together—and Elisabeth would travel with them. Having music around was normal, but she was never forced to play her instrument.

Though music came naturally for Elisabeth, social interaction required strenuous effort. As a child, Elisabeth had difficulty interacting with her peers and was bullied. She noticed that her brain processed information literally and systematically. In conversations, she sometimes lacked the ability to filter her words, and children laughed at her brutal honesty and offbeat comments.

Elisabeth loved nature and wildlife, and she loved spending time at her family's cabin in the countryside. Through nature and music, she was able to express herself and feel peace. But Elisabeth's greatest challenge when growing up was making her feelings understood. When she felt pain from sensory overload from scents or sounds, her family and friends thought she was being overly dramatic. As a young adult, Elisabeth often felt confused and misunderstood. She did not know how to explain to others why communication drained her emotions and caused her to feel exhausted.

Visual movement such as people mingling quickly tired her. She had to remove tags from her clothes—they were like knives on her skin. "The best defense to avoid sensory overload is to not be tired when I expose myself to a challenging environment and to take small breaks throughout the event, like lifting the lid of a kettle to prevent it from boiling over."

When Elisabeth was twenty-three, she learned that her dad had Asperger's. At that time, autism resources were limited—this was the first time Elisabeth had heard the term *Asperger's*. His diagnosis was the beginning of her journey of self-discovery.

When she was twenty-five, her then boyfriend had brain surgery. While recovering, he had no filter, no capacity to compensate for or ability to ignore what bothered him. So everything that caused even the slightest friction in their relationship brutally surfaced in clear verbal messages. Hurt and confused, she contemplated the painful information.

"Thanks to what I'd learned from my father's diagnosis, I realized these qualities could be Asperger's traits." She bought and read all the literature she could find about it. But as there was nothing specifically about females yet, her suspicions were mainly confirmed from relationship books in which one partner had Asperger's (almost always exemplified by the man). Although she had similar, though different, traits than her male counterparts, the relationship issues mirrored her situation exactly.

Broken relationships and mental health deterioration fueled Elisabeth's search for answers. When dating, her autistic quirks could either be celebrated by an open-minded guy or be a repellent if conformity was important to him. "I had always felt I had a 'masculine mind,' failing to follow normal dating norms and to live up to female stereotype expectations."

After researching autism, Elisabeth, at age twenty-seven, discovered she was on the autism spectrum and received a formal diagnosis from a psychotherapist. Seven years later, on Autism Awareness Day, she announced her autism diagnosis publicly and presented a TEDx Talk: "Neurodiversity—the Key That Unlocked My World."

Elisabeth felt freedom when sharing her autism diagnosis. "Hiding your true self is crippling and puts you in a solitary confinement that eats away at your soul. So many people touched by autism stepped out of the shadows and approached me that my feeling of being part of a community really took form."

Elisabeth credits autism for helping her music career as a cellist in the London Philharmonic Orchestra, as it enables her to keep intense focus for long periods of time, to not mind the long hours of social isolation that preparatory work often requires, and to draw on her natural talent for analytical thinking.

Elisabeth's music career has taken her around the world, including to Asia, Europe, and America. While she doesn't enjoy big cities because of the sensory assaults they bring, she does appreciate smaller places such as Switzerland's Lucerne.

Elisabeth met her husband, Damian, through music when he became her orchestra's transport and stage manager. He learned she was autistic on their first date. Damian has learned so much about the autistic mind that he's now "bilingual"—fluent in neurotypical and autistic communication. He also translates her experiences for his friends, with whom she doesn't have to waste energy on hiding her true self. "Damian has an enormous capacity for love and compassion. He's never embarrassed by my quirks, which makes me feel normal and accepted."

Elisabeth's diagnosis has empowered her to develop healthy relationships. Previously, she would feel exhausted trying to blend in by suppressing her autistic instincts. She had created social expectations she couldn't live up to. It was only when she took the approach in relationships that "we" are different and "we" need to understand each other that she made genuine friendships. "My current relationships are based on mutual respect—we are different, and we need to understand each other's neurological differences to fully appreciate each other."[2]

ELISABETH WIKLANDER'S BIOGRAPHY

Swedish-Canadian cellist Elisabeth Wiklander has a master of music degree and played with the Netherlands Philharmonic Orchestra in Amsterdam before obtaining her current position as a member of the London Philharmonic Orchestra. She has taught students at music conservatories in Amsterdam, London, and New York and is engaged in orchestral education as well as her orchestra's community projects and workshops with students, the homeless, the elderly, and the disabled. Elisabeth was diagnosed with Asperger's and is an advocate for neurodiversity, holding the title of Cultural Ambassador for the National Autistic Society in the United Kingdom. She is in high demand for her autism support, lecturing, scientific research, and high-profile media appearances.

REFLECT

1. Nature and music help Elisabeth's mind experience peace. What are some places or activities that cause you to feel calm? How can you use these places or activities to optimize your executive-functioning ability? What environments make you feel anxious or upset? How can you try to adapt to those environments using coping skills or items from your sensory kit?

2. Elisabeth credits autism for helping her music career as a cellist in the London Philharmonic Orchestra. What are three ways autism is a blessing to you? How can you use these strengths to compensate for executive-function deficits?

3. Before she was diagnosed with autism, Elisabeth felt exhausted in her attempts to blend in by suppressing autistic instincts. In some settings, do you try to mask your autism? If so, when do you feel the need to hide your autistic behavior and why? How can you feel comfortable sharing your diagnosis so you don't feel the need to mask your autism?

Chapter 12

Understanding the Twenty Hindrances to Transition

You don't grow out of autism at age eighteen or when you graduate from high school or college. One of the main hindrances for individuals with autism to transition into adulthood is a lack of resources and services.
—Dr. Leann S. DaWalt, director, senior scientist, University Center for Excellence in Developmental Disabilities, Waisman Center

Society and family members often wrongfully misjudge us based on the five markers of the transition to adulthood: finishing college, leaving the parents' home, gainful employment, marriage, and having a family. We feel defeated when we don't attain society's standards of adulthood. When we reach eighteen, many of the resources and services we received, like speech therapy or education programs, are cut off. Adulthood for individuals with autism has less routine than high school and college, making life more difficult and less predictable.

My support team helped me develop the social skills for marriage and employment and overcome the twenty hindrances to transitioning to adulthood. We must remember that autism is a lifelong condition, and we may struggle with some of the hindrances for years or for our whole life. Our support team will provide encouragement when we experience challenges and advice for making decisions and adjustments.

During my fifty-plus interviews of young adults with autism, I noticed some common hindrances they experienced in transitioning to adulthood. I had experienced many of the same roadblocks. As we examine these hindrances, I will provide three tips to overcome each one.

1. The Hindrance of Indecisiveness

We on the spectrum tend to be non-proactive with taking initiative. Instead, rather than making choices, we allow our circumstances to dictate our lives. While writing this book, I learned to be more proactive by making good choices and taking care of my health and well-being.

I had an unusual red/purple circular bull's-eye rash on my leg that looked like Lyme disease from a tick bite or an infection from a spider bite. In the past I would've waited until I felt immeasurable pain before having my doctor examine me. Instead, I faced my fear head-on and set up a doctor's appointment and blood labs. The next day I received a voice message from the medical clinic: "Your labs were all normal." I then had peace of mind rather than a catastrophe mindset telling me, *You're going to die from Lyme disease or experience loss of neurological abilities from the bite.*

When I visit my favorite Mexican café each Friday, keeping with my routines, I always order the same monster steak burrito combo. I started to take initiative by ordering my favorite meal plus a new meal to try, like the chicken tamales or carne asada tacos. This new routine challenges me to enjoy new things, form a new habit, and make decisions without anxiety.

I recommend three ways to kick the habit of indecisiveness. First, don't overthink the outcomes of your choices. Once you've made a decision, go with it. Most minor decisions won't have a major impact on your life. For example, should I eat a hamburger or peanut butter sandwich for lunch? Write down the decision and when you plan to carry it out. This prepares you to accept the outcome of your choice and learn from it.

Second, don't allow fear to prevent you from being proactive. When you try things that you fear, your self-confidence becomes stronger. I fear doctors' appointments, but the more I visit the clinic, the less I fear them. Remember, we tend to regret the things we don't do rather than the things we actually do.

Third, it is better to make mistakes than to be indecisive. We will never have all the insider information to make the perfect choice; therefore, we will make mistakes. When things don't turn out as you expect, you can adjust to the circumstance and move ahead with self-confidence.

2. The Hindrance of the Inability to Connect with People

My uncle David, who had Asperger's, was famous for saying, "I just rub people the wrong way, and I don't seem to connect like everyone else." An illustration of this inability to connect can be seen by comparing electrical outlets in Europe to those in the United States. For our electric shavers or hair dryers to operate in Europe, we need to use a European adapter plug. Without the adapter plug, our electronic devices will not connect to the electric supply.

During the last few years, I have learned the importance of connecting with people in order to achieve my goals. My friend Dave created the name Spectrum Inclusion for my website and organization. My former coworker Heather created my Facebook fan page. These key connections helped me receive speaking engagements and publishers for my books by developing a platform for selling books. Within twenty-four hours of receiving a job offer, I had three attorneys inspecting my contract to warn me of the red flags. These friends and connections protected me from making a wrong financial decision that would have impacted my family.

I suggest three ways to deepen your connection with people. First, schedule quality time with them. Don't become so absorbed in your special interests and projects that you ignore those around you. Set aside time to call a friend that you have not talked to for some time. Perhaps schedule a movie night or to meet for coffee. When your co-workers go out for lunch and invite you, join them. Apply the two-day rule: When you receive an email or message from a friend or connection, respond within forty-eight hours. This conveys your interest in their friendship.

Second, listen closely and take an active interest in your conversations with others. Try not to interrupt or prepare responses in advance. Just listen. Be the listening ear for others as a way to develop deeper connections.

Third, don't zone out by thinking about things you need to get done or daydreaming about your special interests. In college I missed many great connections by focusing on papers I had to write and class projects I needed to finish rather than focusing on the people around me. As King Solomon advised, "Be warned, my son, of anything in addition to them. Of making many books there is no end, and much study wearies the body" (Ecclesiastes 12:12).

We can focus on people by asking them about their lives, families, hobbies, goals, and dreams. We can be present in the moment by not checking our phones, glancing around the room, or searching out other distractions. Remember, your connections are your greatest resource outside of your support team and family to reach your goals.

We on the spectrum tend to shy away from making new connections. We tend to become obsessed with one person instead of seeing qualities of a good friend, like respect, thoughtfulness, and care. We search for friends rather than connecting with those around us by being a friend who listens and cares.

If I had to live my college experience over, I would spend less time studying and reading and would spend more energy building connections—because success is being able to connect. One of my ORU roommates is now a five-time best-selling author on nutrition and founded a company worth $500 million. A member of my sister wing at ORU is a *New York Times* best-selling author on Christianity and culture. My connection ability is no longer like an old pair of Velcro shoes, and as a result, I enjoy closer friendships as well as see more fruit in my career and as a national speaker.

3. The Hindrance of Placing All Our Eggs in One Basket

We on the spectrum tend to have difficulty diversifying and multitasking. Even as a young child, my special interests consumed all my energy and time. Here is a quick overview of my special interests: ages two to seven—art, stuffed animals, and squirrels; ages seven to fourteen—art, animals, and Prairie Pup; ages fourteen to twenty-one—baseball, track, cross-country, books, pets, and video games; ages twenty-one to forty— theology, reading, Bible memory work, pets, movies, and academics; age forty to the present—family, travel, writing, speaking, preaching, reading, memory work, mental health, movies, food, pets, and career.

Whatever my special interest was when I was young had my total attention. Notice that as I aged, my special interests became broader and less restrictive. From ages two to seven, I only had three special interests, but from age forty to now, I have more than ten.

Placing all our eggs in one basket can make life difficult. For example, when my special interests were track and cross-country, I spent so much time running and exercising that my GPA suffered. I was able to receive an athletic scholarship for track and cross-country, which helped prepare me for my next special interest in academics and theology. Having autism, I ran a precarious course. If I would've been injured during my senior year of high school and had not been able to compete in track, having placed all my eggs in that basket, I probably would not have been able to attend a university and you would not be reading a book written by me.

Due to my special interests, I experience severe difficulty transitioning from one activity to another. I find it hard to stop working on a project related to my special interests. Peter Lantz, a professional video game designer with Asperger's, describes our inability to multitask: "If I put my mind to something, it will get done, but the rest of my life always suffers."[1]

I offer three suggestions to overcome the hindrance of placing all your eggs in one basket and having difficulty diversifying and multitasking. First, during work, set aside a couple of short break times for your special interests. Don't allow your special interests to consume you, but gain control over your interests by setting a time for them. Some of my co-workers take fifteen-minute breaks for food or smoking. I take a fifteen-minute break each workday to read books and articles on topics I am currently writing about. This break enables my mind to stay fresh and focused. I feel less anxious after reading, and my labor is more productive.

Second, become an expert at your special interests. When you're an expert, you get paid to do what you love. With our intense focus, we can quickly become experts on any subject that sparks our interests. I have become an expert on the topics of theology, autism, and mental health, and I receive emails daily for paid opportunities to speak on these topics. Some ways you can show your expertise is by hosting a podcast about your special interests, writing a blog, and creating a Facebook fan page.

Third, refine your special interests through life experiences. Get out in the world and enjoy it—don't isolate to your special interests. There are three types of natural growth: biological (physical), intellectual (mind), and experiential (maturity).[2] An example of biological growth is when infants digest food and receive nourishment, which causes them to grow physically. Intellectual growth occurs by time and study.

Experiential growth occurs through life experiences, in addition to overcoming challenges and adjusting to them. This is the hardest type of growth for individuals with autism because it requires us to leave our comfort zone and set routines. But experiential growth enables us to diversify.

My maturity and success in life were a result of experiential growth that came by trying new activities—my special interests diversified. Participating in athletics caused my anxiety and sensory issues to decrease, and my teammates encouraged me to discover new interests such as studying, movies, and reading. As a teenager, attending youth group created in me an interest in the Bible and theology, which led me to pursue college degrees in theology and psychology. Mission trips while in college led to my love of speaking and traveling, and also gave me a love for trying new exotic foods, like spicy Cajun-style toucan in a Pygmy village or a calamari salad on the coast of the Mediterranean Sea. Experiential growth will cause you to balance your time and energy between your job, family, friendships, and special interests.

4. The Hindrance of Craving Routines

A change in routine can throw our whole day off or, worse, lead to a meltdown. The smallest routine change at work or with daily activities can produce severe anxiety or fear. The company at which I am employed changed the method for delivering paycheck stubs from email to needing an account on their website. Not being computer savvy, I called the corporate office, and a tech helped me set up an account. This change in paycheck procedure took an hour out of my writing schedule. Nervous from this change in my routine, I went on an autistic ramble to the tech and had difficulty the rest of the day focusing on writing.

Through this experience I learned three ways to prepare for a change in my routine. First, realize that the only constant in life is change, so be ready to adjust. I do this by keeping the change in perspective and not viewing it as the apocalypse but as an inconvenience to my busy schedule. I ask myself, *Will this matter a week from now? In a year?* This reduces anger about the change and helps me relax.

Second, see change as a learning experience. This switch-up gave me the chance to share about autism with a tech from Puerto Rico and to hear his amazing story of surviving Hurricane Maria. I also learned how to set up an employee service account.

Third, reward yourself for not freaking out because of the change. After setting up the account, I felt unmotivated, so I treated myself to a delicious Mediterranean salmon French bread sandwich. Then I went to Barnes & Noble and had the bookstore attendant take my picture with my third book, *Views from the Spectrum*, which was on their shelf.

5. The Hindrance of Misunderstanding Social Norms

Not understanding social norms causes us to say and do things that offend others. During COVID-19, I sometimes unintentionally offended co-workers by talking about politics related to the pandemic and vaccine.

There are three ways to discern social norms and not put your foot in your mouth by your words or actions. First, before you make a comment about someone, ask yourself, *Would I be embarrassed if someone said that about me?* One of the main reasons I say unfiltered comments is that I am quick to speak without considering the consequences of my words. Having a poor short-term memory and attention span, I am afraid I will forget what I want to say. I can avoid socially inappropriate comments by slowing down, thinking about people's feelings, and realizing that I don't always have to express my opinion. By waiting a few seconds to respond, I am able to understand the flow of the conversation and provide a positive comment that delights the person I am speaking with rather than offends.

Second, learn to be mindful of the people around you by watching their behavior. For example, during a formal event like a wedding or graduation party, watch how people interact with one another and listen to the topics of their conversations. If people are fist-bumping, don't try to shake their hands—fist-bump instead. Wait to get your food until others are served. I made this mistake a few times, and people thought I was a selfish jerk. When in doubt concerning a social rule, write down relevant questions and share them with your support team.

Third, an understanding of social norms comes with experience. Put in the time and learn from life experiences. By attending social events with friends, family members, or co-workers who have good people skills, you will learn to decode social norms for yourself. I learned social skills by attending church groups with my friend Steve. As I watched him interact with young adults, especially females, I learned how to start a conversation and make new connections. The positive attitude I saw in Steve became a quality I have developed.

6. The Hindrance of Extreme Anxiety

Years of anxiety can cause high blood pressure, heart attacks, or strokes. Each day in the United States, thousands die from heart disease, and stress is a known leading risk factor. For us on the spectrum, anxiety comes from deadlines, work, relationships, family issues, finances, fear of the future, or just about anything. I experience anxiety when I have a deadline for a work assignment or when rushing to a speaking event. If you have an anxiety disorder, you should talk with a mental health specialist about your symptoms and receive a diagnosis.

Working full-time, writing books, and having a family can be stressful. I have learned some practical ways to reduce stress in my life. First, don't try to accomplish everything at once, but enjoy the seasons of your life. Living in Michigan, I enjoy the four seasons. As the fall approaches, I love seeing the leaves change their colors from green to red to bright orange. As I drive home from work, I take a scenic wooded route so I can see the majestic leaves shine forth from the oak trees. I find taking time to enjoy life causes my work to be more productive and creative.

Second, stop reading and watching things that make you anxious—because you have no control over them. I limit my time reading social media articles and watching the news because I feel my anxiety level increase—especially with articles on government policy or videos of natural disasters or injustice. Instead, I read books on subjects that interest me and relax by watching comedy movies while eating popcorn with my dog, Rudy. Limiting social media will reduce your anxiety level, and laughter is good for the soul.

Third, don't feel like you have to change the world—remember, you're not God. Too many people with autism are unhappy because they do not accept the circumstances they cannot change or have no control over. This generates unnecessary frustration, disappointment, and suffering. As my dad tells me, "Use your energy on things you have power to change. Stressing out over things you have no control over will only lead to disappointment and an early grave." Some things we have little power to change are work policies, laws, traffic, others' ideas, others' happiness, the past, and the weather. If we want to reduce anxiety, we should focus on the things we can change, such as our mindset, education, health, and work ethic.

7. The Hindrance of Being Easily Distracted When Doing Activities Unrelated to Our Interests

We have 100 percent focus on things related to our special interests. Transitioning to adulthood requires us to do things unrelated to our interests, like washing dishes, paying bills, and cleaning our apartment. Becoming distracted and repeatedly forgetting to pay our rent could lead to an eviction, or neglecting to turn back our clock for daylight saving time could result in us being written up for being late to work.

Transitioning to adulthood required me to learn practical ways to stay focused on tasks I find uninteresting, such as going to dentist appointments and getting oil changes. Here are three ways I learned to stay on task.

First, create a weekly and monthly/yearly priority list. The weekly priority list of tasks is on my refrigerator. This notes all my speaking events, appointments, and small projects for that week. I write the projects in order from least important to most important. Washing dishes is more important than vacuuming because you can't eat without dishes. The monthly/yearly priority list is my calendar. I check my calendar each day so I don't forget any speaking events, days off, or rent due dates. I update the weekly priority list each day when I finish a task and mark it off. While at work, if I remember something I need to do, like create PowerPoints, I write it on a piece of paper, and I add it to my weekly list when I get home. I never miss an event or bill because I have them all written down with a date.

Second, when working on a boring task, such as researching the topic of health and well-being, I set aside time for my research or chore and time for fun. For example, my research time is from 10 a.m. to 2 p.m., and after the four hours of labor, I treat myself to a fun walk to the dollar store or a meal from Lam Taste. I find motivation to stay focused by my rewards. During my research, I don't check social media or my phone but stay focused on the task at hand. When writing a book or an article, I know how many words I need to write before I can take a break.

Third, do the most difficult activities first. By doing this, you will feel more motivated to finish your chore or project. For example, when I work a double shift at the hospital (seventeen hours), I do the more difficult tasks during the morning shift, like extra charts and vitals, so on the second shift I have some time to relax with fewer assignments. Daily routines of finishing your chores will help you stay focused on the things you find less interesting so you can accomplish your goals.

8. The Hindrance of Standardized Tests

Many people with autism have difficulty with standardized educational tests such as the ACT and SAT, which are used to determine eligibility for college and scholarships. This prevents many autistic people gifted in science from receiving a scholarship because they may score poorly on the ACT or SAT in English or reading comprehension.

During my senior year of high school, I barely passed the Michigan Educational Assessment Program (MEAP). The MEAP was developed to measure what Michigan educators believe all students should comprehend in five subjects: mathematics, reading, science, social studies, and writing. I scored poor in mathematics but exceptionally high in reading comprehension and science. In order to pass the MEAP and receive a certificate of completion on my diploma, I had to receive a passing score in all five categories.

The two main reasons individuals with autism receive lower scores on standardized tests are difficulty with generalizing ideas/concepts and skills and abilities that are not evenly distributed for each test category. For example, many students with autism may have an exceptional ability in one subject, like science or mathematics, but a lower-than-average ability in English or reading comprehension, which lowers their score.

Standardized tests are also referred to as generalized tests since they cover many subjects. The *DSM-5* (*Diagnostic and Statistical Manual of Mental Disorders*, fifth edition) states that people with autism experience difficulty with generalization, so why would the US Department of Education, which includes the nonprofit College Board, the ACT, and the ETS (Educational Testing Service), give students with autism a generalized test such as the ACT or SAT when autistics are more specialized in their abilities? Why not give them a test in their area of interests and specialty so they can succeed?

We have difficulty with generalization because we don't have recognition ability. For example, with the ACT test question "Which has a higher population? A. Chicago B. New York C. Detroit D. Los Angeles," most students would answer correctly—B. New York. But if you asked those students what the population of New York is, they would have no clue. These students would reply, "New York is the more recognized city, so that's why I picked it." The autistic students, on the other hand, not having the recognition software program in their brains, would get the question wrong. They would try to figure out the exact population of the four cities and then get frustrated, and this question would have a negative impact on the rest of their test scores.

I offer three pieces of advice in regard to standardized tests. First, find a tutor to help prepare you. I was able to pass the MEAP because my mom hired a tutor to help me with the mathematics section.

Second, receive accommodations to help you do your best. Due to my learning disabilities and autism, when I took the ACT and SAT, I received extended time and a quiet area. You may request such accommodations as help with reading the questions, extended time, or a quiet space for taking the tests.

Third, don't allow a standardized test score to define your intelligence or academic ability. For acceptance to Oral Roberts University graduate school, I had to take the Miller standardized test. I received a very low score on the test. I did not even pass it. Yet I went on to graduate with a master of divinity degree from ORU with a 4.0 GPA, and I was one of only three students to graduate with a perfect GPA.

As part of the autism community, we need to advocate for the US Department of Education to switch from standardized to specialized tests. When you attend graduate school, your degree is in a specialized field, so why is the entrance test standardized? For example, my master's degree is in theology. The specialized test would be on theology, not English or mathematics. As Diane Ravitch, former US assistant secretary of education, wrote, "Sometimes, the most brilliant and intelligent minds do not shine in standardized tests because they do not have standardized minds."[3]

9. The Hindrance of a Limited Perspective

We on the spectrum tend to see our world as black and white, while most of life is in the gray—complex, uncertain, and constantly changing.

My autistic mind is focused and literal, which means I view concepts in absolutes. When I began studying theology as a senior in high school, I was dogmatic in my beliefs and had difficulty examining religious ideas from any perspective other than my own. I debated with anyone who believed differently from me, which created division and made people not listen to my message. I now speak on autism and faith to every denomination and religious background and share a message of God's love, acceptance, and grace.

I learned three methods to change from a black-and-white mindset to more abstract thinking. First, I acknowledge signs of polarized thinking. Some words alert us that our thoughts are extreme—like *always, never, impossible, disaster, hate, ruined, failure,* and *perfect.*[4] I recognize how I view people around me. For example, do I see people as only good or evil, or do I see them as having good and bad characteristics?

An example of applying only bad characteristics is when you meet Tim while waiting in line at McDonald's. He is dressed in oil-stained clothes and cracks dirty blonde jokes. You may perceive Tim to be a womanizer and mentally unstable.

An example of applying only good characteristics is when meeting a pretty young blonde who is outgoing and friendly. Based on these external positive traits, you now perceive her to be athletic, wealthy, trustworthy, and perfect in every way.

Applying all good or all bad characteristics can hinder us from interacting with people we perceive as different. We can learn from people and not prejudge them by listening to their stories.

Second, I find a happy middle ground when I disagree with someone whose ideas are different from mine. Interacting with co-workers and friends often involves negotiation and compromise. Polarized thinking can keep us from seeing things from others' perspectives. When there's a conflict, calmly ask why they think that way. Once we come to an understanding, we can work together and accomplish a task.

Third, I ask myself questions when I find myself thinking with a black-and-white mindset, and I reflect on my life. I ask questions such as, *Does this mistake really make me a failure? Will things never get better? Why do I believe things like this only happen to me?* Next, I reflect on my life and accomplishments. I realize I've been in circumstances like this before and did not sink, but became a stronger person. By seeing the world from a more abstract perspective, I am able to make new friends and experience new opportunities. I no longer prejudge others as devils or angels but as interesting people with stories and adventures.

10. The Hindrance of Labels and Having Others Determine What You Should Pursue in Life

Adulthood is determining your own path and taking chances. I received an email from a mom whose nineteen-year-old son's career counselor told him not to pursue a degree in ministry after the young man told her, "I only want to preach to twenty people." The counselor asked this young man, "What happens when the twenty-first person enters your church?" The young man thought for a moment and replied, "I would have to stop my message because that's too big of a crowd."

Since the sixth grade, this young man's passion was to be a minister, and he felt crushed when the counselor suggested he first work in a post office or a warehouse. This counselor was helping the young man learn skills so he could speak to more than just twenty people and make money to gain independence.

The labels "high functioning" and "low functioning" can be deceiving with autism. It is better to state the person's needs and the accommodations to help them thrive. For example, John's sensory issues require him to wear headphones to block out noise while working on his reports. Instead of saying, "John is high functioning and needs headphones," say, "John has autism and needs headphones to thrive while he works."

When I was a young child, many people who heard I had autism placed labels on me and lowered their expectations. The school experts tried to label me as emotionally impaired and warned my parents that I would never read beyond a seventh-grade level, attend college, excel in sports, or have meaningful relationships.

I have learned three ways to overcome labels and pursue my passions. First, I made it my goal to be friends with positive and like-minded people, those who have the same passions I have in life and understand my special interests. I have found like-minded people through church groups and by attending social events in college. You can join local interest-based groups on Facebook, Meetup.com, and other social media sites. People who have the same interests as you will be less judgmental and will help you refine skills related to your passions.

Second, I never allow labels to define my potential. Many adults with autism still suffer from the negative labels people attached to them when young, such as, "You're lazy" or You're stupid." After I was diagnosed with dyslexia and other learning disabilities, I was determined to be an overcomer. This required perseverance and hard work. Remember, labels are only another person's opinion. One speech therapist told my mom, "Ron's lazy—that's why he cannot pronounce *th* and *l* words." It took me over sixteen years of intense speech therapy to pronounce *th* and *l* words, yet still, when I am worn out, I will mispronounce them in front of an audience.

Third, I chose to follow my own path. During my junior year of high school, I felt called by God to attend Oral Roberts University and be a minister, and I did not allow anyone to persuade me otherwise. Some teachers tried to deter me, saying, "With a 1.7 GPA, a university will only accept you on academic probation." Instead of losing hope, I spent three hours a night studying, and during the next four semesters of high school I averaged a 3.50 GPA and graduated with a 2.5 GPA. I attended a local college my freshman year and raised my GPA to 3.9, and I received an academic scholarship to ORU.

In 2005, when Michigan had an economic downfall and I was unemployed, I searched relentlessly until I received full-time employment in the mental health field. During that time, I still pursued speaking and ministry opportunities.

In order to follow your own path, you need to have a plan and understand your strengths. Your strengths will enable you to compensate for your weaknesses. I had challenges with learning disabilities, but my intense focus enabled me to compensate for those weaknesses.

11. The Hindrance of Lack of Responsibility

Nearly 42 percent of young adults on the autism spectrum never worked for pay during their early twenties, and only about 17 percent of young adults on the spectrum from ages twenty-one to twenty-five have ever lived independently.[5] I interviewed many young adults who lived at home and did not develop responsibility by preparing their own meals, paying bills, or doing household chores. Lack of responsibility prevents these young adults from learning essential life skills to live independently.

In order for me to live independently, I had to take on responsibilities and learn to take care of myself. Here are three ways I became a responsible adult: First, I took advantage of every opportunity. When I was sixteen, I took a driver's education course and had my brothers and mom help me become a safe driver by helping me practice. As an adult, you don't want your parents driving you to a date or job interview. I took on responsibility in college by accepting an unpaid community-outreach position in which I learned to set a monthly schedule and sharpen my leadership skills while working with a team.

Second, I did things for myself. After graduating from college, when I still lived at home, my parents had me clean my room, do family chores each week, and pay my health and auto insurance bills. I developed good spending habits by saving money in my 401(k) and budgeting my finances. My interest in theology motivated me to save money so I could build my own library with more than five thousand books.

I know what you're thinking: *I don't make enough money as a part-time dishwasher at a diner to move out of my parents' home.* You can still take steps to be more responsible and learn new skills by doing chores at home. One friend on the spectrum is a twenty-five-year-old artist. Employed as a grocery bagger, he does not make enough money to move out, so he takes community college classes to learn business skills and has opened an art studio in his mom's basement. He's saving for an apartment with the money he makes selling art.

Third, I did not procrastinate, but completed tasks early. Responsible adults do things in a timely manner. I don't work well under pressure or on a timeline. In college I finished my research papers and class projects before the semester began. The week before fall and summer break, I asked my professors for the class syllabus so I knew the assignments. When I had an appointment, I made sure I was at least twenty minutes early. When you're responsible, people trust you and provide you with more freedom.

12. The Hindrance of Not Standing Up for Ourselves

Some supervisors will take advantage of employees with autism because we often have difficulty saying no. These bosses give us the assignments that no one else wants to do, like cleaning the toilet or taking an aggressive psychotic patient to the emergency room.

After I finished seminary, I worked for a pastor who paid me minimum wage to do yard work and shovel his driveway. When I was new at the hospital and other nursing staff members refused an assignment, the supervisor would assign the task to me. Employees with autism can be easy targets for jokes around the watercooler since we want to avoid conflict and so don't stand up for ourselves. Reduce stress and anxiety by being careful not to let others take advantage of you.

I recommend three ways to stand up for yourself. First, be confident but not arrogant. Confidence comes with experience, while arrogance is acting like we are better than others. I am confident in my strengths and look for opportunities to use them in the workplace. Each workday I lead a mental health group and speak to more than twenty patients. I don't view any task as beneath me. If a patient decorates his walls with feces, I help the housekeeper clean the walls. If a co-worker is struggling to finish his assignments, I lend a helping hand. But I don't allow people to take advantage of my generosity. If that same co-worker wants me to do his work every day, I will have a meeting with my supervisor concerning his work ethic.

Second, be assertive with small things. This will empower you to stand up for yourself under pressure. Due to lack of self-confidence as a teenager, I walked with my head down and back hunched. My dad encouraged me to walk confidently with my head held high and shoulders back. When my neighbor had his surround-sound system blaring while I was working on my book, I politely knocked on his door and asked him to turn it down.

Third, speak up when something is bothering you so you don't have an emotional outburst. Stay calm, but summon the courage to vocalize your concern, as others cannot read your mind. When you stand up for yourself, others will respect you.

13. The Hindrance of an Inefficient Filtering System

It's comical when my eight-year-old daughter, Makayla, makes an unfiltered comment, like, "When Grandpa went to the hospital, he was naked on the gurney." It is not so humorous when a forty-five-year-old with Asperger's says to his female neighbor with a facial outbreak of acne, "Did you get mauled by a hungry grizzly bear?" Words are not neutral. They either tear down or build up. They either heal or hurt. Proverbs 18:21 says, "The tongue has the power of life and death."

As a young adult, I had difficulty filtering my inappropriate comments. But I have learned three valuable lessons to filter my words. First, I ask myself three questions: *Does the comment need to be made? How would I feel if someone said that about me? Is the statement uplifting and positive?* If you're at work, a fourth question is, *Could this comment or joke get me fired or be considered harassment?* By asking these questions, you give yourself a few seconds to think before spewing out potential toxic words.

Second, I reflect on my motives. Is this comment to show off my vast knowledge on the topic or is it to inform my hearer of practical information? I try to stay away from gossip, even if it's true. Spreading gossip makes the person you gossiped about angry and makes those who hear your gossip afraid that you will gossip about them next. If you have a reputation for being a gossiper, your friends and co-workers will view you as not trustworthy and will be reserved in sharing personal information with you. As Proverbs 11:13 states, "A gossip betrays a confidence, but a trustworthy person keeps a secret."

Third, I observe the conversation and setting before speaking. Your topics and tone of conversation will be different at a funeral, birthday party, or office meeting. The conversation style in a birthday party is usually relaxed, while it will be more formal in an office meeting. Take a few minutes to listen to other conversations before sharing. When sharing my special interests in a conversation, I observe the person's response. If I receive a positive vibe and the person says, "Tell me more—that's real interesting," I share a little more. But if the hearer is checking his phone or looking around the room, I end the conversation. By filtering our words, we will be less awkward and better able to contribute to conversations—and we may even make a new friend.

14. The Hindrance of Comparing Ourselves to Others

One thing that hindered my transition to adulthood was comparing my accomplishments with those of my two successful older brothers, who had careers and families more than a decade before I did. I felt discouraged when I saw on Facebook my former college roommates and friends getting married and building successful careers in ministry while I was still single, living at home, and underemployed. In 2005, when I reached my lowest point, I questioned why I chose ORU. That mindset would have continued to hold me back if I had not learned three lessons that helped me to stop comparing myself to others. First, an accomplishment delayed does not mean an accomplishment denied. It may simply take longer to accomplish the goal of moving into an apartment or becoming a professional video game designer. I was in my thirties before I was gainfully employed, and I did not become a published author until I was in my forties. When you feel as if you will never reach your goals or as if life has passed you by, make a short list of things you can do daily to inch closer to the finish line. In my thirties when I was single, I made a goal to go on a date every week and attend at least one singles event a month until I had a girlfriend. Within three years of moving at a snail's pace, I was engaged.

Second, I learned to market my uniqueness. Temple Grandin says, "I am different, not less."[6] On the Asperger's Facebook page, a member posted the question, "Do you dress more like a senior citizen or kid?" We on the spectrum dance to our own beat by dressing different— Temple Grandin in her cowboy outfit—or having enthusiasm for unusual habits and hobbies. By marketing my uniqueness of Prairie Pup and Honey Badger and posting pictures of these stuffed animals around the country and with celebrities, I have received speaking engagements and a social media fan following.

I was reminded of the power of marketing uniqueness when I did a book signing at a Barnes & Noble store. After I finished signing, a children's author entered dressed as a wizard from his fantasy novel— children flocked to him as their parents rushed to purchase copies of his book. Be creative and think of ways to make your uniqueness pleasant.

Third, celebrate the successes of friends and colleagues. When a coworker introduces you to his new girlfriend, be happy for him. If a friend publishes a book, take part in her enthusiasm. If someone shares great news with you, keep the focus on them instead of turning it back to yourself. Don't complain about your circumstances by comparing your misfortune to a friend's achievement. Keep a positive perspective; don't be jealous of others' success, but be grateful for family and friends.

15. The Hindrance of a Lack of Real-Life Experience for Navigating the Unknown

Anthropologists refer to the cultural transition to adulthood as the "rite of passage." I call it falling from the eagle's nest and taking flight. The rite of passage has a three-part structure—separation, liminality, and reincorporation. "A young person undergoing a coming-of-age rite of passage must leave her 'normal world' (separation) and enter into a situation where she experiences the free-fall of being no longer a child but not yet an adult (liminality)." During this period, she takes on more responsibility. Liminality could be going away to college or moving out of the family home. "Once the initiate has successfully mastered the liminal phase, she returns to the normal world as an adult (reincorporation), having 'leveled up' with skills that are needed to function as a healthy member of the community."[7]

Notice the difficulties in these three phases: the separation—causes anxiety; the liminality—learning new skills when we struggle to generalize concepts learned in previous stages; and finally reincorporation—a new beginning of adulthood, which means a change in our routine and an overload of responsibilities, with minimal support.

Most people with autism don't go through this nicely packaged rite of passage when transitioning to adulthood, but rather encounter a dangerous battlefield with barbed-wire trenches and hidden land mines. Our transition is less smooth and more herky-jerky, much like our childhood development.

In my transition journey, I discovered three ways to gain life experiences to prepare for the unknown future of adulthood. First, I had mentors who helped me acquire skills by learning, doing, and teaching. The main qualities I sought in mentors were patience, a gentle spirit, and the ability to teach well. I had five mentors who inspired me to become the person I am today. My first mentor was my dad, who taught me the importance of hard work and perseverance. While in college, my mentors were Dr. Jack Van Impe and Professor Dr. Daniel

Grimes, who encouraged my love for the Scriptures and for the people I serve.

In 2014 Les Stobbe, an established literary agent with over sixty years of experience, took a chance on me although I was an unknown author without a social media platform. He coached me in writing and grammar, cheered me on when I was discouraged, and refined my book proposal and manuscript. A year later Les negotiated with an acquisitions editor, and I received my first book contract.

My current mentor is Dr. Laurence A. Becker, the producer of the documentary *Fierce Love and Art*, which is narrated by Temple Grandin and features nine artists with autism stories, including mine. Dr. Becker is a fountain of wisdom on education, art, nutrition, and autism, and his living room is filled with original artwork by savants and prodigies. When I am in my eighties, I hope to have this same passion and energy to travel the country and inspire others.

Second, I gained knowledge by reading articles and books on autism. I improved my social skills by reading autobiographies of individuals on the spectrum—including Temple Grandin, Carly Fleischmann, and John Elder Robison—and meeting others with autism at conferences and events. By learning from their challenges, I am more equipped to navigate my own journey. Talk with other young adults with autism and listen to their insights. Check out books from the library to gain more knowledge. Read the three books I list at the end of each chapter.

Third, I've come to understand my world by traveling and experiencing other cultures. By doing missionary work among indigenous people in three countries, I've learned how each culture has unique social norms and taboos. In Bulgaria, I was preaching and stimming with my hands. I tapped my open left hand over my closed-fisted right hand. In response to my hand motions, the Bulgarian congregation scowled at me, and the pastor took a deep breath. Ignorant of the social culture of Bulgaria, I did not realize that my hand motion was the equivalent of holding up the middle finger in the United States.

Life experiences like travel and social activities help us better interpret social norms and see things from a new perspective.

16. The Hindrance of a Lack of Direction in Life

Many individuals with autism float from job to job or stay at the same company for decades with little opportunity for promotion or personal growth. They don't have a career path in mind and they grapple with formulating the steps needed to accomplish their career goals. In the workplace, their social interactions exhaust them, as does attempting to mask their sensory issues and quirks. This makes goals harder to accomplish.

During my ministry and mental-health field careers, I formed three principles I follow when I lack direction and feel exhausted. First, a solid work ethic will open new opportunities. Every now and then a supervisor will ask us to do something that is not in our job description. By doing these extra assignments, we communicate our commitment to the job. We can impress our bosses by keeping ourselves busy when things are slow. For example, when the patients are in group, I keep busy by helping my co-workers finish their charts or folding patients' laundry. Doing only our job requirements communicates to management that we're not fully committed and don't desire to move to the next level.

People with a good work ethic arrive on time for work. One of the main reasons people are fired is tardiness and missing too many workdays. You will win the respect of your co-workers by arriving on time and being ready to work. When supervisors see your solid work ethic, they will offer you promotions. Through promotions you will gain more knowledge and skills, which help define your strengths. I learned I had leadership skills by being put in leadership positions.

Second, when I feel lost in life, I reinvent myself by using my gifts to serve others. I learned this from my co-worker Joe. When the economy crashed in Michigan, Joe, who was then working in the automobile industry and was earning a six-figure income, found himself unemployed. In response, he reinvented himself at age fifty by going back to college to be a nurse. He decided on this career after discovering a hidden talent for compassion while caring for his ill mother-in-law. Joe and I have been working together now for twelve years.

People with autism have difficulty with change and especially with reinventing themselves after a loss. A book title on reinventing after a crisis sums it up best: *A Paradise Built in Hell.* The premise of Rebecca Solnit's book is that after a disaster like Hurricane Katrina, 9/11, or an economic downfall, we may need to reinvent ourselves with a new career that requires new skills. After the economic crash in 2004, like Nurse Joe, I had to reinvent myself by changing my career from youth ministry to mental health. I evaluated the things I was good at (communication, leading groups, and following routines) and realized that mental health was a good fit. I reinvented myself by taking additional psychology classes. These classes, along with other life experiences, prepared me to write about autism. Life in this post-COVID-19 world may require you to reinvent yourself by going back to school or finding a new job.

Third, I learned that when I stay focused and alert, good things happen. I stay focused by writing down my goals and accepting only opportunities that relate to my passions. My two main passions are writing books and speaking on autism and faith. When I am offered an opportunity outside my strengths and interests, I politely turn them down. By staying focused on writing and speaking, good things happen, such as opportunities to interview famous athletes and celebrities in the autism community and speak around the country.

17. The Hindrance of a Lack of Self-Sufficiency, Causing a Dependence on Parents and Loved Ones for Your Needs

I interviewed many young adults with autism who still rely on their parents to pay their bills, prepare their meals, and do their laundry.

I learned these skills by performing family chores as a child and attending college out of state. Haley Moss, author of *The Young Autistic Adult's Independence Handbook*, shares:

> The first time I did laundry in the dorms, I put all of my dirty clothes in the dryer and wondered why they were still soapy—and warm. It took a few moments to realize the washer and dryer were not the same design as the ones at home, and I had mixed up the washer and the dryer. I felt like I had failed at being an independent adult, and that somehow my independent adult card would be revoked. This feeling of independence being ripped away from young autistic people—especially those who spent their childhoods under the watchful eye of overprotective relatives or other trusted grown-ups—is not uncommon.[8]

Even neurotypicals need to ask for help from loved ones from time to time. Humans are not wired like the bobcat, who leaves her young after three months to fend for themselves. After moving out of my parents' house, I found three resources that helped me gain more reward points on my independent-adult card.

First, parents are a great source of knowledge and practical insight. Just because you moved out of your parents' house doesn't mean you shouldn't seek their expertise when making major career decisions or heed their tips on dating. I still call my dad when I need advice on purchasing a vehicle or resolving a workplace conflict. He has over ninety years of life experience. In college, when I struggled with loneliness while living 930 miles from home, I'd call my parents to cheer me up. My mom still gives me pointers for raising my daughter, Makayla. Make sure to thank your parents for the wisdom you've gleaned from them.

Second, self-sufficiency comes through using the knowledge you've acquired. As you apply knowledge, you gain wisdom. You can learn to do home repairs or prepare meals by watching YouTube videos or taking community college courses. Co-workers and friends who are great cooks can help you be a better chef. Use the resources and connections around you. Start with a simple step and then work your way up to the hard thing at your own pace. This prevents you from becoming too stressed and possibly giving up. By being teachable with a hunger to discover new things, you will become more self-sufficient.

Third, don't overtax your support team by being codependent. If you exceed the limit on your credit card, don't call your support team to bail you out. The purpose of your support team is to provide you with advice and encouragement. Assign different roles to your support-team members based on their expertise and experience. For example, your parents can help you deal with housing issues. Your older brother, a businessman, can teach you to budget finances. Your former college roommate can give you dating tips.

Self-sufficiency does not make us an independent island, but rather makes us aware of when and how to ask for help from others. We should not feel shame when we need help.

18. The Hindrance of Lack of Financial Planning

Many young adults with autism make poor decisions with money because they never learned to budget their finances and save for the future. One of my college buddies on the spectrum activated his first credit card, which had a 25 percent interest rate, and purchased a $3,500 TV. Not wise. Ouch.

Here are three ways I make money work for me so I can retire when I turn sixty-five. First, I set up checking and savings accounts at my bank and put money in my 401(k) each paycheck. When I was twelve years old, my dad set up a bank account with me. He had me save 10 percent of the money I earned from mowing the lawn and chores. This set a habit of money management, and I currently save 20 percent of my income.

You also will want to set up checking and savings accounts with a bank. Checking is used for everyday transactions such as depositing and withdrawing money to pay your bills. Most checking accounts don't earn interest. Make sure to keep track of your spending so you don't overdraw money and have to pay penalty fees. Use your checkbook to record each deposit and withdrawal to protect against overdrafts. Keep your checkbook in a safe place so people don't write checks in your name and steal your money.

A savings account is better than checking because you earn interest on your money. The interest rate is referred to as annual percentage yield ("APY" on your statement). Some savings accounts require you to maintain a minimum balance or pay a fee. This can add up quickly, so understand the obligations and requirements in the account contract. Choose a bank that is nearby and offers the best interest rate and the lowest minimum balance on its savings accounts. If you use an ATM, find out the transaction fees and where the free ATMs are located.

Before opening an account, set up an appointment to talk with an adviser or bank teller to get information on their checking and savings accounts. Six questions you should ask: Is there a minimum balance to maintain? What is the overdraft fee? What is the interest rate? What is the app like? Are there any hidden account fees? What are the different account options, and are you offering any specials?

Now that you have an account, save money each month. You can begin small with twenty dollars a month. This will equal $240 for the year. Every four months, evaluate your finances and, if possible, increase the amount you save—make saving a lifelong habit.

If you have a job, research the retirement benefits your employer offers. You can get this information from human resources. Most companies offer a 401(k) and will match all or part of your contribution. A 401(k) is a retirement savings plan sponsored by an employer.

Second, I budget my money by tracking my spending. I make a spreadsheet and list my bills and everything I purchased during the month, along with the price. Each month, I have to pay auto insurance, rent, utilities, internet, and groceries. I include this on my spreadsheet as essential spending, along with any medical bills or car repairs. Rent, food, health and auto insurance, utilities, and gas are my most important budget priorities.

Video games, Starbucks coffee, Netflix, and cable television are nonessentials, so you can live without them. If you're spending more money each month on food or gas than you expected, find areas to cut back on, like eating at restaurants or going to movies. This will help you stay on budget. If you sign up for a free trial, set a reminder to unsubscribe before the trial period ends.

Remember, small purchases add up quickly. I pay for everything with cash or check, and this causes me to think twice before I make a purchase. When I order food at a restaurant, I save money by drinking water and choosing a less expensive meal. If you use a credit card, pay the balance each month so you don't find yourself in debt or paying late fees. Mark on a calendar when your bills are due. Always check your monthly statement for overcharges and unexplained charges. By checking, you can correct these overcharges. A credit card can build up your credit for major purchases like a house or vehicle, but can also ruin your credit if you spend money out of control—so be responsible with the plastic in your wallet.

Use a budget tool like Mint. This will help you manage your entire financial life. Mint shows how much money you have in your account(s), what your spending habits are, your credit score, and how to create a budget. Best of all, this app is free. On the other hand, if using a budget app isn't the best fit for you, NerdWallet offers great suggestions for downloadable spreadsheets to help you manage your money with a hands-on approach.

It's important to know the difference between good and bad debt. Good debt is the kind that can actually help you get closer to your goals by helping increase either your potential or net worth. Examples of good debt are student loans and home mortgages. An example of bad debt is purchasing things with your credit card that you don't need or can't afford.

Third, I make extra cash on the side to save for the future. I hustled cash in college by going dorm to dorm at the end of each semester and asking students if I could have their unwanted textbooks. I then sold the textbooks back to the school bookstore for cash. ORU dress code required male students to wear ties, so at the end of the year, I'd ask seniors for their ties, and the next semester, I sold those ties to the incoming freshmen for ten dollars each. I currently make extra cash by speaking at churches and hosting autism workshops around the country. Work with your support team to come up with creative ways to make extra cash using your gifts, or if you have debt, ways to pay it off.

19. The Hindrance of Lack of Transportation

Only 34 percent of teens with autism get a driver's license, compared to 83 percent of teens without autism.[9] Driving can be challenging for us on the spectrum due to motor coordination challenges, delayed decision-making skills, problems with executive functioning when multitasking, and ADHD affecting our ability to concentrate on the road. In America, unlike in Europe, we don't have a mass transportation system that makes travel easier for those who don't have driver's licenses.

I passed driver's education and received my permit when I was fifteen and my driver's license at sixteen, but it took me years to master the road. When I was nineteen, I made a left turn and totaled my parents' car and injured my knee. I have now gone more than a decade without any traffic tickets or accidents. I have learned three valuable lessons to being a safe and responsible driver.

First, driving skills come with practice. When I began driving, I had trouble maintaining my speed and staying in my lane. I hated driving on the highway, especially during rush-hour traffic. I disliked driving with vehicles buzzing by or with people talking in my car, because I couldn't concentrate. My biggest fear driving pre-GPS and Google Maps was being lost or stranded on the side of the road in the pitch-dark. After years of experience, I now feel confident driving on the highway and with people in the back seat, but I still feel nervous when parallel parking.

You can learn to drive by taking a driver's education program or private lessons. My dad had me practice driving with him in an empty parking lot. When you begin, use a vehicle you feel comfortable driving. It is easier to learn to drive a car that has an automatic transmission, as well as learning in a compact car, which has fewer blind spots than most larger vehicles. Once I received my permit, I went driving with my mother and brothers. I started by driving back roads, and then after I gained some experience, I moved up to the highways. Beginning drivers should not drive in a car filled with people or with someone who is a critical backseat driver.

Armani Williams, the first NASCAR driver diagnosed with autism, encourages autistics: "Don't be afraid of learning something new. Once you put in the hard work and commitment to learning the basics of working the steering wheel, the gas, and brake pedal, it will become easier and you will become more comfortable on the road, freeways, or even on the racetrack, if you want to be a race car driver."[10]

Second, safe drivers obey the rules of the road and maintain their vehicles. One strength autistic people bring to driving is that we tend to be rule followers. Following the rules requires us to learn what the different signs on the road mean, when to yield, and how much distance to keep between vehicles. Remember to drive slower in bad weather conditions such as snow, ice, and rain, which make braking difficult. Minimize distractions by not texting or eating and drinking. If you need to make a phone call, pull over or use hands-free technology. Keep your vehicle safe to be on the road by regular maintenance, repairs, brake and light inspections, and tire rotations. Every three months or three thousand miles, get an oil change, and replace your shocks and struts every fifty thousand to one hundred thousand miles. Some service centers provide a free inspection with an oil change. Safe driving and regular vehicle maintenance will save you money on auto insurance and repairs.

Third, know what to do during a traffic stop and after an accident. When driving, always have your driver's license or permit accessible. Keep a copy of your motor vehicle registration and auto insurance in both your glove compartment and your wallet. If an officer pulls you over, remain calm and comply with his requests. The officer is only doing his job by enforcing the law, and traffic stops can put him on high alert. Staying calm and complying will ease the tension. Don't argue with the officer by stating, "I was not speeding" or "You have no right to pull me over." Even if you disagree with your alleged violation, being obedient will make the ordeal go more smoothly, and the officer may let you off with just a warning.

Don't admit guilt. If the officer asks you if you know why she is pulling you over, respond by stating, "No. Can you please tell me why?" Never get out of your car and approach the officer. Leaving your car will be perceived as a threat. This final advice is a no-brainer. Do not drive off or attempt to avoid being pulled over. This could lead to a high-speed pursuit, which can be life-threatening for the driver, passengers, the police, and anyone else who happens to be on the road.

After an auto accident, first check that everyone is okay. Call 911 if anyone is injured and requires medical attention. If you're able, drive your car to the side of the road and turn on your hazard lights. If you're unable to move your car, leave the vehicles where they are. If necessary, walk to safety. Wait for the police to arrive. In the meantime, gather the other driver's name, phone number, address, and insurance information, and be sure to write down the other car's license plate number. If your phone is available, take pictures of the person's driver's license, insurance info, and license plate. Also, take a few notes, such as the direction the vehicles were heading and the street names, and any nearby cross streets. If possible, photograph the scene. Finally, report the accident to your insurance company.

If you decide not to drive or are unable to receive a driver's license, learn the bus routes in your area or the subway or trolley schedules in your city. An expensive alternative for transportation is Uber or taxi. A reliable form of transportation makes employment and attending college or social events easier.

20. The Hindrance of Not Getting a Good Night's Sleep

Many individuals with autism struggle with insomnia and not getting enough sleep—often taking longer to fall asleep and struggling to stay asleep. Some causes of this are depression, anxiety, ADHD, sensory issues, medications, or staying up late playing our favorite video game or watching TV.

During high school and college, I had a set sleep schedule. I went to bed on weeknights at 10:00 p.m. and rose at 7:00 a.m., and on the weekends I stayed up until midnight and woke up by 8:00 a.m. After graduating from college, I had no set routine and began to stay up later, going to bed at 11:30 p.m. and getting up for work at 5:55 a.m. I often felt tired in the morning, was unmotivated, and lacked self-care. I also had more health problems.

It took a while to get my sleeping routine on track, but I gleaned three important things about a good night's sleep. First, I studied the benefits of a good night's sleep, which included improving memory ability and problem-solving, balancing emotions, and providing repairs and maintenance throughout the body—and how to take advantage of them.

REM sleep improves memory ability by transporting our short-term memories from the hippocampus to our long-term secure vault in the cortex.[11] Our brain does not record memories like a video camera filming each detail precisely as it occurs. Rather, it's like a print shop, shaping our memories and designing them to fit nicely into different categories so we can use our memories to learn from our past and interact with our world in the present. This enables us to make quick decisions based on past experiences and not go through thousands of memory videos to recognize how things relate, which would slow down the decision-making process. Since our brain does not record memories like a video, if we don't get enough sleep, some memories can be lost forever.

Sleeping enables us to remember and comprehend what we learned in class. When studying for a test, we will remember 20 percent more information if we had three straight nights of eight or more hours of sleep before taking an exam.[12]

Sleeping calms our emotions and helps us regulate them, and a good night's sleep allows me to be more creative in my writing and to discover new ways to solve problems. When I have a major decision or I feel a lack of creativity, I find that when I "sleep on it," the answers seem to come to me or I get a new idea for a chapter.

Second, I developed a sleep schedule of eight hours a night. Go to bed and get up at the same time each day. Keep this schedule on weekends and holidays—don't deviate from the routine more than one hour. Consistency reinforces our body's sleep-wake cycle. My routine is to turn off electronic devices two hours before bedtime and brush my teeth before I hop into bed. Electronic devices with blue LED light will affect your melatonin production, causing you to be less tired. We should not eat or exercise within two hours of bedtime, and avoid falling asleep watching TV. Don't keep your cell phone near your bed or use an alarm clock with a light—checking your digital clock can be a source of anxiety. And do your best to help calm your body before bed. Read a paperback book, listen to soothing music. Think happy thoughts. Turn your room thermometer down below seventy degrees. If you don't fall asleep right away, do something else relaxing, then return to bed when you feel tired.

Third, I don't allow worry or anxiety to steal a good night's sleep from me. Before I go to bed, I give all my anxieties and fears to God.

As Philippians 4:6 says, "Do not be anxious about anything, but in every situation, by prayer and petition, with thanksgiving, present your requests to God." When I am struggling to fall asleep or stay asleep, I apply the thirteen sleeping techniques mentioned in the "Living Healthy on the Spectrum" chapter. A hot bath also helps me fall asleep worry-free.

When I don't have time for a hot bath, I splash cold water on my face and hands. This causes my temperature to decrease a few degrees to sleep level. I find the best method for improving my sleep is going to bed and waking up at the same time every day. Our sleep impacts our physical and mental health. Therefore, if you have difficulty with sleep, contact your doctor.

Closing Thoughts

You can have a great life with autism and thrive, but there will be challenges. Your support team can provide you with guidance when you encounter these twenty hindrances. Stay focused and positive, realizing that transition is never easy and takes time. Sleeping eight hours a night will empower you to be productive and creative, solve problems easier, eat healthier, live longer, and have endurance to transition to adulthood.

REFLECT

1. I examine twenty hindrances to transitioning to adulthood. Which three of these hindrances have you experienced? How have you attempted to overcome them?

2. Write a list of your personal top five hindrances in transition. What makes these five hindrances a challenge for you? When have you encountered them? How can your support team help you with these hindrances?

3. What are some of your fears in transitioning to adulthood? How can your support team help you feel more confident when facing these fears?

FUN ACTIVITIES

With your group or a friend, write on the top of a piece of poster board, in big letters, "My Challenges for Transitioning to Adulthood." On the left side of the poster board, list the five challenges or fears you have with transitioning to adulthood. Next to the challenges or fears, paste or tape a picture representing that challenge. You can get the pictures online or from magazines, or draw the pictures yourself. For example, if one of your five challenges or fears is transportation, you can paste or draw a picture of a car or bus. If the challenge is sleep, you can paste or draw a picture of the moon, a stuffed animal you sleep with, or a bed. For the challenge of lack of direction, you can paste or draw a map, blueprints, or a compass.

On the right side of the poster board and next to each challenge or fear, write the strengths and skills you have to overcome these challenges and the help you will need from your support team. On the bottom of the poster board, write, "It's not what we accomplish in life that matters most, but what we overcome."

After finishing this activity, discuss your challenges and fears for transitioning with your group and support team. Place the "My Challenges for Transitioning to Adulthood" poster on your bedroom wall to help you navigate the journey with confidence.

FURTHER READING

The Young Autistic Adult's Independence Handbook, by Haley Moss
How to Adult, a Practical Guide: Advice on Living, Loving, Working, and Spending like a Grown-Up, by Jamie Goldstein
Adulting: How to Become a Grown-up in 535 Easy(ish) Steps, by Kelly Williams Brown

Kayla Cromer's Story
Everything's Gonna Be Okay—
Overcoming Life's Obstacles

*Being on the spectrum and having other learning differences,
I am used to working harder and have a great drive to succeed. I interpret things differently, which helps with analyzing scripts, engulfing myself into roles, to achieve realism . . .
and make strong choices.*

—KAYLA CROMER

KAYLA CROMER IS FROM A small town in northern California. She was
raised in a home surrounded by love. Both her parents worked, so her
grandparents took care of her after school. Her grandparents fostered a
lot of rescue animals, which she adored. Outdoor adventures were her
favorite, especially camping.

From an early age, Kayla had to overcome many learning challenges. Even though she put a lot of effort into her studies, she had
difficulty keeping up with academics and taking standardized tests.
During pre-K, she was tested for learning disabilities and received tu-
toring because she struggled with reading, writing, math, and social
cues. Soon after, she was diagnosed with dyslexia and then Asperger's.

Kayla's parents encouraged her in her education and helped cultivate her unique gifts. She was a visual learner and was highly creative.

Her dad would pick up appliances from Goodwill for her to take apart. Her mom always kept an eye out for art contests for Kayla to enter.

Her parents knew she had the desire to succeed, so they enrolled her in a school that supported students with learning differences, to help her achieve her goals. Her mom even quit her job and would drive Kayla one-hundred-plus miles daily to this school. "We sacrificed as a family," she says, "and it saved me. I am forever thankful!"

Growing up, Kayla loved to spend Saturday mornings watching *SpongeBob SquarePants* with her dad. She couldn't get enough of TV series like *Law and Order: SVU* and *America's Most Wanted* and movies like *Pirates of the Caribbean*, *The Hunger Games*, *Lord of the Rings*, and the Harry Potter series, and the Disney movies. Adventure, horror, sci-fi, and true crime are her favorite genres.

Academics were a challenge for Kayla, but acting and modeling came naturally. "Becoming a model and actress just kind of happened. Modeling really helped me gain poise, which in turn has helped me as an actress."

Mentors and teachers in the modeling and film industries empowered Kayla for her career. One acting teacher suggested that she should embrace her genuine self. "That has really helped me open up as an actress. I also used to study the poses of actresses who booked international beauty campaigns for brands like Chanel, Lancôme, and Dior. That helped me in my modeling career."

Kayla persevered and was inspired by other actresses and models with disabilities. "Seeing Keira Knightley make movies and flourish as an actress, even though she struggled with dyslexia, really inspired me to act." Her parents also encouraged her to do her best, have good character, and treat people with kindness. These qualities were instrumental to Kayla's success. Her modeling career picked up after a photo of her went viral, resulting in her being signed to a contract.

Asperger's has empowered Kayla to be an overcomer in life. "Easy isn't something I know. For me personally, my hard work and dedication help me dig deep into scripts and characters. I see things other people won't see."

Kayla still experiences obstacles as she transitions to adulthood. "My fear of driving. I started off on country roads and moved on from there. I knew it was something I had to conquer! Now I drive everywhere in Los Angeles traffic! I think it would be cool to drive across the country on a road trip one day."

Kayla has a few similarities with her character Matilda from *Everything's Gonna Be Okay*. "We both can be hysterical without knowing it. We are both strong-willed and accept our differences and advocate for ourselves. We love our families and want to fit in socially with others and find love."

Everything's Gonna Be Okay enables Kayla to be an advocate for the autism community. "The TV series, Freeform, and Disney have amplified my voice. Disney is very dedicated to inclusion too. The exposure has led to many media opportunities to speak about autism."

Kayla offers advice to young adults with autism who desire to act or model: "For modeling, I would say to build your confidence up with home photo shoots and see if you like it. Approach small boutiques and offer to model for free for their social media posts. Stay away from modeling school scams and submit to legit modeling agencies.

"For acting, I would suggest joining community or school theater classes. Both areas have opportunities in front of and behind the camera. Explore all those options. Once you find your passion, learn everything you can and pursue it!"

Kayla looks forward to new challenges and opportunities as she transitions to adulthood. She is passionately career focused. She is currently paving a path for herself and recently added a management team. "I want to pursue feature films and book neurotypical roles to show my range. I want to continue with my career, get married to a kind man, buy a house with land, have rescue animals, and travel for work and pleasure."

Kayla's dream role is to play a character in a Marvel series or movie or a film involving a physical transformation. "I love fitness! To physically train for an adventure-type film would be a dream come true! Totally amazing! I would work my tail off!"[13]

KAYLA CROMER'S BIOGRAPHY

Kayla Cromer is the daughter of Reno and Pam Cromer. Kayla has always had a love for acting. Watching *Pirates of the Caribbean: The Curse of the Black Pearl* ignited her passion. A photo from a San Francisco photo shoot soared across social media and launched her modeling career. Cromer has appeared on magazine covers and periodicals nationwide.

Kayla appeared in an episode of TLC's *Ghost Brothers* as a guest investigator and recently finished filming *Apparition*. She has been cast in the feature film *Okinawa* as Sniper's wife. Kayla wrapped the pilot episode of Freeform's & Avalon Entertainment's *Everything's Gonna Be Okay* as the female lead, Matilda.

REFLECT

1. To become an actress and model, Kayla had to overcome many obstacles. What are some challenges you are currently experiencing in transitioning to adulthood? How can you, like Kayla, approach these challenges with confidence?

2. Kayla persevered and was inspired by other actresses and models with disabilities. Who are some people with autism or disabilities who have inspired you to overcome? What lessons have you learned from these individuals and how can you apply them to your life?

3. Asperger's has empowered Kayla to be an overcomer in life. How has autism empowered you to overcome obstacles? Do you feel there are hindrances in transitioning to adulthood? If so, what are the hindrances and how can your support team help you in those areas?

Epilogue

I might hit developmental and societal milestones in a different order than my peers, but I am able to accomplish these small victories on my own time.

—HALEY MOSS, author, advocate, and attorney with autism

ON JANUARY 21, 2022, AMAZON Prime released *As We See It*, which follows Jack (Rick Glassman), Harrison (Albert Rutecki), and Violet (Sue Ann Pien), three roommates on the autism spectrum struggling with employment, making friends, and finding romance while navigating the strange world of adulthood with help from Mandy (Sosie Bacon), a counselor/life coach. The three main stars identify as being neurodivergent in real life. It took me only two days to binge-watch the eight episodes.

As We See It highlights the complexity and vastness of the autism spectrum by following each character's struggles with transitioning to adulthood and the accommodations they require. Jack, who has Asperger's, struggles with filtering his comments and keeping a job, while Harrison has a phobia of leaving the apartment, and his only friend is a young boy who lives upstairs. Violet is obsessed with finding a boyfriend on dating apps and has difficulty dealing with her complicated relationship with her older brother, who is her guardian.

Likewise, you will have your own challenges in transitioning and will need some accommodations along the way.

In my forties, I still experience new challenges with adulthood. While writing each chapter, I faced the very issues I was writing about. I found myself living and learning from my book. As I completed the "Living Healthy on the Spectrum" chapter, I experienced abdominal pain and used the list of the eight things to share with your primary physician for a health concern. The week I began writing "Advocating for Your Accommodations," I received a summons to jury duty in the mail, requiring me to freshen up my advocacy skills. Three hours into writing "Navigating the Social Nuances of Interviewing," a businessman contacted me and asked me to travel to Florida for a job interview for a position as a speaker and advocate to the autism community. After the interview in Florida, while writing "Making Wise Decisions That Influence Your Life," the company sent me a contract for the job. When I saw red flags in the contract, I used the seven steps of the decision-making process to decide not to accept the offer.

After I finished this book, I felt gratitude for my support team, who empowered me with the resources and practical knowledge to help me transition to adulthood more smoothly and enjoy life. Two qualities that are helpful while transitioning to adulthood are maintaining a positive attitude and taking life as it comes.

I was reminded of the importance of a positive attitude and not being overwhelmed by life after reading *The Luck Factor* by Richard Wiseman. The premise of Richard's book is that lucky people experience luck due to their positive perspective, friendliness, and lack of anxiety—three qualities people with autism struggle with. Lucky people focus on the present, and their relaxed personalities enable them to notice opportunities in life and take advantage of them.

Opportunity happens by our connection with others. Richard Wiseman writes, "Lucky people are effective at building secure, and long-lasting, attachments with the people that they meet. They are easy to get to know and most people like them. They tend to be trusting and form close friendships with others. As a result, they often keep in touch with a much larger number of friends and colleagues than unlucky people, and time and time again, this network of friends helps promote opportunity in their lives."[1]

We on the spectrum often feel unlucky because we are unaware of the opportunities around us. Our anxiety and lack of focus in the present moment cause us to miss opportunities and not connect with others. Instead of seeing the people around us who open unexpected doors of opportunity, we worry and focus on the problems in our lives.

By trying new things, lucky people build connections. My eight-year-old daughter, Makayla, does not like change and only enjoys eating at two restaurants, McDonald's and Ram's Horn, where she goes with her grandparents. A big part of adulthood is variety. If we can change up our routine by trying new things, our luck can change and we can create new connections.

The final quality we can gain from lucky people is self-confidence. They have a hope complex. Often we on the spectrum exhibit learned hopelessness—if we think we will fail, we don't even try. When we hit a bump in the road—our car breaks down, we get an unexpected bill, we perform poorly on a test, a relationship goes sour, we're fired from a job—we feel like a failure and ask, "Why do I have such horrible luck?"

Studies have shown that people with a more positive expectation in life tend to take the steps to ensure a healthy lifestyle. They exercise more, eat a balanced diet, set up annual physical and dental exams, and pay attention to medical advice, while people who are anxious are more prone to accidents and have difficulty concentrating on what they are doing, causing them to miss out on opportunities.[2]

While finishing my fourth book, I learned to slow down and enjoy the moment by playing a "Vampire Chase Human" game with Makayla or eating a family meal with electronics off. Enjoying the moment causes me to have the three C's of a cat: cool, calm, and collected.

When problems arise, I remain calm, gather my thoughts, and come up with a solution. I collect my thoughts by writing down the problem and the steps to solve it.

When my wife's 2010 Ford Focus did not start due to negative-digit weather, I had my neighbor help me jump-start the car. When the car would not remain running without the jumper cables, I realized it was not the battery but the alternator, which would require me to take the car to the auto shop. Here's how I wrote down the problem:

Car not starting
1. Check battery by using jumper cables.
2. Ask neighbor to help me jump-start my car to see if the problem is the battery.
3. If car is still not running after using jumper cables, take to an auto shop to diagnose.
4. Contact auto shop and set up an appointment to check out car.
5. Call local towing companies and compare prices for tow.
6. Choose towing company and have them tow car to shop.
7. Pay auto shop for repairs and the towing company bill.

I find that writing down the steps to a problem causes me to stay collected and feel less anxious. Transitioning to adulthood will present you with many new challenges. Writing them down can help you brainstorm solutions and know the steps in the proper order.

In my more than forty years of life, I can testify that transitioning to adulthood is not for the fainthearted, but requires guts and courage. It takes guts to keep getting up after you make mistakes or feel like a failure, and it takes courage to maintain a positive attitude when your milestone list takes longer than it does for your brothers or peers. Popcorn is prepared in the same pot, at the same heat, and in the same oil—yet the kernels do not all pop at the same time; so don't compare your transition to adulthood with others.

I have more than five thousand quotes memorized, so I will end with one of my favorites. Steve "Pre" Prefontaine, an American long-distance runner from Oregon who competed in the 1972 Summer Olympics, stated, "A lot of people run a race to see who is fastest. I run to see who has the most guts."[3] Transition to adulthood with guts.

REFLECT

1. I share two lessons I learned while writing this book: the benefits of maintaining a positive attitude and taking life as it comes. What are two lessons you've learned from this book and how can you apply them to your life?
2. After reading this book, what are three things you can work on with your support team that will help you gain more independence?
3. I describe my struggles in adulthood and the joys I experienced: graduating from college, getting married, and having a family. What do you desire most to accomplish in life, and how can you, with the help of your support team, make this goal a reality?

FUN ACTIVITIES

The purpose of this activity is to set small goals and record the steps required to reach lifelong accomplishments and dreams. Your dream in life could be a long-term relationship or marriage, obtaining a driver's license and going on a two-week road trip, graduating from college, a career related to your interests and passions, or traveling the world. Talk with your group or a friend and decide what your long-term goal is. Try to make your goals as specific as possible.

For example, with a long-term relationship goal, make this specific by stating the qualities you desire in a romantic partner or activities you'd like him or her to enjoy. Don't make your goal generic, like to "be happy" or "travel more." To make "be happy" specific, rework it to something like "have a career I enjoy in video game design" or "have a friend who I can go to movies with on Friday nights." You can make the "travel more" goal specific by deciding where you'd like to travel and when you hope to travel there.

On poster board, draw a staircase leading up to your lifelong goal or dream. At the bottom of the staircase write a short-term goal. On the middle step of the staircase write down a second goal related to the first goal, but that is a little more difficult to obtain. On the top of the staircase, record your lifelong goal or dream. The first two goals need to relate to your lifelong goal. If your goal is a long-term relationship with a partner who loves animals, make your first goal something like "volunteer at an animal shelter, and each day I volunteer, talk to at least one new person." Once you meet someone you're interested in and he or she shows an interest in you, the second goal could be to "invite him or her to a movie or a fun event like the zoo."

Once you've been dating for a few months, your final goal could be to "make a commitment to exclusively date each other."

On the steps leading up the staircase above each goal, write notes about the things you learned while moving up the stairs toward your long-term goal. For example, the notes on the long-term goal of a relationship could read, "I learned that people love to talk about themselves and share their stories" or "I discovered that giving a compliment is a great way to begin a conversation." Write on the top of the poster board "Reaching for My Dreams" and hang it on your bedroom wall.

FINAL ACTIVITY

Write a one-page summary describing in detail how you envision your life in a year, in five years, and in ten years. For each time period, share what you hope to be doing for a career and how you will be spending your free time. For each time period, also note accomplishments you hope to reach and how you hope to reach them. This activity will help you focus your priorities. It will give you a blueprint for creating the life you desire and motivate you to transition to adulthood.

FURTHER READING ────────────────

Becoming an Autism Success Story, by Anita Lesko

From Foster Care to Millionaire: A Young Entrepreneur's Story of Tragedy and Triumph, by Cody McLain

Bad Choices Make Good Stories: My Life with Autism, by Dylan Volk

Acknowledgments

IT TOOK A TEAM EFFORT to write and publish *Adulting on the Spectrum*. I'd like to acknowledge those who encouraged and empowered me to write:

- My literary agent, Bob Hostetler, and the Steve Laube Agency team.
- The Art of Autism and its founder, Debra Muzikar. I originally published the stories in this book in the Art of Autism, and I write a monthly blog for their site (the-art-of-autism.com).
- Brittany Stonestreet for editing the manuscript with her keen eye for detail, grammar, punctuation, and for providing me with valuable feedback and recommendations for the content.

A special thanks to people whose inspiring stories are featured in the chapters: Sydney Holmes, Jackie Anne Blair, Juliana Fetherman and Michael Fetherman, Armando Bernal, Xavier DeGroat, Amy Gaeta, Tiffany Fixter, Father Matthew Schneider, Cody McLain, Tal Anderson, and Kayla Cromer.

A special thanks to Dr. Barry M. Prizant, author of *Uniquely Human: A Different Way of Seeing Autism*, for writing the foreword.

Thanks to the professionals and individuals in the autism community whom I interviewed: Andrew Duff, Andrea Reger, Angela Marquez, Eric Chessen, Sarah Broady, Erin McKinney, Stephanie C.

Holmes, Eric Michael Garcia, Jim Hogan, Haley Moss, Mikhaela Ackerman, Mark Fleming, Anthony Ianni, Michael Bernick, Desiree Kameka Galloway, Wendela Whitcomb Marsh, Dr. Leann S. DaWalt, Dr. Jackie Marquette, Dr. Lara Honos-Webb, Dr. Lawrence Fung, Dr. Tony Attwood, Dr. Temple Grandin, and the countless others who also contributed.

David Sharif, a disability advocate and friend in the autism community (May 28, 1997–April 23, 2022)—RIP. I enjoyed interviewing you and appreciated your insight on autism and college life. You will be greatly missed, but your advocacy and love will live on.

My thanks to present and former staff at Kregel Publications for their continual encouragement and desire to advance the gospel of Christ: Jerry Kregel, Catherine DeVries, Rachel Kirsch, Dori Harrell, Paul Miller, Sarah J. De Mey, Janyre Tromp, Steve Barclift, and Katherine Chappell.

I would like to thank my students at Destiny School of Ministry, and Pastor Lee and Dr. Yvonne Matlock, under whose leadership I have taught for the past twenty years—they have demonstrated the true heart of a pastor.

Finally, I would like to thank my family, co-workers at Havenwyck Hospital, and friends for their encouragement on my writing journey.

And I especially want to thank Jesus Christ for giving me the wisdom, strength, and grace to finish this book.

Notes

Introduction

1. Jesse A. Saperstein, *Getting a Life with Asperger's: Lessons Learned on the Bumpy Road to Adulthood* (TarcherPerigee, 2014), 122.
2. *The Autobiography of Saint Thérèse of Lisieux: The Story of a Soul*, trans. John Beevers (Image Books, 2001), 2.

Chapter 1: Leaving the Nest

1. Names and details are altered to protect identities.
2. Jesse Saperstein, interview by Ron Sandison, June 10, 2015. Used with permission.
3. Zosia Zaks, *Life and Love: Positive Strategies for Autistic Adults* (AAPC, 2006), 32.
4. Zaks, *Life and Love*, 42.
5. Temple Grandin, keynote presentation at the World Autism Conference and Exposition, Loveland, CO, December 2, 2023.

Chapter 2: Living Healthy on the Spectrum

1. Maheswari S. Senthil, "Four Things to Know About the Third-Deadliest Cancer," Loma Linda University, March 11, 2019, https://news.llu.edu/patient-care/four-things-know-about-third-deadliest-cancer-0.

2. Moneek Madra et al., "Gastrointestinal Issues and Autism Spectrum Disorder," *Child and Adolescent Psychiatric Clinics of North America* 29, no. 3 (2020), http://doi.org/0.1016/j.chc.2020.02.005.

3. "Testicular torsion occurs when a testicle rotates, twisting the spermatic cord that brings blood to the scrotum. The reduced blood flow causes sudden and often severe pain and swelling. . . . Testicular torsion usually requires emergency surgery. If treated quickly, the testicle can usually be saved. But when blood flow has been cut off for too long, a testicle might become so badly damaged that it has to be removed." "Testicular Torsion," Mayo Clinic, February 24, 2022, https://www.mayoclinic.org/diseases-conditions/testicular-torsion/symptoms-causes/syc-20378270.

4. Zosia Zaks, *Life and Love: Positive Strategies for Autistic Adults* (AAPC, 2006), 115.

5. Matthew Walker, *Why We Sleep: Unlocking the Power of Sleep and Dreams* (Scribner, 2017), 149.

6. Arianna Huffington, *The Sleep Revolution* (Harmony Books, 2016), 110.

7. Brian C. Tefft, "Acute Sleep Deprivation and Culpable Motor Vehicle Crash Involvement," *Sleep* 41, no. 10 (2018), https://doi.org/10.1093/sleep/zsy144.

8. Walker, *Why We Sleep* (Scribner, 2017), 5, 138.

9. Eric J. Olson, "Lack of Sleep: Can It Make You Sick?," Mayo Clinic, November 28, 2018, https://www.mayoclinic.org/diseases-conditions/insomnia/expert-answers/lack-of-sleep/faq-20057757.

10. DaiWare, "The Link Between High Blood Pressure and Circadian Rhythm," Medium, January 15, 2018, https://medium.com/@DaiWare_Inc/the-link-between-high-blood-pressure-and-circadian-rhythm-d43fad080eb7.

11. Huffington, *The Sleep Revolution*, 113–14.
12. Michael O'Riordan, "Younger Type 2 Diabetes Patients Face Higher Mortality and CVD Risks," TCTMD, April 10, 2019, https://www.tctmd.com/news/younger-type-2-diabetes-patients -face-higher-mortality-and-cvd-risks.
13. Kathleen Drinan and Phillip LoSavio, "Sleep Prevention and Heart Disease: Everything You Need to Know," UChicago Medicine, January 10, 2024, https://www.uchicagomedicine.org/fore front/heart-and-vascular-articles/how-sleep-deprivation-and -sleep-apnea-impact-heart-health.
14. Eric Suni and Ealena Callender, "How Sleep Deprivation Affects Your Heart," Sleep Foundation, April 25, 2024, https://www .sleepfoundation.org/sleep-deprivation/how-sleep-deprivation -affects-your-heart.
15. Stephanie Watson and Kristeen Cherney, "The Effects of Sleep Deprivation on Your Body," Healthline, August 23, 2024, https:// www.healthline.com/health/sleep-deprivation/effects-on-body #effects.
16. Walker, *Why We Sleep* (Scribner, 2017), 35.
17. "Autism and Obesity: Common Ground and Origins?," Children's Health Defense, October 2, 2018, https://childrens healthdefense.org/news/autism-and-obesity-common-ground -and-origins/.
18. "Autism and Obesity," Children's Health Defense.
19. Katrina L. Piercy and Richard P. Troiano, "Physical Activity Guidelines for Americans from the US Department of Health and Human Services," *Circulation: Cardiovascular Quality and Outcomes* 11, no. 11 (2018), https://doi.org/10.1161/CIRCOUT COMES.118.005263.
20. Eric Chessen, interview by Ron Sandison, November 11, 2021. Used with permission.
21. "5 Best Workouts Ever; No Gym Needed," *The Business Standard*,

June 19, 2023, https://www.tbsnews.net/bangladesh/health/5-best -workouts-ever-no-gym-needed-652446.

22. Carla Maria Avesani et al., "Ultraprocessed Foods and Chronic Kidney Disease—Double Trouble," *Clinical Kidney Journal* 16, no. 11 (2023): 1723–36, http://doi.org/10.1093/ckj/sfad103.

23. Nuri Faruk Aykan, "Red Meat and Colorectal Cancer," *Oncology Review* 9, no. 288 (2015): 42, http://doi.org/10.4081/oncol .2015.288.

24. Carl J. Lavie et al., "In Reply—Impact of a High-Shrimp Diet on Cardiovacular Risk," Mayo Clinic Proceedings, February 2021, http://doi.org/10.1016/j.mayocp.2020.10.028.

25. Jackie's story first appeared on *The Art of Autism* and is used here with permission. Ron Sandison, "How Jackie Ann Blair's Autism Helps Her Be a Better Nurse," *The Art of Autism*, September 17, 2020, https://the-art-of-autism.com/how-jackie-anne-blairs -autism-helps-her-be-a-better-nurse/.

Chapter 3: Building and Maintaining Friendships

1. Ami Klin, "Imagining a Better World for Children with Autism," International Mental Health Research Symposium presentation, October 26, 2018, posted January 18, 2019, by Brain & Behavior Research Foundation, YouTube, https://www.you tube.com/watch?v=UBfeE8YWp3o.

2. Dylan Volk, *Bad Choices Make Good Stories: My Life with Autism* (D & A Publishing, 2018), 125.

3. Ron Sandison, "The Hidden Rules of Communication: How to Create a Lasting Impression," *The Art of Autism*, June 7, 2020, https://the-art-of-autism.com/the-hidden-rules-of-communi cation-how-to-create-a-lasting-impression/.

4. Vanessa Van Edwards, *Captivate: The Science of Succeeding with People* (Penguin Random House, 2017), 121.

5. Tony Beshara, *Acing the Interview: How to Ask and Answer the*

Questions That Will Get You the Job! (HarperCollins Leadership, 2008), 87.

6. Temple Grandin and Sean Barron, *Unwritten Rules of Social Relationships: Decoding Social Mysteries Through the Unique Perspectives of Autism* (Future Horizons, 2005), 206.

7. Jed Baker, *Preparing for Life: The Complete Guide for Transitioning to Adulthood for Those with Autism and Asperger's Syndrome* (Future Horizons, 2005), 5.

8. Judy Endow, *Learning the Hidden Curriculum: The Odyssey of One Autistic Adult* (AAPC, 2012), 13.

9. Daniel Tammet, *Born on a Blue Day: Inside the Extraordinary Mind of an Autistic Savant* (Free Press, 2006), 141.

10. "An Active Social Life Is Good for Your Health," *Swedish Blog*, May 1, 2019, https://blog.swedish.org/swedish-blog/a-healthy-social-life-is-good-for-your-health.

Chapter 4: Avoiding the Pitfalls of Dating

1. Zosia Zaks, *Life and Love: Positive Strategies for Autistic Adults* (AAPC, 2006), 245.

2. *Dumb and Dumber*, written by Peter Farrelly, Bennett Yellin, and Bob Farrelly, directed by Peter Farrelly and Bob Farrelly (New Line Cinema, 1994), Internet Movie Database, https://www.imdb.com/title/tt0109686/quotes/.

3. Stephen M. Shore, *Beyond the Wall: Personal Experiences with Autism and Asperger Syndrome* (Future Horizons, 2003), 54.

4. Lindsey Sterling, *The Social Survival Guide for Teens on the Autism Spectrum: How to Make Friends and Navigate Your Emotions* (Callisto Teens, 2020), 37.

5. Emily A. Vogels, "10 Facts About Americans and Online Dating in 2019," Pew Research Center, February 6, 2020, https://www.pewresearch.org/short-reads/2020/02/06/10-facts-about-americans-and-online-dating/.

Chapter 5: Overcoming a Hopeless Complex

1. Courtney E. Ackerman, "Learned Helplessness: Seligman's Theory of Depression," PositivePsychology.com, March 24, 2018, https://positivepsychology.com/learned-helplessness-seligman-theory-depression-cure/.

2. Dylan Volk, *Bad Choices Make Good Stories: My Life with Autism* (D & A Publishing, 2018), 37.

3. Jack F. G. Underwood et al., "Neurological and Psychiatric Disorders Among Autistic Adults: A Population Healthcare Record Study," Cambridge University Press, October 3, 2022, http://doi.org/10.1017/S0033291722002884.

4. Alix Generous, interview by Ron Sandison, quoted in *Views from the Spectrum: A Window into Life and Faith with Your Neurodivergent Child* (Kregel, 2021), 165. Used with permission.

5. Volk, *Bad Choices Make Good Stories*, 63.

6. Temple Grandin and Sean Barron, *Unwritten Rules of Social Relationships: Decoding Social Mysteries Through the Unique Perspectives of Autism* (Future Horizons, 2005), 10.

7. Wendy Lawson, *Understanding and Working with the Spectrum of Autism: An Insider's View* (Jessica Kingsley Publishers, 2001), 118–19.

8. Xavier's story first appeared on *The Art of Autism* and is used here with permission. Ron Sandison, "Xavier DeGroat: The First White House Intern Diagnosed with Autism," *The Art of Autism*, March 6, 2021, https://the-art-of-autism.com/xavier-degroat-the-first-white-house-intern-diagnosed-with-autism/.

Chapter 6: Advocating for Your Accommodations

1. Haley Moss, *The Young Autistic Adult's Independence Handbook* (Jessica Kingsley Publishers, 2021), 172.

2. Ron Sandison, *Views from the Spectrum: A Window into Life and Faith with Your Neurodivergent Child* (Kregel, 2021), 37.
3. Areva Martin, *The Everyday Advocate: Standing Up for Your Child with Autism* (Penguin Books, 2010), 52.
4. Jenara Nerenberg, *Divergent Mind: Thriving in a World That Wasn't Designed for You* (HarperOne, 2021), 211.

Chapter 7: Learning the Ins and Outs of the Workplace

1. Lindsey Ford, "People with Autism Often Have Difficulty Finding Employment. This Nonprofit Links Them to Trade Jobs," Rocky Mountain PBS, April 24, 2024, https://www.rmpbs.org/blogs/rocky-mountain-pbs/tact-nonprofit-autism-denver.
2. Names and details are altered to protect identities.
3. "Employment Statistics," Autism Society, accessed December 9, 2024, https://autismsociety.org/employment/.
4. Marcia Scheiner, *An Employer's Guide to Managing Professionals on the Autism Spectrum* (Jessica Kingsley Publishers, 2017), 54.
5. Brian R. King, *Strategies for Building Successful Relationships with People on the Autism Spectrum: Let's Relate!* (Jessica Kingsley Publishers, 2011), 158.
6. Dr. Jackie Marquette, interview by Ron Sandison, May 6, 2021. Used with permission.
7. Angela Mahoney, interview by Ron Sandison, "Tips for Successful Employment for Those on the Autism Spectrum," *The Art of Autism*, July 26, 2017, https://the-art-of-autism.com/tips-for-successful-employment-for-those-on-the-autism-spectrum/.
8. Anita Lesko, "How Childhood Jobs Prepared Me for Success as an Autistic Adult," The Mighty, April 27, 2023, https://themighty.com/topic/autism-spectrum-disorder/how-childhood-jobs-prepared-me-for-success-as-an-autistic-adult/.
9. Much of the content in this section was originally published in

Ron Sandison, "5 Practical Ways to Help Adults with Autism Gain Employment," MySLP Today, April 1, 2016, https://myslp .today/5-practical-ways-help-adults-autism-gain-employment. Used with permission.

10. *2016 Deloitte Impact Survey: Building Leadership Skills Through Volunteerism* (Deloitte, 2016), https://www2.deloitte.com/us/en /pages/about-deloitte/articles/citizenship-deloitte-volunteer -impact-research.html.

11. Rudy Simone, *Asperger's on the Job: Must-Have Advice for People with Asperger's or High Functioning Autism and Their Employers, Educators, and Advocates* (Future Horizons, 2010), 3–4.

12. Dr. Jackie Marquette, interview by Ron Sandison, May 6, 2021. Used with permission.

13. Ron Sandison's translation of the verse, based on the NIV.

14. Ron Sandison, "Empowering Individuals with Autism for Employment Disability," church conference talk in Cleveland, Ohio, posted May 15, 2023, by Key Ministry, YouTube, https:// www.youtube.com/watch?v=GO6FZHOs87Q.

15. Judy Endow, *Learning the Hidden Curriculum: The Odyssey of One Autistic Adult* (AAPC, 2012), 89.

16. Mark Fleming, interview by Ron Sandison, "Gym Owner and Trainer Mark Fleming: Helping Others on the Autism Spectrum Become Physically Fit," *The Art of Autism*, January 23, 2020, https:// the-art-of-autism.com/gym-owner-and-trainer-mark-flem ing-helping-others-on-the-autism-spectrum-become-physically -fit.

17. Tiffany Fixter's story first appeared in *Autism Parenting Magazine* and is used here with permission. Ron Sandison, "Meet a Brewery Owner Helping Autistic Adults Build Careers," *Autism Parenting Magazine*, July 8, 2024, https://www.autismparenting magazine.com/brewery-helps-autistic/.

Chapter 8: Navigating the Social Nuances of Interviewing

1. Tony Beshara, *Acing the Interview: How to Ask and Answer the Questions That Will Get You the Job!* (HarperCollins Leadership, 2008), 11.
2. Beshara, *Acing the Interview*, 45.
3. Andrea Reger, "How Many Applications Does It Take to Get a Job?," *Hire Lehigh*, Lehigh University, December 6, 2021, https://www.hirelehigh.com/post/how-many-applications-does-it-take-to-get-a-job/.
4. Stephan Maldonado, "20 Common Resume Buzzwords (and What to Use Instead)," Vault, January 16, 2019, https://vault.com/blogs/resumes-cover-letters/20-common-resume-buzzwords.
5. Andrea Reger, interview by Ron Sandison, May 28, 2021. Used with permission.
6. Nelson Schwartz, "In Hiring, a Friend in Need Is a Prospect, Indeed," *New York Times*, January 27, 2013, https://www.nytimes.com/2013/01/28/business/employers-increasingly-rely-on-internal-referrals-in-hiring.html.
7. Beshara, *Acing the Interview*, 167.
8. Kim Parker, "When Negotiation Starting Salaries, Most U.S. Women and Men Don't Ask for Higher Pay," Pew Research Center, April 5, 2023, https://www.pewresearch.org/short-reads/2023/04/05/when-negotiating-starting-salaries-most-us-women-and-men-dont-ask-for-higher-pay/.
9. Father Matthew's story first appeared on *The Art of Autism* and is used here with permission. Ron Sandison, "Father Matthew Schneider Navigating Life as Priest on the Autism Spectrum," *The Art of Autism*, August 13, 2021, https://the-art-of-autism.com/father-matthew-schneider-navigating-life-as-priest-on-the-autism-spectrum/.

Chapter 9: Making Wise Decisions That Influence Your Life

1. Lawrence R. Sutton, *Teaching Students with Autism in a Catholic Setting* (Loyola Press, 2020), 25.
2. The elements of habits—cue, behavior, and reward—are commonly understood and widely used by many book and article writers.
3. Dave Martin, *Make That, Break That: How to Break Bad Habits and Make New Ones That Lead to Success* (Inspire, 2021), 182.
4. Anthony Ianni, *Centered: Autism, Basketball, and One Athlete's Dreams* (Red Lightning Books, 2021) 108.

Chapter 10: Managing Emotions and Sensory Issues

1. "Specific Phobia," National Institute of Mental Health, accessed October 19, 2024, https://www.nimh.nih.gov/health/statistics/specific-phobia.
2. "What Are Anxiety Disorders?," American Psychiatric Association, accessed December 10, 2024, https://www.psychiatry.org/patients-families/anxiety-disorders/what-are-anxiety-disorders. A "social phobia" is now called "social anxiety disorder," as noted in this APA article.
3. Sue Sutton, *Living Fulfilled Lives: Empowering People with Learning Disabilities* (Sarah Grace Publishing, 2018), 74.
4. Theresa Hamlin, *Autism and the Stress Effect: A 4-Step Lifestyle Approach to Transform Your Child's Health, Happiness and Vitality* (Jessica Kingsley Publication, 2016), 44.
5. "You Guessed It: Long-Term Stress Can Make You Gain Weight," Cleveland Clinic, March 1, 2023, https://health.clevelandclinic.org/stress-and-weight-gain.
6. Jory Fleming and Lyric Winik, *How to Be Human: An Autistic Man's Guide to Life* (Simon & Schuster, 2021), 152.
7. Mark Moss et al., "Modulation of Cognitive Performance and Mood by Aromas of Peppermint and Ylang-Ylang," *International*

Journal of Neuroscience 118, no. 1 (2008) 59–77, http://doi
.org/10.1080/00207450601042094.

8. Tal's story first appeared in *Autism Parenting Magazine* and is
used here with permission. Ron Sandison, "Meet Tal Anderson,
Star of *Atypical*," *Autism Parenting Magazine*, October 8, 2021,
https://www.autismparentingmagazine.com/atypical-actress
-tal-anderson/.

Chapter 11: Managing the Mind for Organization and Executive Functioning

1. "The Link Between Alcoholism and Autism," Vertava Health,
accessed March 8, 2024, https://vertavahealth.com/alcohol
/autism-link/.

2. Elisabeth's story first appeared on *The Art of Autism* and is used
here with permission. Ron Sandison, "Elisabeth Wiklander,
Cellist with the London Philharmonic Orchestra (LPO), Talks
About Her Autism and Neurodiversity," *The Art of Autism*,
June 30, 2020, https://the-art-of-autism.com/elisabeth-wiklander
-cellist-with-the-london-philharmonic-orchestra-lpo-talks-about
-her-autism-and-neurodiversity/.

Chapter 12: Understanding the Twenty Hindrances to Transition

1. Peter Lantz, interview by Ron Sandison, quoted in *Views from
the Spectrum: A Window into Life and Faith with Your Neurodivergent Child* (Kregel, 2021), 47. Used with permission.

2. The elements of growth—biological, intellectual, and experiential—are commonly understood and widely used by many book
and article writers.

3. Diane Ravitch, keynote address, January 21, 2015, PS3 in Green-
wich Village, New York, quoted in Jennifer Neufeld, "Parents Band
Together to End a 'Test-Obsessed System,'" *Observer*, January 23,

2015, https://observer.com/2015/01/parents-band-together-to-end
-a-test-obsessed-system.

4. Rebecca Joy Stanborough, "How Black and White Thinking Hurts You (and What You Can Do to Change It)," Thrive
Global, February 4, 2020, https://community.thriveglobal.com
/black-and-white-thinking-damage-communication-psychol
ogy-research/.

5. Ann Roux et al., *National Autism Indicators Report: Transition
into Young Adulthood* (Life Course Outcomes Research Program, A.J. Drexel Autism Institute, Drexel University, 2015),
https://doi.org/10.17918/NAIRTransition2015.

6. Temple Grandin, *The Way I See It: A Personal Look at Autism &
Asperger's* (Future Horizons, 2008), 9.

7. Betty Ray, "How to Help Young People Transition into Adulthood," *Greater Good Magazine*, October 21, 2019, https://
greatergood.berkeley.edu/article/item/how_to_help_young
_people_transition_into_adulthood.

8. Haley Moss, *The Young Autistic Adult's Independence Handbook*
(Jessica Kingsley Publishers, 2021), 14.

9. Allison E. Curry et al., "Longitudinal Study of Driver Licensing
Rates Among Adolescents and Young Adults with Autism Spectrum Disorder," *Autism* 22, no. 4 (2018): 479–88, https://doi
.org/10.1177/1362361317699586.

10. Armani Williams, interview by Ron Sandison, quoted in *Views
from the Spectrum*, 239. Used with permission.

11. Matthew Walker, *Why We Sleep: Unlocking the Power of Sleep
and Dreams* (Scribner, 2017), 111.

12. Arianna Huffington, *The Sleep Revolution: Transforming Your
Life, One Night at a Time* (Harmony Books, 2017), 221.

13. Kayla's story first appeared on *The Art of Autism* and is used here
with permission. Ron Sandison, "An Interview with Kayla Cromer, Autistic Actress on Everything's Gonna Be Okay," *The Art of*

Autism, June 11, 2021, https://the-art-of-autism.com/an-interview
-with-kayla-cromer-autistic-actress-on-everythings-gonna-be
-okay/.

Epilogue

1. Richard Wiseman, *The Luck Factor: Changing Your Luck, Changing Your Life: Four Essential Principles* (Arrow Books, 2004), 45.

2. Wiseman, *The Luck Factor,* 112.

3. Mark Remy, *The Runner's Rule Book: Everything a Runner Needs to Know—and Then Some* (Rodale, 2009), 12.

About the Author

 RON SANDISON works full-time in the medical field and is a professor of theology at Destiny School of Ministry. He is an advisory board member of the Art of Autism and the Els Center of Excellence. Ron has a master of divinity from Oral Roberts University and is the author of *A Parent's Guide to Autism: Practical Advice. Biblical Wisdom* and *Views from the Spectrum: A Window into Life and Faith with Your Neurodivergent Child*. Ron has fifteen thousand Bible verses memorized, including twenty-two complete books of the New Testament. He speaks at seventy events each year, including twenty-five education conferences. He is the founder of Spectrum Inclusion, which empowers young adults with disabilities for employment. Ron and his wife, Kristen, reside in Rochester Hills, Michigan, with their daughter, Makayla. His website is spectruminclusion.com. You can contact him at sandison456@hotmail.com.

Also available from Ron Sandison

This heartfelt and inspiring book highlights the stories of twenty remarkable young adults with autism, showcasing their achievements with the unwavering support of their families and faith in God. The author, an adult with autism himself, offers a unique perspective on the potential gifts and talents autism can bring. Along with personal stories, the book includes expert insights, parenting advice, and Scripture, offering a blend of encouragement, practical tips, and a celebration of autism, faith, and possibility.